Gender

READERS IN CULTURAL CRITICISM
General Editor: *Catherine Belsey*

Posthumanism	*Neil Badmington*
Reading the Past	*Tamsin Spargo*
Reading Images	*Julia Thomas*
Gender	*Anna Tripp*

Readers in Cultural Criticism
Series Standing Order
ISBN 0–333–78660–2 hardcover
ISBN 0–333–75236–8 paperback
(*outside North America only*)

You can receive future titles in this series as they are published by placing a
 standing order.
Please contact your bookseller or, in case of difficulty, write to us at the address below
with your name and address, the title of the series and the ISBN quoted above.

Customer Services Department, Macmillan Distribution Ltd, Houndmills, Basingstoke,
Hampshire RG21 6XS, England

Gender

Edited by Anna Tripp

palgrave

Introduction, selection and editorial matter
© Anna Tripp 2000

First published 2000 by
PALGRAVE
Houndmills, Basingstoke, Hampshire RG21 6XS and
175 Fifth Avenue, New York, N.Y. 10010
Companies and representatives throughout the world

PALGRAVE is the new global academic imprint of St. Martin's Press LLC
Scholarly and Reference Division and Palgrave Publishers Ltd (formerly
Macmillan Press Ltd).

ISBN 0-333-77036-6 hardback
ISBN 0-333-77037-4 paperback

This book is printed on paper suitable for recycling and
made from fully managed and sustained forest sources.

A catalogue record for this book is available
from the British Library.

Library of Congress Cataloging-in-Publication Data
Gender / edited by Anna Tripp.
      p. cm.—(Readers in cultural criticism)
   Includes bibliographical references and index.
   ISBN 0-333-77036-6 (cloth)—ISBN 0-333-77037-4 (pbk.)
   1. Sex role. 2. Sex differences. 3. Feminist theory. I. Tripp, Anna. II. Series.

HQ1075 .G425 2000
305.3—dc21
                                                      00-042076

10   9   8   7   6   5   4   3   2   1
09 08 07 06 05 04 03 02 01 00

Printed and bound in Great Britain by Creative Print & Design (Wales), Ebbw Vale

TO MAELON AND TONY HOLYLAND

Contents

General Editor's Preface

Culture is the element we inhabit as subjects.

Culture embraces the whole range of practices, customs and representations of a society. In their rituals, stories and images, societies identify what they perceive as good and evil, proper, sexually acceptable, racially other. Culture is the location of values, and the study of cultures shows how values vary from one society to another, or from one historical moment to the next.

But culture does not exist in the abstract. On the contrary, it is in the broadest sense of the term textual, inscribed in the paintings, operas, sculptures, furnishings, fashions, bus tickets and shopping lists which are the currency of both aesthetic and everyday exchange. Societies invest these artefacts with meanings, until in many cases the meanings are so 'obvious' that they pass for nature. Cultural criticism denaturalises and defamiliarises these meanings, isolating them for inspection and analysis.

The subject is what speaks, or, more precisely, what signifies, and subjects learn in culture to reproduce or to challenge the meanings and values inscribed in the signifying practices of the society that shapes them.

If culture is pervasive and constitutive for us, if it resides in the documents, objects and practices that surround us, if it circulates as the meanings and values we learn and reproduce as good citizens, how in these circumstances can we practise cultural *criticism*, where criticism implies a certain distance between the critic and the culture? The answer is that cultures are not homogeneous; they are not even necessarily coherent. There are always other perspectives, so that cultures offer alternative positions for the subjects they also recruit. Moreover, we have a degree of power over the messages we reproduce. A minor modification changes the script, and may alter the meaning; the introduction of a negative constructs a resistance.

The present moment in our own culture is one of intense debate. Sexual alignments, family values, racial politics, the implications of economic differences are all hotly contested. And positions are taken up not only in explicit discussions at political meetings, on television and in the pub. They are often reaffirmed or challenged implicitly in films and advertisements, horoscopes and lonely-hearts columns. Cultural criticism analyses all these forms in order to assess their hold on our consciousness.

There is no interpretative practice without theory, and the more sophisticated the theory, the more precise and perceptive the reading it makes possible. Cultural theory is as well defined now as it has ever been, and as strongly contested as our social values. There could not, in consequence, be a more exciting time to engage in the theory and practice of Cultural Criticism.

Catherine Belsey
Cardiff University

Acknowledgements

The editor and publishers wish to thank the following for permission to use copyright material:

Catherine Belsey, for 'A Future for Materialist Feminist Criticism' in Valerie Wayne (ed.), *The Matter of Difference: Material Feminist Criticism of Shakespeare*, Harvester/Wheatsheaf (1991), pp. 257–70, by permission of the author; Homi K. Bhabha, for 'Are You a Man or a Mouse?' in Maurice Berger, Brian Wallis and Simon Watson (eds), *Constructing Masculinity* (1995), pp. 127–34. Copyright © 1995, by permission of Routledge, Inc; Judith Butler, for material from Judith Butler, *Bodies That Matter: On the Discursive Limits of 'Sex'* (1993), pp. 223–42, by permission of Routledge, Inc; Diane Elam, for material from Diane Elam, *Feminism and Deconstruction: Ms en Abyme* (1994), pp. 42–58, by permission of Routledge; Anne Fausto-Sterling, for 'How to Build a Man', in Maurice Berger, Brian Wallis and Simon Watson (eds), *Constructing Masculinity* (1995), pp. 127–34. Copyright © 1995, by permission of Routledge, Inc; Stephen Heath, for 'Joan Riviere and the Masquerade' in Victor Burgin, James Donald and Cora Kaplan (eds) *Formations of Fantasy* (1986), pp. 45–61, by permission of Routledge; Chandra Talpade Mohanty, for 'Under Western Eyes: Feminist Scholarship and Colonial Discourses' in Mohanty, Russo and Torres (eds), *Third World Women and the Politics of Feminism* (1991), pp. 51–80, by permission of Indiana University Press; Adrienne Rich, for 'Toward a More Feminist Criticism' from Adrienne Rich, *Blood, Bread, and Poetry: Selected Prose 1979–1985*, Virago (1987), pp. 85–99. Copyright © 1986 by Adrienne Rich, by permission of the author, W. W. Norton & Company, Inc and Virago Press Ltd; Joan Riviere, for 'Womanliness as a Masquerade' in Victor Burgin, James Donald and Cora Kaplan (eds), *Formations of Fantasy* (1986), pp. 35–44, by permission of Routledge; Jacqueline Rose, for material from Jacqueline Rose, *Sexuality in the Field of Vision* (1986), pp. 83–103, by permission of Verso; Jonathan Rutherford, for material from Jonathan Rutherford, *Forever England: Reflections on Masculinity and Empire* (1997), pp. 139–63, by permission of Lawrence & Wishart; Lynne Segal, for material from Lynne Segal, *Slow Motion: Changing Masculinities Changing Men*

(1990), pp. 1–25, by permission of Virago Press Ltd; Virginia Woolf, for material from *A Room of One's Own*, Ch. 2. Copyright © 1929 by Harcourt, Inc and renewed 1957 by Leonard Woolf, by permission of The Society of Authors as the literary representative of the Estate of the author and Harcourt Inc.

Every effort has been made to trace the copyright holders but if any have been inadvertently overlooked the publishers will be pleased to make the necessary arrangement at the first opportunity.

1

Introduction

Anna Tripp

What does it mean to be a woman? What does it mean to be a man? Is there a basic 'male nature' and a basic 'female nature' which remain unchanged throughout human history and across different cultures? If so, what are the defining characteristics of a 'real man' or a 'natural woman'? Or, alternatively, are our notions of 'femininity' or 'masculinity' in fact context-specific and variable, constructed by and circulated within particular cultural formations and signifying practices? If so, what are the processes and mechanisms by which our understandings and experiences of femininity and masculinity are produced, maintained or changed?

The essays collected in this anthology explicitly address these questions, setting them in a range of theoretical and political contexts and presenting a variety of possible responses. However, such questions are by no means limited to the sphere of academic writing. They are at large in our culture – inflecting all fields of activity, representation and enquiry – and the ways in which they have been answered in the past, are being answered at present and might be answered in the future have a crucial bearing on our lives. Moreover, if questions of gender are not explicitly addressed in any given context – at work, in the home, in science, education, law, politics – then assumptions about gender will operate on an unspoken or unconscious level, lurking within and silently shaping our beliefs and behaviour.

GENDER AS ESSENCE OR CONSTRUCT?

Early in 1999 a programme on BBC Radio 4 called *In Our Time* featured a debate between the Darwinian philosopher, Helena Cronin, and the feminist Germaine Greer.[1] Cronin's argument is that there are profound psychological differences between women and men, and that these can be explained by Darwin's theories of evolution. Over evolutionary time, she claims, natural selection has favoured on the one hand 'those men who have competed like mad to get mates' and on the other those women who have been cautious and 'judicious' in their choice of sexual partner. According to Cronin, this means that 'Men are *by nature* more competitive, ambitious, status-conscious,

dedicated, single-minded and persevering than women ... This is a two mil-
lion year-old fact [and] we should accept it.'[2] Here Cronin is articulating
what might be called an *essentialist* model of sexual difference, maintaining
as she does that there are certain ways of thinking and behaving which are
'essentially' manly, and certain ways of thinking and behaving which are
'essentially' womanly. In this model, women and men are deemed to have
innate and distinct characteristics which remain fundamentally unchanged
and unchangeable throughout history and across cultures.

Cronin grounds her arguments in her interpretation of the work of Charles
Darwin, but nineteenth-century science is of course not the only point of
reference for essentialist models of sexual difference. For instance, the Old
Testament defines the destiny of women as follows: 'Unto the woman God
said, "I will greatly multiply thy sorrow and thy conception; in sorrow thou
shalt bring forth children; and thy desire shall be to thy husband and he shall
rule over thee".'[3] If this is what it means to be a woman, then heaven help us.
The woman is not told that her *duty* will be to her husband; she is told that
her *desire* will be to her husband. A duty is an externally imposed obligation
– and might not prove so difficult to resist – but a desire is most often
experienced as something which comes from inside of us, as an intimate
and inextricable part of ourselves. In defining who we are, we often invoke
what we want: our goals and ambitions, our likes and dislikes. In this way,
Genesis presents a god-given definition not just of how a woman is required
to behave, but also of what, in essence, she *wants* and *is*.

Germaine Greer, countering Cronin's essentialist position, proposes a very
different understanding of differences between women and men:

> I ... agree that masculinity is very different from femininity ... but I also
> believe that men work very hard at *creating* masculinisms ... There's a lot
> of aspects of the way they behave which are highly cultural and extremely
> protean, [and] could change pretty quickly ... Things cannot *not* fit with
> biology ... that's obvious ... the point is that culture does its own thing
> with biology, [and] it could have done any one of a number of things.[4]

What Greer does here is separate sex – 'biological' maleness or femaleness –
from gender – signified by the nouns 'masculinity' and 'femininity'. In
Greer's model, gender is understood to be a variable and unstable cultural
construct. The ways in which women and men think, behave and interact,
Greer argues, will often have a great deal more to do with the particular
culture in which they live than with nature, and will vary significantly
from culture to culture and from one period of history to another. Different
cultures interpret so-called biological 'facts' in a variety of different ways: for
example, as Chandra Talpade Mohanty argues in her essay in this anthology, 'that women mother in a variety of societies is not as significant as *the*

value attached to mothering in these societies.[5] In political terms, Cronin's model is a conservative one: if human behaviour and psychology can only be changed significantly by evolution, then we cannot seriously expect to alter either within the space of a human lifetime. Greer's model is more radical and open: human beings are social creatures, endlessly adaptable and inventive – and, if particular constructions of gender are the products of particular cultural circumstances, then constructions of gender are susceptible to political intervention and can change as rapidly as cultures do. As Liz Yorke, another feminist critic, writes:

> Things have changed and are changing in ways that seemed inconceivable, 'unthinkable', even as recently as the sixties. I remind myself that what is 'unthinkable' now may eventually become acceptable ways of thinking for the future – for both women and men.[6]

In this way, a particular cultural context – through its language, vocabularies and signifying practices, through its customs and conventions, through its social structures, institutions and technologies – will encourage certain ways of thinking and behaving and preclude others. And since all of these things are to a greater or lesser extent subject to change, so too are our understandings and experiences of what it means to be women and men.

THE SEX/GENDER DISTINCTION

If it is indeed the case that our understandings of ourselves and the world are enabled and delimited by – amongst other things – the language and vocabularies available to us, it is interesting to note that the analytical category of 'gender', in the sense that Germaine Greer uses it above, only passed into common English usage relatively recently.[7] It was not until the latter part of the twentieth century that it became widely acceptable to make a distinction between 'sex' – denoting anatomical or biological 'maleness' or 'femaleness' – and the term 'gender' – denoting the distinct sets of characteristics culturally ascribed to maleness and femaleness and signified by the adjectives 'masculine' and 'feminine'.[8] Meanings are never stable or static, and a glance at any dictionary which includes etymologies will show that 'gender', like all words, has a long, complex and evolving history, signifying different things at different times (as well as different things at the same time).

For the first two-thirds of the twentieth century, 'gender' was most widely used as a technical term specific to the study of grammar. The 1966 edition of *The Oxford Dictionary of English Etymology* defines it as '(Gram.) any of the three "kinds", masculine, feminine and neuter, of nouns, adjectives, and pronouns'.[9] For example, in French, the gender of the noun *glaçage* (icing) is masculine, while the gender of the noun *patinoire* (ice rink) is feminine. So, until the late 1960s, 'gender' was generally understood to have a fairly narrow and uncontroversial meaning, and, moreover, to have less relevance in English (which does not routinely gender nouns or adjectives) than in other languages.

ROBERT STOLLER: SEX AND GENDER

1968 is treated by many commentators as the year in which a definitive shift took place and the modern meaning of 'gender' emerged in the English language. It was during this year that the American psychoanalyst Robert Stoller published a book called *Sex and Gender*, in which he clearly differentiates between these two terms.[10] In his 'Preface' he makes the crucial claim that:

> [O]ne can speak of the male sex or the female sex, but one can also talk about masculinity and femininity and not necessarily be implying anything about anatomy or physiology. Thus, while sex and gender seem to common sense to be practically synonymous, and in everyday life to be inextricably bound together, one purpose of this study will be to confirm the fact that the two realms (sex and gender) are not at all inevitably bound in anything like a one-to-one relationship, but each may go in its quite independent way.[11]

'Feminine' or 'masculine' forms of behaviour, Stoller contends in relation to various case histories, may have less to do with biological sex than with cultural conventions and conditioning. He argues that 'gender ... [is] primarily culturally determined; that is, learned postnatally ... This cultural process springs from one's society.'[12] In this way, from the late 1960s onwards, it began to be possible to use the term 'gender' to signify all those culturally produced assumptions, expectations, conventions and stereotypes concerning 'appropriate' demeanour and 'normal' behaviour for women and for men.

FEMINISMS

The late 1960s and early 1970s was also the period in which a new wave of Anglo-American feminism gained critical mass, and writers such as Germaine Greer, Ann Oakley and Kate Millett set about theorising and politicising the newly available analytical category of gender.[13] These feminists emphasised not only the cultural construction of gender, but the cultural construction of *gendered inequality*: in other words, the ways in which gender constitutes power relations.[14] Oakley, Millett and Greer all identified the society in which they were living as patriarchal: that is, structured in ways that tend to privilege men's interests over women's interests.

Now as we enter the twenty-first century, it seems undeniable that feminism has made profound differences to the ways in which Western cultures understand gender. However, when talking about feminism, it is also important to recognise that it has never represented a single, unified 'theory of gender'. As Catherine Belsey puts it, 'There are many ways to be a feminist.'[15] Feminism – if it can be referred to in the singular at all – consists of many different theories, practices, perspectives and agendas – and this will be evident from a reading of the diverse selection of feminist essays in this anthology.

FEMINISM, MODERNISM AND POSTMODERNISM

In 1929 Virginia Woolf published her pioneering feminist work, *A Room of One's Own*. Employing the experimental strategies of literary modernism, this is a witty, ironic and exploratory narrative, shuttling between a number of different personae and perspectives and mapped onto a series of allegorical journeys and encounters in 'Oxbridge' and London. The section included in this anthology is entitled 'Women and Fiction', a typically ambiguous signpost, concerned as it is with both women's literary output and the 'fictions' written about women.

Woolf lived and wrote long before a formal distinction between sex and gender was readily available or widely recognised, yet this distinction is in some ways implicit in her argument. Her feminist analysis has distinctly materialist leanings and a keen awareness of the role of history, culture and language in the production of cultural understandings of what it means to be a woman or a man. For example, she is particularly concerned with the differences, both qualitative and quantitative, between men's and women's literary output in the past. These, she argues, have nothing to do with fundamental or essential differences between women and men, but are due to what she calls 'grossly material things'.[16] Women's opportunities and talents are limited and circumscribed, she forcefully asserts, by unequal access to education, careers and political processes, leisure time and adequate living conditions.

In the section anthologised here, the narrator goes into the British Library in search of 'the truth' about women.[17] However, research among the supposedly 'learned' and 'unprejudiced'[18] works in this library reveals that 'the truth about women' is plural, contradictory and ultimately evasive, dispersed through reams of text and years of argument. 'Woman' turns out to be a protean cultural construct, obsessively created and debated within a series of different discourses or 'fictions'.

Woolf analyses variable cultural constructions of 'Woman' from within the context of British modernism. In the latter part of the twentieth century, postmodern theorists have advocated an even more thoroughgoing scepticism towards the existence of universal, transcultural or ahistorical truths and essences: Elizabeth Spelman, for example, asserts that 'the more universal the claim one might hope to make about women...the more likely it is to be false'.[19] Jean-François Lyotard, one of the writers primarily associated with postmodern scepticism, also adds the vital corollary that 'the right to decide what is true is not independent of the right to decide what is just'.[20] Taking this into account, one might begin to suspect that claims regarding 'the truth about women' articulated in the name of science, religion or in other influential discourses might be profoundly political after all, since the power to define a person or group goes hand in hand with the power to control that person or group, in legislating what is and is not appropriate and acceptable behaviour. Gender is an ongoing effect of meanings and definitions culturally produced and circulated, and, crucially, these definitions have very real material consequences in our lives.[21]

GENDER AND BINARY OPPOSITIONS

In modern English usage, it is common to hear women and men described as 'opposite sexes'. This is a linguistic habit which, through repetition, has come to seem natural, but which, some feminist critics have argued, demands closer scrutiny. Why are we 'opposite', as opposed to, say, 'adjacent', or simply 'different'? In the parable of the girl and the boy on the train in her essay 'Gender or Sex?', Diane Elam identifies what she calls a 'binary logic' at work in our understandings of gender, suggesting that 'we satisfy our prescribed gender role more through a knowledge of what we are not than what we are'.[22] From this perspective, gender is not a free-standing identity; it is constructed in relationship, and we come to our understandings of masculinity and femininity through a process of differentiation. One is masculine precisely by not being feminine, and vice versa; thus masculinity must simultaneously repudiate and rely on a notion of femininity as its defining and constitutive difference.

Binary logic, according to the French feminist Hélène Cixous, is a crucial characteristic of Western patriarchal thought, both generating and underpinning gendered power relations.[23] Binarism structures reality into a series of 'either/or' oppositions, for example as active/passive, culture/nature, rational/irrational, public/private. Within each of these oppositions, one term will tend to be privileged over the other, with the subordinate term typically aligned with femininity. Although it is integral to many of our habitual modes of thought and expression, and thus difficult to escape, binary thought can be seen as both reductive and restrictive: it attempts to polarise plurality, complexity and nuance into a simple question of either/or, collapsing a multiplicity of variations into a single opposition. In the light of these considerations, it is not surprising that it has become a primary object-ive of many feminists to destabilise and deconstruct rigid binary construct-ions of gender, the stabilisers of patriarchal power.

RESISTANCE?

Given the ways in which Western patriarchal cultures attempt to normalise or naturalise culturally constructed gender roles, and to fix gender into a rigid binary oppositional structure – and given that these understandings of gender are deeply ingrained in habits of thought and expression (as in the phrases 'a real man' or 'a member of the opposite sex') – in what ways might those involved in radical gender politics go about challenging such constructions?

Most if not all of the writers in this anthology would agree that it is not possible simply to cast off or step outside of cultural constructions of gender. Gender may be a construct, but gender also *constructs us*. In fact, it is possible to argue that our concept of the human subject is always already gendered, and the intelligibility of human subjects depends on their identi-fication with a specific gender: other people are always 'he' or 'she' to us, never 'it'. As Judith Butler puts it in *Bodies That Matter*, 'the "I" neither precedes nor follows the process of . . . gendering but emerges only within and as the matrix of gender relations themselves'.[24] In these ways, gender functions for us as a cultural typology, setting parameters for signification and interpretation, and cultural understandings of gender difference would seem to be inevitably and inextricably present in the ways in which we make sense of ourselves, others and the world in general.

Does this condemn us then to cultural determinism, leaving no room to resist the gender norms imposed on us by our culture? Most of the writers in this anthology tackle this question, either directly or indirectly, and examine ways out of this dilemma. As Woolf shows in her inconclusive search for 'the truth about women', constructions of gender are never singular or fully coherent, and are thus fundamentally unstable.[25] Meaning is never fixed: as we have seen, the term 'gender' means different things at different times and different things at the same time – and the same goes for the meanings of 'feminine' and the meanings of 'masculine'. Thus there always exists within a culture the possibility that these things can and will be interpreted differently. It is the inconsistencies, instabilities and contradictions of the cultural mean-ings we encounter and internalise which can provide the impetus for change.

For example, Joan Riviere's discussion of the dilemmas suffered by pro-fessional women in the early twentieth century demonstrates that conventions of feminine behaviour may at times come into conflict with the demands of other roles played by the same person.[26] It is easy to see that internalised conflict may have negative effects: after all, the living out of contradiction is pathologised in Riviere's case histories. However, in other instances and different contexts this frustration might be channelled in more positive directions, becoming the motivation for political action and analysis: Catherine Belsey argues that one of the primary forces inspiring feminism is 'the anger which is a consequence of those contradictions lived materially as women's experience'.[27]

Neither femininity nor masculinity are fixed, coherent or static constructions. We are none of us simply one thing; we are none of us wholly or exclusively 'feminine' or 'masculine'. Gender is never, so to speak, unadulterated: it is always already inflected and intersected by differences of generation, class, 'race', ethnicity, sexuality and so on. In spite of exasperated complaints from both sexes, women are patently not 'all the same', and neither are men: understandings of femininity and masculinity as homogeneous and fixed binary opposites are not sustainable. Gender differences are inevitably complicated by other differences, and cannot ultimately be separated out from these. It seems an obvious but important fact that not all women are equally oppressed and not all men benefit equally from the arrangements of a patriarchal culture. This is a consideration which some feminists, in their understandable eagerness to find common ground between women, have perhaps failed to take fully into account. It is a problem associated especially with middle-class, liberal, reformist feminists in affluent Western cultures, and one which is addressed in detail by Adrienne Rich and Chandra Talpade Mohanty in their essays here. Both of these writers suggest that, for feminists, the possibilities of communication and solidarity should never be taken for granted, but must be forged, as the outcome of a painstaking attention to and respect for 'the differences among us'.[28]

Rich, Mohanty and others show that the construction of gender is marked by differences *between* cultures and differences *within* cultures. It is also subject to *historical* differences. Woolf's piece, for example, ends on a speculative note, considering the radical transformations that may take place in the lives of women a hundred years into the future. Because social values and realities change from one historical period to another, what is held to be indisputably 'true' about women or men at one point in history may be contested at another. Close attention to historical differences is an immensely productive strategy for feminism: as Gillian Beer puts it, 'we need to be alert to the processes of gender formation and gender change ... we shall better discover our own fixing assumptions if we value the *unlikeness* of the past'.[29] Such an awareness counters the inertia of day-to-day common sense and empowers those engaged in a politics of transformation.

FEMINISM AND PSYCHOANALYSIS

Arguably, feminism and psychoanalysis represent two of the most radical attempts in twentieth-century Western culture to theorise sexual and gender difference – and, over the years, they have had a distinctly uneasy, on–off, love–hate relationship. Certain feminists have angrily rejected psychoanalysis as an insidious instrument of patriarchy; others, however, have sought to re-evaluate and appropriate the strategies and insights of Freudian and post-Freudian theory to aid their analysis of the gendering process to which, in varying ways, all human beings are subjected.

Kate Millett is a persuasive example of the former tendency. In *Sexual Politics* (1971) she denounces Freud's equation of masculinity with activity and femininity with passivity, and pours eloquent scorn on his notion of penis envy, in which the female is seen as destined by her anatomy to experience a sense of lack and inferiority.[30] Three years later Juliet Mitchell countered with a book called *Psychoanalysis and Feminism* in which she argues that psychoanalysis does not have to be seen as *advocating* a patriarchal society, but simply as *describing* one, and can provide a useful analysis of its structures and mechanisms.[31] Shifting Millett's emphasis, Mitchell points to Freud's notion of undifferentiated infant sexuality, arguing that in this way Freud's work allows us to recognise we are not born 'masculine' or 'feminine', nor are we born heterosexual: these things are rather *acquisitions* made by human subjects as they are integrated into a particular type of human culture.

Possibly the single most important aspect of psychoanalytic theory to feminism, however, has been the notion of the unconscious, and the ways in which it undermines rationality, subjectivity and meaning, rendering them inherently unstable. In the early twentieth century – when Freud first became fashionable among Anglophone intellectuals – Virginia Woolf sought to play out in her writing the disturbing effects of the unconscious on orthodox understandings of character and communication; in the second half of the twentieth century, theorists like Jacqueline Rose have developed this line of enquiry with greater hindsight and rigour. It is through the notion of the unconscious that psychoanalysis can provide an effective antidote to cultural determinism and its disempowering assumption that gender norms are inevitably and effectively internalised. Psychoanalysis provides feminism with useful material because it explores the many difficulties and failures of this process, identifying what Rose memorably calls 'a resistance to identity at the very heart of psychic life'.[32] Freudian and post-Freudian psychoanalysis emphasise the ways in which the unconscious divides subjectivity against itself, continually undermining and disrupting any assumption of a unified and stable sexual identity. In these ways, what feminism may have to gain from an alliance with psychoanalysis is the possibility of viewing femininity as neither a set of natural attributes nor as a cultural *fait accompli*, but rather as a laborious and sometimes bungled acquisition.

FEMINISMS: AN INTERIM SUMMARY

Essentialist models of sexual and gender difference (like that articulated by Cronin) argue that women and men have innate and distinct characteristics which are – for those who know how to look – detectable beyond or beneath the distortions and vagaries of culture. For a theorist such as Cronin, political attempts to deny the 'true nature' of either sex (for example, women's 'natural' inclination to settle down and raise a family and men's 'natural' competitiveness and promiscuity) will be doomed to failure. Feminists, however, have sought, in a variety of ways, to contest such understandings of gender. For instance, while essentialists invoke notions of nature and what is 'natural' in order to authorise their positions, others have countered that these very notions of 'nature' and 'the natural' are in fact culturally mediated or constructed, historically variable and ideologically motivated. As Gillian Beer succinctly puts it, '[t]he words "nature" and "natural" are perhaps the most artful in language. They soak up ideology like a sponge'.[33] If a culture can effectively represent a particular mode of behaviour as 'only natural', then this leaves little space for argument or resistance; it is more damning, after all, to be labelled 'unnatural' than simply 'unconventional'. However, what seems to be 'normal', 'natural' or attractive feminine or masculine behaviour in one culture at one particular time may seem strange, even ridiculous, in another context. Jonathan Culler explains that: 'We do have massive evidence that one language makes "natural" or "normal" thoughts that require a special effort in another... Different languages divide up the world differently.'[34] In this way, a close attention to historical, cultural and linguistic difference, such as that advocated and practised by many of the writers in this anthology, has the potentially radical effect of *denaturalising* the constructions of gender we have come to take for granted. Analyses of the specific cultural, psychological and linguistic *processes* by which individual subjects are gendered also help to show that gender is not something we are born with – or even something that can be acquired once and for all – but is rather the effect of a series of ongoing negotiations between subject and context which are never settled or complete. Furthermore, an exploration of the differences and contradictions *within* identity leads us to understand gender as something which can never be stable, coherent or unequivocal – and is thus always open to change.

MASCULINITIES

Feminism is perhaps most centrally concerned with the construction, the nuances and the implications of what it means to be a woman within a specific context in a given culture at a particular historical moment. However, as we have seen, it has also been proposed that gender is not so much an essence – not even so much an identity – as a *relation*. In any individual context, femininity is intelligible through its differences to masculinity, and vice versa. If this is the case, then feminist redefinitions of what it means to be a woman will have a knock-on effect on understandings and experiences of what it means to be a man. Perhaps not surprisingly then, in the last two decades or so, there has been a surge of interest in masculinity as a complex and changing cultural construction. Some of this work on masculinities has been carried out in the service of feminism (such as Lynne Segal's essay in this anthology); some might be seen as complementary to feminism (Homi Bhabha's 'Are You a Man or a Mouse?', for example), while some represents a hostile reaction to what have been seen as feminism's emasculating effects (Jonathan Rutherford discusses this 'backlash' in 'Mr Nice (and Mr Nasty)'). What is clear is that, while feminism has played a pioneering role in the articulation, politicisation and development of questions of gender, the field of enquiry into gender is broader than feminism.

However, even today, an invitation to students to consider the construction of gender in a literary text will often produce a reading of the ways in which the text represents its female characters. There are good reasons for this: while three decades of feminism have given us ample critical equipment to analyse the conventions and constrictions of femininity, arguably we are still much less used to dissecting masculinity as a specific cultural construct. Masculinity has long and often been represented as the human norm – and conventionally masculine qualities (such as vigour, courage, rationality, authority, mastery, independence) have been seen simultaneously as universal 'human' ideals. As Holly Devor puts it in her book *Gender Blending*:

> In patriarchally organised societies, masculine values become the ideological structure of the society as a whole. Masculinity thus becomes 'innately' valuable and femininity serves as a contrapuntal function to delineate and magnify the hierarchical dominance of the masculine.[35]

This point is neatly illustrated in the (now old-fashioned) English phrase 'the world and his wife', where 'the world' is seen as masculine; the masculine is the universal case; the feminine is the particular, the adjunct, the after-thought. 'He' – the masculine pronoun – has in the past been understood to subsume both men and women. In this manner it could be argued that masculinity takes up a great deal more space than femininity, and – at least until recently – has had a 'goes-without-question' clause attached to it. Masculinity has been – much like white skin in most contexts in the West – 'unmarked' and unremarked, simultaneously pervasive and evasive, presented as the standard or universal case.

It is in response to this state of affairs that Homi Bhabha begins his essay in this anthology by stating that '[t]o speak of masculinity in general . . . must be avoided at all costs'.[36] It is only relatively recently that masculinity, like femininity, has been analysed as a complex, plural and protean cultural product, where before it was often taken for granted as something singular and monolithic. A comparison between the three essays on masculinity in this anthology will reveal some of the forms and directions this analysis has taken. At any given historical moment, it seems that understandings and experiences of masculinity are riddled with contradictions and anxieties – contradictions and anxieties distilled in Bhabha's title, 'Are You a Man or a Mouse?'. Masculinity is no more stable, free-standing or internally coherent than femininity: produced through ongoing processes of identification and differentiation, it is continually threatened by that which defines it. As Evelyn, a character in Angela Carter's fascinating 1977 novel *The Passion of New Eve*, learns, 'to be a *man* is not a given condition but a continuous effort'.[37]

THE SEX–GENDER DISTINCTION REVISITED

Since the sex–gender distinction has been put into cultural circulation, its precise nature, relevance and implications have been vigorously disputed. What *is* the relationship between sex and gender? What is the relationship between femaleness and femininity? What is the relationship between maleness and masculinity? For a theorist like Helena Cronin, the former naturally and more or less inevitably entails the latter, whereas for many of the Anglo-American feminists writing from the 1960s onwards, gender was often seen as a pernicious regime of cultural definitions and values imposed upon sexed bodies. Germaine Greer argued, on *In Our Time*, that gender is a culturally and historically variable interpretation of sexual difference. Recently, however, certain theorists have begun to question the clarity and usefulness of the sex–gender distinction. Perhaps sex, far from being a 'given' and stable base onto which the variable constructions of gender are grafted, is itself more protean, more culturally mediated or shaped, and more difficult to isolate from gender than might at first be supposed?

In her hugely influential book *Gender Trouble*, first published in 1990, Judith Butler asks:

> Can we refer to a 'given' sex or a 'given' gender without first inquiring into how sex and/or gender is given, through what means? And what is 'sex'

anyway? Is it natural, anatomical, chromosomal, or hormonal, and how is a feminist critic to assess the scientific discourses which purport to establish such 'facts' for us?[38]

In recent years a number of critics have set out to address these questions. Thomas Laqueur and Suzanne J. Kessler have both done interesting work in this area, as has Anne Fausto-Sterling, whose essay 'How to Build a Man' is included in this anthology.[39] While it is now virtually a truism that gender is 'cultural' and sex is 'biological' and 'anatomical', writers like Kessler and Fausto-Sterling explore the ways in which biology and medicine are themselves activities carried out by women and men whose ways of thinking, modes of expression and institutional practices are enabled and shaped by the pre-existing categories and conventions of their cultural context and historical moment. For example, as Kessler argues, 'doctors make decisions ... on the basis of shared cultural values that are unstated, perhaps even unconscious, and therefore considered objective rather than subjective.'[40] Such decisions, it transpires, may even be surgically imposed upon newborn infants who do not fit neatly into the preconceived categories of 'female' or 'male'. In other words, gender stereotypes inform understandings of sexual difference in medical science, and, in a number of influential but often invisible ways, theory and practice in this field will actualise and perpetuate patriarchal and heterosexual conventions, not simply recognising but also policing and constructing a binary model of sexual difference.

MASQUERADE AND PERFORMATIVITY

Joan Riviere was a contemporary of Freud's, and her essay 'Womanliness as a Masquerade' (1929) became an important point of reference for many theorists of gender in the 1990s. In this essay she discusses case studies of women who, because of the contradictory demands made of them in their social context (for example a demand to be 'feminine' and self-effacing at the same time as a demand to be an articulate, assertive and competent professional), experience anxieties and instabilities of identity. These women, she argues, may put on a show or 'masquerade' of disarming girlishness, in order to defuse perceived disapproval from those around them. She gives an example – unfortunately still recognisable to women 70 years later – of a 'capable housewife' who 'puts on the semblance of a rather uneducated, foolish and bewildered woman' when dealing with builders in her own home.[41] She then goes on to ask how one would distinguish 'between genuine womanliness and the "masquerade"' and comes to the intriguing conclusion that they may be, in fact, 'the same thing'.[42] If womanliness is no more or less than a masquerade, this of course prompts the question of what is *behind* the mask. Riviere gives us a model of feminine identity as an ongoing charade or anxious performance which – though 'real in its effects'[43] – is never firmly grounded, never anything other than precarious. These lines of enquiry have been taken up by late twentieth-century gender theorists – for example by Judith Butler, who, since the beginning of the 1990s, has become extraordinarily influential in this field.

Butler replaces Riviere's notion of masquerade with that of gender as a *performative*, and in so doing rewrites conventional understandings of the sex–gender distinction. She proposes in the preface to her 1993 book, *Bodies That Matter*, that 'there is no prediscursive "sex" that acts as a stable point of reference... in relation to which the cultural construction of gender proceeds... sex is already gender, already constructed... the "materiality" of sex is forcibly produced'.[44] For Butler, 'women' and 'men' no longer function as stable and foundational categories of analysis, pre-existing the cultural imposition of gender. In Diane Elam's concise formulation of Butler's position, 'sex is... the retrospective projection of gender, its fictional origin'.[45] Western patriarchies produce and naturalise the notion of an immutable binary structure called 'sex' which is supposed to predate and underpin culture; thus they designate 'as an *origin* or *cause* those identity categories that are in fact the *effects* of institutions, practices [and] discourses'.[46] From this point of view, sexual identity does not precede gender; a sense of sexual identity is produced and reproduced through the repetitive performance or citation of the codes and conventions of gender in our culture. Being a man or a woman is, as Butler memorably asserts, 'a kind of persistent impersonation that passes as the real'.[47] Sex is 'real-ised' as an effect of discourse and 'cultural performance'.[48]

QUEER THEORY

Western patriarchal cultures tend to imagine masculinity and femininity as a conceptual 'couple', existing in a 'naturally' complementary binary opposition – and gender norms are produced and caught up in what Judith Butler, in her earlier work, calls a 'heterosexual matrix'.[49] The heterosexist and homophobic character of many habitual modes of interpretation, behaviour and expression has been thoroughly and convincingly analysed by lesbian and gay critics over the course of many decades – but, in the 1990s, a new body of work known as queer theory emerged which seemed in some ways to represent a departure from some of the more traditional premises and strategies of lesbian and gay studies.[50] Eve Kosofsky Sedgwick's *The Epistemology of the Closet*[51] and Judith Butler's *Gender Trouble*, both published in 1990, have often been identified as important catalysts – but queer theory also has deep roots in the work of French philosopher Michel Foucault, in particular his 1976 book, *The History of Sexuality, Volume I: An Introduction*, which traces intimate relationships between sexuality and discursive practices, knowledge and power.[52]

In so far as it is possible to generalise, queer theory turns away from gay and lesbian identity politics[53] and extends an anti-essentialist and deconstructive approach from gender to sexuality. As Peter Widdowson and Peter Brooker put it:

> Queer studies 'queries' orthodoxies and promotes or provokes...uncertainties...disrupt[ing] fixed or settled categorisation...[Q]ueer theory seeks...to question all...essentialising tendencies and binary thinking.[54]

For example, queer theory exposes the constructedness and historical specificity of our notions of 'the homosexual' and 'the heterosexual'. It is possible to argue that it was only in the late nineteenth century, with the advent of the pseudo-science of sexology, that the notion of homosexuality was 'invented'. As Joseph Bristow points out:

> Only by the 1890s had sexuality and its variant prefixed forms become associated with types of sexual person and types of erotic attraction. The *Supplement* to the *OED* records that both the words heterosexuality and homosexuality first entered the English language in an 1892 translation of the well-known study, *Psychopathia Sexualis*, by...Richard von Krafft-Ebing.[55]

This is not of course to claim that homosexual practices did not take place before the late 1800s, but the idea of 'the homosexual' – something which one could 'be', and as a term which could explain one's entire identity – did not exist in its modern form before then. Thus queer theory offers an understanding of sexuality not as something god-given, natural or innate, but instead as a series of culturally and historically specific classifications, definitions, moralisations and contestations. Modern Western cultures *produce* a notion of the 'deviant' or 'queer' in order to shore up a sense of heterosexual 'normality', a 'queerness' which the 'straight' must then simultaneously deny and depend on as its constitutive difference. One of queer theory's most effective strategies is to work the contradictions and anxieties inherent in these constructions – exploiting, for example, the way in which, as Butler puts it, 'homosexual desire...panics gender'.[56] In other words, queer theory takes what has been stigmatised by a culture as 'perverse' and uses this as a lever to decentre, deconstruct or 'query' notions of 'the natural' and 'the normal'.

THE FUTURE?

If the identity categories to which people have referred in order to define themselves are seen as lacking essential homogeneity and stable foundations, then where does this leave those involved in radical politics? For example, how can feminists organise around their supposedly common identity as women once the very category 'women' has been deconstructed, revealed as a variable and unstable production characterised by linguistic, cultural and historical difference rather than natural unity? While this state of affairs has produced panic in some quarters, others have welcomed the potential for perhaps unlimited transformation of subjects and societies which this loss of anchorage releases.

Of course, to recognise that gender is a product not of a natural inner essence but of our place within a cultural and symbolic system is only a first step. And since gender plays such an integral part in the formation and intelligibility of subjects, it is not possible simply to transcend or opt out of existing structures of gender and sexual difference: if they are to be changed, they must be changed *from inside*. In other words, we cannot rely on a politics which hopes to 'liberate' a pre-social woman or man presumed to exist somewhere beneath or beyond culture: we must reinvent subjects *within* culture by reimagining existing constructions of sex and gender.

A number of contemporary critics have begun the work of subverting and reimagining the binary structures and 'heterosexual matrix' within which sex and gender are currently produced. Such work attempts to move away from understandings of femininity and masculinity as bipolar identities irrevocably rooted in biological sex, and often places new emphasis on the mutability and blendability of masculinity and femininity. For example, Marjorie Garber has worked on the transgressive effects of bisexuality and cross-dressing, both of which produce what she terms 'category crises' in historical understandings of sex, sexuality and gender. She defines a category crisis as 'a failure of definitional distinction, a borderline that becomes permeable, that permits of border crossings from one (apparently distinct) category to another'.[57] Diane Elam, the author of the final essay in this anthology, invokes scenarios in which 'sex/gender combinations ... sexualities ... [and] sexual differences would proliferate'[58] – and Holly Devor, in her fascinating study *Gender Blending: Confronting the Limits of Duality*, expands on this:

> Members of society might be taught to value adaptability and flexibility rather than obedience to gender roles, so that the most respected and socially valued personality types would be those which were able to make use of any behaviours which served their purposes in any situation. ... Men and women, masculinity and femininity, would be seen as immature stages in the process of reaching a blended gender identity and display.[59]

Speculative and utopian though such thinking is, it remains vitally important to radical gender politics. It gives an exhilarating sense that, however rigid and repressive particular cultural constructions of sex and gender might be, they are always haunted by future possibilities and possible futures.

2

Women and Fiction

Virginia Woolf

The scene, if I may ask you to follow me, was now changed. The leaves were still falling, but in London now, not Oxbridge; and I must ask you to imagine a room, like many thousands, with a window looking across people's hats and vans and motor-cars to other windows, and on the table inside the room a blank sheet of paper on which was written in large letters WOMEN AND FICTION, but no more. The inevitable sequel to lunching and dining at Oxbridge seemed, unfortunately, to be a visit to the British Museum. One must strain off what was personal and accidental in all these impressions and so reach the pure fluid, the essential oil of truth. For that visit to Oxbridge and the luncheon and the dinner had started a swarm of questions. Why did men drink wine and women water? Why was one sex so prosperous and the other so poor? What effect has poverty on fiction? What conditions are necessary for the creation of works of art? – a thousand questions at once suggested themselves. But one needed answers, not questions; and an answer was only to be had by consulting the learned and the unprejudiced, who have removed themselves above the strife of tongue and the confusion of body and issued the result of their reasoning and research in books which are to be found in the British Museum. If truth is not to be found on the shelves of the British Museum, where, I asked myself, picking up a notebook and a pencil, is truth?

Thus provided, thus confident and enquiring, I set out in the pursuit of truth. The day, though not actually wet, was dismal, and the streets in the neighbourhood of the Museum were full of open coal-holes, down which sacks were showering; four-wheeled cabs were drawing up and depositing on the pavement corded boxes containing, presumably, the entire wardrobe of some Swiss or Italian family seeking fortune or refuge or some other desirable commodity which is to be found in the boarding-houses of Bloomsbury in the winter. The usual hoarse-voiced men paraded the streets with plants on barrows. Some shouted; others sang. London was like a workshop. London was like a machine. We were all being shot backwards and forwards on this plain foundation to make some pattern. The British Museum was another department of the factory. The swing-doors swung open; and there one stood under the vast dome, as if one were a thought in the huge bald forehead which is so splendidly encircled by a band of famous names. One went to the counter; one took a slip of paper; one opened a volume of the catalogue, and..... the five dots here indicate five separate minutes of stupefaction, wonder and bewilderment. Have you any notion of how many books are written about women in the course of one year? Have you any notion how many are written by men? Are you aware that you are, perhaps, the most discussed animal in the universe? Here had I come with a notebook and a pencil proposing to spend a morning reading, supposing that at the end of the morning I should have transferred the truth to my notebook. But I should need to be a herd of elephants, I thought, and a wilderness of spiders, desperately referring to the animals that are reputed longest lived and most multitudinously eyed, to cope with all this. I should need claws of steel and beak of brass even to penetrate the husk. How shall I ever find the grains of truth embedded in all this mass of paper? I asked myself, and in despair began running my eye up and down the long list of titles. Even the names of the books gave me food for thought. Sex and its nature might well attract doctors and biologists; but what was surprising and difficult of explanation was the fact that sex – woman, that is to say – also attracts agreeable essayists, light-fingered novelists, young men who have taken the M.A. degree; men who have taken no degree; men who have no apparent qualification save that they are not women. Some of these books were, on the face of it, frivolous and facetious; but many, on the other hand, were serious and prophetic, moral and hortatory. Merely to read the titles suggested innumerable schoolmasters, innumerable clergymen mounting their platforms and pulpits and holding forth with loquacity which far exceeded the hour usually alloted to such discourse on this one subject. It was a most strange phenomenon; and apparently – here I consulted the letter M – one confined to the male sex. Women do not write books about men – a fact that I could not help welcoming with relief, for if I had first to read all that men have written about women, then all that women have written about men, the aloe that flowers once in a hundred years would flower twice before I could set pen to paper. So, making a perfectly arbitrary choice of a dozen volumes or so, I sent my slips of paper to lie in the wire tray, and waited in my stall, among the other seekers for the essential oil of truth.

What could be the reason, then, of this curious disparity, I wondered, drawing cartwheels on the slips of paper provided by the British taxpayer for other purposes. Why are women, judging from this catalogue, so much more interesting to men than men are to women? A very curious fact it seemed, and my mind wandered to picture the lives of men who spend their time in writing books about women; whether they were old or young, married or unmarried, red-nosed or hump-backed – anyhow, it was flattering, vaguely, to feel oneself the object of such attention, provided that it was not entirely bestowed by the crippled and the infirm – so I pondered until all such frivolous thoughts were ended by an avalanche of books sliding down on to the desk in front of me. Now the trouble began. The student who has been trained in research at Oxbridge has no doubt some method of shepherding his question past all distractions till it runs into his answer as a sheep runs into its pen. The student by my side, for instance, who was copying assiduously from a scientific manual, was, I felt sure, extracting pure nuggets of the essential ore every ten minutes or so. His little grunts of satisfaction indicated so much. But if, unfortunately, one has had no training in a university, the question far from being shepherded to its pen flies like a frightened flock hither and thither, helter-skelter, pursued by a whole pack of hounds. Professors, schoolmasters, sociologists, clergymen, novelists, essayists, journalists, men who had no qualification save that they were not women, chased my simple and single question – Why are some women poor? – until it became fifty questions; until the fifty questions leapt frantically into midstream and were carried away. Every page in my notebook was scribbled over with notes. To show the state of mind I was in, I will read you a few of them, explaining that the page was headed quite simply, WOMEN AND POVERTY, in block letters; but what followed was something like this:

Condition in Middle Ages of,
Habits in the Fiji Islands of,
Worshipped as goddesses by,
Weaker in moral sense than,
Idealism of,
Greater conscientiousness of,
South Sea Islanders, age of puberty among,
Attractiveness of,
Offered as sacrifice to,
Small size of brain of,
Profounder sub-consciousness of,
Less hair on the body of,
Mental, moral and physical inferiority of,
Love of children of,
Greater length of life of,
Weaker muscles of,
Strength of affections of,
Vanity of,
Higher education of,
Shakespeare's opinion of,
Lord Birkenhead's opinion of,
Dean Inge's opinion of,

La Bruyère's opinion of,
Dr Johnson's opinion of,
Mr Oscar Browning's opinion of, . . .

Here I drew breath and added, indeed, in the margin, Why does Samuel
Butler say, 'Wise men never say what they think of women'? Wise men never
say anything else apparently. But, I continued, leaning back in my chair and
looking at the vast dome in which I was a single but by now somewhat
harassed thought, what is so unfortunate is that wise men never think the
same thing about women. Here is Pope:

Most women have no character at all.

And here is La Bruyère:

Les femmes sont extrêmes, elles sont meilleures ou pires que les
hommes –

a direct contradiction by keen observers who were contemporary. Are they
capable of education or incapable? Napoleon thought them incapable. Dr
Johnson thought the opposite.[1] Have they souls or have they not souls?
Some savages say they have none. Others, on the contrary, maintain that
women are half divine and worship them on that account.[2] Some sages hold
that they are shallower in the brain; others that they are deeper in the
consciousness. Goethe honoured them; Mussolini despises them. Wherever
one looked men thought about women and thought differently. It was
impossible to make head or tail of it all, I decided, glancing with envy at
the reader next door who was making the neatest abstracts, headed often
with an A or a B or a C, while my own notebook rioted with the wildest
scribble of contradictory jottings. It was distressing, it was bewildering, it
was humiliating. Truth had run through my fingers. Every drop had
escaped.

I could not possibly go home, I reflected, and add as a serious contribution to the study of women and fiction that women have less hair on
their bodies than men, or that the age of puberty among the South Sea
Islanders is nine – or is it ninety? – even the handwriting had become in
its distraction indecipherable. It was disgraceful to have nothing more
weighty or respectable to show after a whole morning's work. And if I could
not grasp the truth about W. (as for brevity's sake I had come to call her) in the
past, why bother about W. in the future? It seemed pure waste of time to
consult all those gentlemen who specialise in woman and her effect on whatever it may be – politics, children, wages, morality – numerous and learned as
they are. One might as well leave their books unopened.

But while I pondered I had unconsciously, in my listlessness, in my desperation, been drawing a picture where I should, like my neighbour, have been writing a conclusion. I had been drawing a face, a figure. It was the face and the figure of Professor von X engaged in writing his monumental work entitled *The Mental, Moral, and Physical Inferiority of the Female Sex*. He was not in my picture a man attractive to women. He was heavily built; he had a great jowl; to balance that he had very small eyes; he was very red in the face. His expression suggested that he was labouring under some emotion that made him jab his pen on the paper as if he were killing some noxious insect as he wrote, but even when he had killed it that did not satisfy him; he must go on killing it; and even so, some cause for anger and irritation remained. Could it be his wife, I asked, looking at my picture? Was she in love with a cavalry officer? Was the cavalry officer slim and elegant and dressed in astrakhan? Had he been laughed at, to adopt the Freudian theory, in his cradle by a pretty girl? For even in his cradle the professor, I thought, could not have been an attractive child. Whatever the reason, the professor was made to look very angry and very ugly in my sketch, as he wrote his great book upon the mental, moral and physical inferiority of women. Drawing pictures was an idle way of finishing an unprofitable morning's work. Yet it is in our idleness, in our dreams, that the submerged truth sometimes comes to the top. A very elementary exercise in psychology, not to be dignified by the name of psycho-analysis, showed me, on looking at my notebook, that the sketch of the angry professor had been made in anger. Anger had snatched my pencil while I dreamt. But what was anger doing there? Interest, confusion, amusement, boredom – all these emotions I could trace and name as they succeeded each other throughout the morning. Had anger, the black snake, been lurking among them? Yes, said the sketch, anger had. It referred me unmistakably to the one book, to the one phrase, which had roused the demon; it was the professor's statement about the mental, moral and physical inferiority of women. My heart had leapt. My cheeks had burnt. I had flushed with anger. There was nothing specially remarkable, however foolish, in that. One does not like to be told that one is naturally the inferior of a little man – I looked at the student next me – who breathes hard, wears a ready-made tie, and has not shaved this fortnight. One has certain foolish vanities. It is only human nature, I reflected, and began drawing cartwheels and circles over the angry professor's face till he looked like a burning bush or a flaming comet – anyhow, an apparition without human semblance or significance. The professor was nothing now but a faggot burning on the top of Hampstead Heath. Soon my own anger was explained and done with; but curiosity remained. How explain the anger of the professors? Why were they angry? For when it came to analysing the impression left by these books there was always an element of heat. This heat took many forms; it showed itself in satire, in sentiment, in curiosity, in reprobation. But there was another element which was often present and could not immediately be identified. Anger, I called it. But it was anger that had gone underground and mixed itself with all kinds of other emotions. To judge from its odd effects, it was anger disguised and complex, not anger simple and open.

Whatever the reason, all these books, I thought, surveying the pile on the desk, are worthless for my purposes. They were worthless scientifically, that is to say, though humanly they were full of instruction, interest, boredom, and very queer facts about the habits of the Fiji Islanders. They had been written in the red light of emotion and not in the white light of truth. Therefore they must be returned to the central desk and restored each to his own cell in the enormous honeycomb. All that I had retrieved from that morning's work had been the one fact of anger. The professors – I lumped them together thus – were angry. But why, I asked myself, having returned the books, why, I repeated, standing under the colonnade among the pigeons and the prehistoric canoes, why are they angry? And, asking myself this question, I strolled off to find a place for luncheon. What is the real nature of what I call for the moment their anger? I asked. Here was a puzzle that would last all the time that it takes to be served with food in a small restaurant somewhere near the British Museum. Some previous luncher had left the lunch edition of the evening paper on a chair, and, waiting to be served, I began idly reading the headlines. A ribbon of very large letters ran across the page. Somebody had made a big score in South Africa. Lesser ribbons announced that Sir Austen Chamberlain was at Geneva. A meat axe with human hair on it had been found in a cellar. Mr Justice —— commented in the Divorce Courts upon the Shamelessness of Women. Sprinkled about the paper were other pieces of news. A film actress had been lowered from a peak in California and hung suspended in mid-air. The weather was going to be foggy. The most transient visitor to this planet, I thought, who picked up this paper could not fail to be aware, even from this scattered testimony, that England is under the rule of a patriarchy. Nobody in their senses could fail to detect the dominance of the professor. His was the power and the money and the influence. He was the proprietor of the paper and its editor and sub-editor. He was the Foreign Secretary and the Judge. He was the cricketer; he owned the racehorses and the yachts. He was the director of the company that pays two hundred per cent to its shareholders. He left millions to charities and colleges that were ruled by himself. He suspended the film actress in mid-air. He will decide if the hair on the meat axe is human; he it is who will acquit or convict the murderer, and hang him, or let him go free. With the exception of the fog he seemed to control everything. Yet he was angry. I knew that he was angry by this token. When I read what he wrote about women I thought, not of what he was saying, but of himself. When an arguer argues dispassionately he thinks only of the argument; and the reader cannot help thinking of the argument too. If he had written dispassionately about women, had used indisputable proofs to establish his argument and had shown no trace of wishing that the result should be one thing rather than another, one would not have been angry either. One would have accepted the fact, as one accepts the fact that a pea is green or a canary yellow. So be it, I should have said. But I had been angry because he was angry. Yet it seemed absurd, I thought, turning over the evening paper, that a man with all this power should be angry. Or is anger, I wondered, somehow, the familiar, the attendant sprite on power? Rich people, for example, are often angry because they suspect that the poor want to seize their wealth. The professors, or patriarchs, as it might be more accurate to call them, might be angry for that reason partly, but partly for one that lies a little less obviously on the surface. Possibly they were not 'angry' at all; often, indeed, they were admiring, devoted, exemplary in the relations of private life. Possibly when the professor insisted a little too emphatically upon the inferiority of women, he was concerned not with their inferiority, but with his own superiority. That was what he was protecting rather hot-headedly and with too much emphasis, because it was a jewel to him of the rarest price. Life for both sexes – and I looked at them, shouldering their way along the pavement – is arduous, difficult, a perpetual struggle. It calls for gigantic courage and strength. More than anything, perhaps, creatures of illusion as we are, it calls for confidence in oneself. Without self-confidence we are as babes in the cradle. And how can we generate this imponderable quality, which is yet so invaluable, most quickly? By thinking that other people are inferior to oneself. By feeling that one has some innate superiority – it may be wealth, or rank, a straight nose, or the portrait of a grandfather by Romney – for there is no end to the pathetic devices of the human imagination – over other people. Hence the enormous importance to a patriarch who has to conquer, who has to rule, of feeling that great numbers of people, half the human race indeed, are by nature inferior to himself. It must indeed be one of the chief sources of his power. But let me turn the light of this observation on to real life, I thought. Does it help to explain some of those psychological puzzles that one notes in the margin of daily life? Does it explain my astonishment of the other day when Z, most humane, most modest of men, taking up some book by Rebecca West and reading a passage in it, exclaimed, 'The arrant feminist! She says that men are snobs!' The exclamation, to me so surprising – for why was Miss West an arrant feminist for making a possibly true if uncomplimentary statement about the other sex? – was not merely the cry of wounded vanity; it was a protest against some infringement of his power to believe in himself. Women have served all these centuries as looking-glasses possessing the magic and delicious power of reflecting the figure of man at twice its natural size. Without that power probably the earth would still be swamp and jungle. The glories of all our wars would be unknown. We should still be scratching the outlines of deer on the remains of mutton bones and bartering flints for sheep skins or whatever simple ornament took our unsophisticated taste. Supermen and Fingers of Destiny would never have existed. The Czar and the Kaiser would never have worn crowns or lost them. Whatever may be their use in civilised societies, mirrors are essential to all violent and heroic action. That is why Napoleon and Mussolini both insist so emphatically upon the inferiority of women, for if they were not inferior, they would cease to enlarge. That serves to explain in part the necessity that women so often are to men. And it serves to explain how restless they are under her criticism; how impossible it is for her to say to them this book is bad, this picture is bad, this picture is feeble, or whatever it may be, without giving far more pain and rousing far more anger than a man would do who gave the same criticism. For if she begins to tell the truth, the figure in the looking-glass shrinks; his fitness for life is diminished. How is he to go on giving judgement, civilising natives, making laws, writing books, dressing up and speechifying at banquets, unless he can see himself at breakfast and at dinner at least twice the size he really is? So I reflected, crumbling my bread and stirring my coffee and now and again looking at the people in the street. The looking-glass vision is of supreme importance because it charges the vitality; it stimulates the nervous system. Take it away and man may die, like the drug fiend deprived of his cocaine. Under the spell of that illusion, I thought, looking out of the window, half the people on the pavement are striding to work. They put on their hats and coats in the morning under its agreeable rays. They start the day confident, braced, believing themselves desired at Miss Smith's tea party; they say to themselves as they go into the room, I am the superior of half the people here, and it is thus that they speak with that self-confidence, that self-assurance, which have had such profound consequences in public life and lead to such curious notes in the margin of the private mind.

But these contributions to the dangerous and fascinating subject of the psychology of the other sex – it is one, I hope, that you will investigate when you have five hundred a year of your own – were interrupted by the necessity of paying the bill. It came to five shillings and nine pence. I gave the waiter a ten-shilling note and he went to bring me change. There was another ten-shilling note in my purse; I noticed it, because it is a fact that still takes my breath away – the power of my purse to breed ten-shilling notes automatically. I open it and there they are. Society gives me chicken and coffee, bed and lodging, in return for a certain number of pieces of paper which were left me by an aunt, for no other reason than that I share her name.

My aunt, Mary Beton, I must tell you, died by a fall from her horse when she was riding out to take the air in Bombay. The news of my legacy reached me one night about the same time that the act was passed that gave votes to women. A solicitor's letter fell into the post-box and when I opened it I found that she had left me five hundred pounds a year for ever. Of the two – the vote and the money – the money, I own, seemed infinitely the more important. Before that I had made my living by cadging odd jobs from newspapers, by reporting a donkey show here or a wedding there; I had earned a few pounds by addressing envelopes, reading to old ladies, making artificial flowers, teaching the alphabet to small children in a kindergarten. Such were the chief occupations that were open to women before 1918. I need not, I am afraid, describe in any detail the hardness of the work, for you know perhaps women who have done it; nor the difficulty of living on the money when it was earned, for you may have tried. But what still remains with me as a worse infliction than either was the poison of fear and bitterness which those days bred in me. To begin with, always to be doing work that one did not wish to do, and to do it like a slave, flattering and fawning, not always necessarily perhaps, but it seemed necessary and the stakes were too great to run risks; and then the thought of that one gift which it was death to hide – a small one but dear to the possessor – perishing and with it my self, my soul, – all this became like a rust eating away the bloom of the spring, destroying the tree at its heart. However, as I say, my aunt died; and whenever I change a ten-shilling note a little of that rust and corrosion is rubbed off; fear and bitterness go. Indeed, I thought, slipping the silver into my purse, it is remarkable, remembering the bitterness of those days, what a change of temper a fixed income will bring about. No force in the world can take from me my five hundred pounds. Food, house and clothing are mine forever. Therefore not merely do effort and labour cease, but also hatred and bitterness. I need not hate any man; he cannot hurt me. I need not flatter any man; he has nothing to give me. So imperceptibly I found myself adopting a new attitude towards the other half of the human race. I was absurd to blame any class or any sex, as a whole. Great bodies of people are never responsible for what they do. They are driven by instincts which are not within their control. They too, the patriarchs, the professors, had endless difficulties, terrible drawbacks to contend with. Their education had been in some ways as faulty as my own. It had bred in them defects as great. True, they had money and power, but only at the cost of harbouring in their breasts an eagle, a vulture, for ever tearing the liver out and plucking at the lungs – the instinct for possession, the rage for acquisition which drives them to desire other people's fields and goods perpetually; to make frontiers and flags; battleships and poison gas; to offer up their own lives and their children's lives. Walk through the Admiralty Arch (I had reached that monument), or any other avenue given up to trophies and cannon, and reflect upon the kind of glory celebrated there. Or watch in the spring sunshine the stockbroker and the great barrister going indoors to make money and more money and more money when it is a fact that five hundred pounds a year will keep one alive in the sunshine. These are unpleasant instincts to harbour, I reflected. They are bred of the conditions of life; of the lack of civilisation, I thought, looking at the statue of the Duke of Cambridge, and in particular at the feathers in his cocked hat, with a fixity that they have scarcely ever received before. And, as I realised these drawbacks, by degrees fear and bitterness modified themselves into pity and toleration; and then in a year or two, pity and toleration went, and the greatest release of all came, which is freedom to think of things in themselves. That building, for example, do I like it or not? Is that picture beautiful or not? Is that in my opinion a good book or a bad? Indeed my aunt's legacy unveiled the sky to me, and substituted for the large and imposing figure of a gentleman, which Milton recommended for my perpetual adoration, a view of the open sky.

So thinking, so speculating I found my way back to my house by the river. Lamps were being lit and an indescribable change had come over London since the morning hour. It was as if the great machine, after labouring all day had made with our help a few yards of something very exciting and beautiful – a fiery fabric flashing with red eyes, a tawny monster roaring with hot breath. Even the wind seemed flung like a flag as it lashed the houses and rattled the hoardings.

In my little street, however, domesticity prevailed. The house painter was descending his ladder; the nursemaid was wheeling the perambulator carefully in and out back to nursery tea; the coal-heaver was folding his empty sacks on top on each other; the woman who keeps the greengrocer's shop was adding up the day's takings with her hands in red mittens. But so engrossed was I with the problem you have laid upon my shoulders that I could not see even these usual sights without referring them to one centre. I thought how much harder it is now than it must have been even a century ago to say which of these employments is the higher, the more necessary. Is it better to be a coal-heaver or a nursemaid; is the charwoman who has brought up eight children of less value to the world than the barrister who has made a hundred thousand pounds? It is useless to ask such questions; for nobody can answer them. Not only do the comparative values of charwomen and lawyers rise and fall from decade to decade, but we have no rods with which to measure them even as they are at the moment. I had been foolish to ask my professor to furnish me with 'indisputable proofs' of this or that in his argument about women. Even if one could state the value of any one gift at the moment, those values will change; in a century's time very possibly they will have changed completely. Moreover, in a hundred years, I thought, reaching my own doorstep, women will have ceased to be the protected sex. Logically they will take part in all the activities and exertions that were once denied them. The nursemaid will heave coal. The shopwoman will drive an engine. All assumptions founded on the facts observed when women were the protected sex will have disappeared – as, for example (here a squad of soldiers marched down the street), that women and clergymen and gardeners live longer than other people. Remove that protection, expose them to the same exertions and activities, make them soldiers and sailors and engine-drivers and dock labourers, and will not women die off so much younger, so much quicker, than men that one will say, 'I saw a woman to-day', as one used to say, 'I saw an aeroplane'. Anything may happen when womanhood has ceased to be a protected occupation, I thought, opening the door. But what bearing has all this upon the subject of my paper, Women and Fiction? I asked, going indoors.

3

A Future for Materialist Feminist Criticism?

Catherine Belsey

I

I am delighted, if slightly unnerved, to find myself classified as a materialist feminist critic. This new identity seems more significant, more challenging and above all more collective than being a feminist critic with materialist inclinations or, worse, what I feared I was, a feminist fumbling with and puzzled by questions about the materiality of culture and cultural history. But the readiness with which we reach for categories can be worrying: classification is dangerous to the degree that it creates an illusion of clarity, and seems at a stroke to do away with the fumbling and the puzzles. For that reason, it seems important to explore the implications of my new-found identity and feminism's latest political category.

What [. . .] is materialist feminism? What is materialist feminist criticism? Or, more politically, less essentially, what might they be? What might we make them, make out of them?

The now classic essay by Judith Newton and Deborah Rosenfelt emphasises the repudiation of idealism that characterises materialist feminism. Not quite conceding that 'materialist' is a euphemism for the unacceptable, unspeakable 'Marxist', but not quite denying it either, Newton and Rosenfelt emphasise materialist feminism's concern with the social and the economic, as opposed to the purely psychological, and with historical difference, as opposed to the universal and essential categories of 'woman' or 'patriarchy'.[1] Idealism fails to take account of the power of social class and social institutions to determine differences between women, as well as between women and men. It fails to do justice to the different forms of oppression which exist at specific historical moments. Middle-class feminism has had to come to terms with its own idealist tendencies, evident in its failure to engage the commitment of working-class women; white, western feminism is gradually learning to listen to black women and women of colour, whose oppressions are also culturally, historically and economically

29

specific. Materialism stresses the specificity of struggle because it attends to the social and economic conditions which both permit and promote conflicts of interest. [...]

II

But materialism as Newton and Rosenfelt define it is not concerned exclusively with the economy. In Marxism, too, since Althusser, 'economism' – belief that the economy is the sole or final determinant of history – has been regarded as unduly limiting. Althusser's famous concept of 'determination in the last instance', however precarious, was an effort to overcome the reductiveness of some Marxist readings of history, a reductiveness that Marx himself did not share. In the end Althusser's work probably generated more questions than anwers, but the incisiveness of the questions he posed made it impossible to return to an economistic innocence. In Marxist criticism, the days when the truth of the text could be read off from the author's class position had gone for good. The lived experience of individuals was no longer seen as directly determined by their place in the relations of production. On the contrary, individual experience was understood to be the complex effect of a number of interacting forces, among them culture, in the broadest sense of that term. Culture, itself a complex phenomenon, was not independent of the economy, but it was not merely an expression of it either. Resident in what was thinkable at a specific historical moment, culture was now a material practice. And it followed that from now on the categories of 'experience' and 'meaning' and 'mode of address' would be understood to be within the range of concerns of a materialist analysis.

Materialist feminism takes advantage of this theoretical development, and in consequence makes possible a *rapprochement* in theory that feminists have surely never doubted in practice. Much work in feminism has been concerned with the role of language in reinforcing patriarchy and keeping women in their (sexual, domestic, subordinate) place. Studies of he-man vocabulary, of gender-differentiated forms of address, and differential terms of abuse and praise, revealed consistent asymmetries which reproduced the inequalities of power between the sexes. The prevalence of this work in the seventies in particular made it possible for hardline Marxists to sneer at the illusion that power was purely discursive or that oppression was merely a matter of language. But those words, 'purely' and 'merely', give the whole game away. To privilege the material-as-economic over meaning and culture is simply to reaffirm, by reversing it, the conventional idealist opposition between consciousness and the 'real' world.

At least since the seventeenth century, women who have written in protest about the injustices of a male-dominated society have recognised the social construction of gender difference. How else, after all, can we account for our continued subordination? If it is not natural, and therefore inevitable, it must be cultural, an effect of visual images, of social and educational processes, of differential ways of talking to little girls and little boys, of definitions internalised and *lived*. We have all learned to read these signifying practices from the earliest age. Culture exists, in a word, as meanings. But the cultural meanings of man and woman, experienced at the level of consciousness, have also been lived precisely as material practices; not only as rape and violence, but as the slower, more tedious and more insidious oppression of women's bodies by regimes of beauty, by corsetry and crippling footwear, by marital availability, domestic labour and continual childbirth.

These differential cultural meanings, and the modes of address which naturalise the power relations between men and women, are learned, but learned so young that they seem transparent. They seem so, that is, until they come into contradiction with other cultural meanings; the 'rights', for instance, of the individual, regardless of sex, to life, liberty and the pursuit of happiness. Feminism is born of the anger which is a consequence of those contradictions lived materially as women's experience.

The proposition that 'experience' is an effect and not an origin, a cultural construct and not the source of truth, could presumably only be doubted by women whose commitment to feminism has never wavered for a moment, or who have simply not yet lived very long. To have lived long enough to have been an adolescent in the fifties is for many of us to have experienced in the deepest areas of our identity a yearning to wear circular skirts, tight, wide belts and three-inch heels (however inappropriate any of this might have been in our own specific instances). For my part it is also to have experienced fantasies of myself as an earth-mother, working at a trestle table to produce apple pies that would gratify hordes of rosy-cheeked and smiling children. Mercifully, in my case it is at the same time to have been sent to a girl's school that firmly regarded such notions as unmitigated nonsense, and to a women's college where it had apparently never occurred to anyone that a rational human being could think of higher education as the prerogative of men. If these contradictions led to difficulties in later life, they did at least allow me to account in theoretical terms for my experimental transition from flared jeans as the only imaginable clothing to flared jeans as the most hideous garment ever devised. And if, to complete the list of contradictions, I invoke my experience to provide evidence that experience is not reliable as a source of knowledge, I do so only in order to suggest that whether we can learn from experience depends on what we make of it, on what theories we bring to bear on it in order to make it make sense, on how we make it produce a knowledge for us.

III

If materialist feminism treats experience as the location of cultural meanings, and if it regards meaning as a material practice, it necessarily acknowledges the importance of literary criticism in the production of feminist analysis and feminist cultural history. Fiction is a crucial site of cultural meaning in its political and historical difference. If the meaning of woman is not an unchanging and universal essence but a cultural construct, feminism moves and alters with and between cultures. Most of the societies we know about have been decisively (though in diverse ways) patriarchal, and in consequence woman has been the difference that specifies the limits – and the limitations – of man. Shakespeare's culture is no exception, and Shakespeare's plays reveal with great subtlety the shifts that language is put to in defence of a Renaissance masculinity which so engrosses meaning to itself that it constantly risks the exclusion of its defining other.

It is the figure of Hamlet who so insistently worries at the question, 'What is a man?' (IV. iv. 33),[2] but perhaps *Macbeth* is the play that struggles most resolutely to produce an answer. In *Macbeth* a man is at various moments daring, not a coward (I. vii. 47–51), humane and not a regicide (I. vii. 46–7); he is human, a part of nature, properly daunted by the supernatural (III. iv. 99–103, 107–8); he is violent (IV. iii. 220); he is also capable of human feeling, tears (IV. iii. 221). The definitions and redefinitions lay claim to include nearly all human-kindness in their scope, so that only a tiny, domestic corner is left for the proper, admissible, socially acceptable meaning of woman.

Woman means mother. It means Lady Macduff playing innocently with her son, engaging and vulnerable, and only marginally less naïve than the child she is unable to protect (IV. ii. 30–85). It means breasts and milk (I. v. 44–5) and giving suck (I. vii. 54–5), all of them inevitably and hideously repudiated by a woman who wants to intervene in the public world of history. And the play lays bare the tragic consequences of this system of differences – in the figure of Lady Macbeth unsexed and driven mad, in Macbeth manly and ultimately despairing, and finally in Macduff fulfilling the requirements of *his* manhood, by ominously reiterating Macbeth's own initial display of masculinity, as he too presents the state with the severed head of a traitor.

Macbeth charts the disintegration of a culture which is haunted by images of women who will not stay in place: women with beards, in possession of forbidden knowledge, who vanish into air, and who refuse to confine themselves to the single, narrow meaning that difference allots to them at a specific cultural and historical moment. It displays a world where no earthly power can hold the meaning of woman in its patriarchally legitimated place, where the signified breaks free of its moorings and shows itself unfixed, differed and deferred by a signifier which cannot master it. The play magnificently demonstrates the instabilities of a patriarchy which confines woman to motherhood and promises to man everything else that it means to be human.

IV

Since culture is a material practice, and since literary criticism is a component part of culture, it follows that feminist criticism is itself a cultural phenomenon. Feminist criticism cannot in these circumstances be defined in advance, identified in its essential nature eternally and universally, sought out in earlier epochs and recognised in its unchanging correctness. Feminist criticism takes a position at and in relation to a specific cultural and historical moment. And in that sense it is necessarily a product of its own present. At the same time, it is also an intervention in the power relations which prevail at that present, and in that sense feminist criticism is inevitably political.

Our present is postmodern. That is to say, it participates in the crisis of epistemology which has informed western culture since the aftermath of the Second World War.[3] Both the Holocaust and Hiroshima produced a crisis of confidence in the Enlightenment version of history as a single narrative of the progressive enfranchisement of reason and truth. Where in these hideous episodes, and where in the subsequent squaring up of the superpowers, equipped with their apocalyptic arsenals, were reason and truth to be found? Instead, two hundred years after the Enlightenment prevailed in the West, history was seen to be an effect of conflicting interests after all, but interests defined on all sides as absolute certainties.

The postmodern condition is characterised in consequence by a deep distrust of absolutes, a scepticism about truth, and what Lyotard calls 'incredulity toward metanarratives'.[4] Postmodernity calls into question the knowledges and the histories produced by the Enlightenment. It doubts those humanist ways of interpreting the world and the past which have promoted Man as the hero of history, and thus served to legitimate existing forms of domination. The postmodern undermines rationalist and empiricist modes of knowing, and therefore denaturalises the supremacy of the free West. And, most important for feminists, on all those accounts it dethrones masculinity.

It would appear, therefore, that the postmodern is precisely the condition of the most recent flowering of feminist analysis, that feminism and postmodernism share a scepticism which is both epistemological and political. The Enlightenment commitment to truth and reason, we can now recognise, has meant historically a single truth and a single rationality, which have conspired in practice to legitimate the subordination of black people, the non-Western world, women: liberal Enlightenment history, a story of the emancipation of the people, has in practice neglected the emancipation of black people, the non-western world, women. None of these groups has any political interest in clinging to the values which have consistently under-valued *them*. The plurality of the postmodern, by contrast, discredits supre-macism on the part of any single group. It celebrates difference of all kinds, but divorces difference from power. Postmodernism is in all these senses the ally of feminism.

Nevertheless, it has been argued that feminism and postmodernism are inevitable enemies, that feminism itself is precisely an impossibility in our postmodern condition. In *Gynesis*, her brilliant discussion of the discursive allocation of the feminine, the putting into discourse of woman, Alice Jardine makes a strong case for the incompatibility of feminism and the postmodern. Her argument is that insofar as feminism is a commitment to Woman, to the discovery of the truth about Woman, the uncovering of her real, authentic self, feminism refuses to take account of the postmodern problematisation of universal truth. It merely reproduces the founding humanist move, replacing Man with Woman, as humanism crucially replaced God with Man. And in so far as feminist criticism is about women characters in fiction, or about women writers, the postmodern undermines its deepest commitments. When postmodern writing calls into question the whole concept of character, and poststructuralist criticism proclaims the death of the author, what tasks remain for feminist critics? What can we do with our denunciations of female stereotypes in fiction, when the truth about women with which we contrast them no longer seems to hold? And what becomes of feminist history in a world where we have lost our faith in the grand historical narrative, complete with virtuous and heroic protagonists who carry forward a single struggle towards a defined and shared ideal which is also a closure, the end, in every sense, of history?[5]

I do not believe that feminism is incompatible with the postmodern. There are forms of feminism that attribute to unchanging Woman a single history, which is one of unremitting struggle to break or to evade the oppressions of patriarchy. There are modes of feminist criticism that are wholly Woman-centred, which isolate women writers, are content to discuss female char-acters or depend on a contrast between fictional stereotypes and the truth about women. And it is important to recognise that we may be able to learn something from all of them. But a materialist feminism might, I believe, differentiate itself from them, is indeed compelled to do so by the logic of its own recognition of the materiality, which is to say in this instance the historicity, of culture. Feminism is above all about relations of difference. Its concern is with gender relations which are also power relations. Femin-ism is a politics, and its modes of resistance are as protean as the patriar-chal practices it contests. Resistance is always a relation of difference, a differentiating relation, and the politics of feminism works in the gaps difference produces, in the interstices between specific operations of power and submission.

Woman in patriarchy is a difference and feminism is a commitment to that difference – and at the same time to a separation of difference from power. Woman is no more a transcultural essence than Man: the two terms are interlinked and interdependent. The feminist protest is about power, not anatomy; it is about specific struggles, not a universal human condition. Materialist feminism points out that historically difference has implied domination, and that the subordination of women has no grounding in nature, or indeed in anything other than patriarchal appropriations of control in the service of self-interest.

Patriarchal power is not an essence either: it is not singular or constant or unalterable.[6] Feminist histories tell of changes in gender relations, not all of them either advances or retreats, losses or victories. On the contrary, feminism records a series of specific stories (the *petits récits* of Lyotard's *Postmodern Condition*), which recount false starts, duplicities and betrayals, as well as gains which turn out to present more problems than they solve. I think, for example, and in no particular order, of witchcraft, the advent of the contraceptive pill and the sexual revolution of the sixties, the reign of Queen Elizabeth I, and early psychoanalysis, with its pre-eminent attention to women. Are these episodes gains or losses in the feminist struggle? How could we classify them in a single grand narrative of emancipation, complete with heroic conquests and specified goals? Do they not each in their turn incur resistances? And how would we classify these? Feminism at any specific moment invades and occupies the terrain between domination and subordination, but the terrain itself is constantly shifting and is often uncertainly defined. Many of the stories feminism recounts lack the happy *obviousness* which would characterise history as one grand romance, with a single virtuous figure at its centre, remorselessly confronting dangers and defeating dragons.

Feminism is first and foremost a politics: and that means taking up a position. But feminism in its current mode is also a constitutive element of our postmodern condition: and that means recognising plurality, acknowledging that there are many ways to be a feminist. A materialist feminism, acknowledging its own historical specificity, recognises its postmodern location and in consequence endorses and incites heterogeneity. Feminist politics may take different forms, may be implemented in a range of different practices, and this difference can be perceived as a strength and not a weakness. Unlike some other kinds of radical politics, feminism has no need to be forever defining and delimiting its territory, purifying its doctrines, policing the edges of truth and denouncing heresy. Feminism is a commitment, but not in my view a commitment to an essence; it tells stories, but not a single history of vice and virtue locked in perpetual opposition.

Materialist feminist history is supple, subtle and complex: it has no place for a unitary and univocal metanarrative.

Equally, our readings of texts are supple, subtle and complex. The postmodern attends not only to the plurality of possible practices, including reading practices, but also to the heterogeneity of the text itself. Within the *Macbeth* I have already outlined there resides a second, related but distinct, network of meanings, which offers another signified for Renaissance patriarchy, and links it with Renaissance humanism, to display something of the oppression inscribed in that ostensibly liberating moment. In *Macbeth* it is the difference within the term *man*, and the corresponding difference within the text, which generate the tragedy. If *woman* means mother and giving suck, as I have suggested, it is nonetheless Macbeth himself who is too full of the milk of human kindness (I. v. 14). In that concession, Lady Macbeth identifies her husband's weakness and the audience recognises his humanity. Human kindness, humane as well as generically human, metaphorically includes milk, incorporating the difference that specifies woman and so defines man. Macbeth, we are to understand at this moment, is everything a human being might be, allowing after all no place, no specificity of any kind, for woman. The murder of the unresisting, unprotesting, unoffending Lady Macduff might almost be read as an emblem of that encroachment, as manhood expands to fill all the available human space, leaving no room for her.

By contrast the resisting, protesting, offending Lady Macbeth demands a place, an identity and a specificity which is not masculinity, but an unsexing that takes her altogether outside the realm of the human, beyond all visitings of nature (I. v. 42). It is from there, from a place outside the natural, that she seduces her husband to his own destruction by exploiting the plurality of manhood.

In the event, Lady Macbeth cannot survive in this extra-human realm, and there is finally little to choose between her destiny and Lady Macduff's. Only the witches, whose identity is neither clearly gendered nor unequivocally human (I. iii. 41–3, 45–7, 53), can flourish in a culture which places the meaning of woman at once outside man, as his silent and submissive difference, and inside man as his humane and humanising kindness. On this reading, the villainous Lady Macbeth is at the same time the victim of a humanism which makes humanity synonymous with man, and which cannot in consequence afford to let women live.

The heterogeneous text is one which is not readily coopted on behalf of either subversion or containment. Materialist feminists, I believe, have no need to take sides in the debates between new historicists and cultural materialists on that issue. All texts exceed their own unitary projects; all texts release new interpretations as we bring to bear on them different – and differential – reading practices. That is not to say that they mean whatever we like, but that in the first place, a debate about whether a play 'really' supports or challenges the monarchy is, from a feminist perspective, neither here nor there. And in the second place, that debate only reiterates, with whatever elegance and subtlety, the proposition that meaning is single and univocal, and available to be pinned down by 'correct' reading.[7] The concerns of materialist feminist criticism, I have suggested, are elsewhere.

V

Acknowledging the materiality of culture, and its own identity as an intervention in its cultural moment, materialist feminist criticism also implies a self-consciousness about style. In one sense, this attention to the signifier is itself a postmodern gesture: the empiricism familiar since the Enlightenment to most of the English-speaking world famously repudiates rhetoric and proclaims the plain style as adequate and appropriate to its purpose of speaking out the unvarnished, extra-textual, extra-linguistic truth. Postmodernism, by contrast, is unable to find a place for meaning independent of representation, or presentation, as Lyotard more exactly calls it, since the 're' of representation precisely proposes the autonomy of the signified, affirms a state of pure intelligibility, of untrammelled conceptuality, anterior to signification.[8] It is in France, therefore, where this understanding of language has a stronger hold, that feminism has most insistently posed the question, 'how should women write?' And, of course, the answers French feminists have offered have not always seemed persuasive to their English-speaking readers.

At the same time, however, we know now that the plain style was never as plain as it pretended, and that it was always a good deal more stylish than its adherents acknowledge. Locke, who distrusts the duplicity of metaphor, is full of metaphors, and is more persuasive in consequence. But then Locke never really believed in the existence of pure conceptuality in the first place.[9] And in any case, the proclaimed but illusory plainness was not transparency but precisely a pretence of unmediated access to a presence, an intelligibility, which was always elsewhere – though at the beck and call, we were to construe, of the writer.

In practice feminists, especially since Virginia Woolf, have never ignored the question of their own mode of address, because we know that, as women, we cannot be sure of an audience unless we set out to enlist one. The project has always been to find for feminism a distinctive voice, or preferably voices, designed to ensure attention, without repeating the familiar, authoritarian, patriarchal gestures in the process. (Vituperation, for instance is one obvious patriarchal gesture, intended to humiliate an opponent; obscurantism is another). And feminist fiction has been even more self-consciously eager to find a narrative mode which does justice to its cause.

How *should* women write? Materialist feminism would perhaps begin by modifying the question. Since the writing that concerns us is not the expression of an interiority, but a political intervention that sets out to be effective, the crucial question seems to be, how should *feminists* write? And the answer is, persuasively, of course. And pleasurably – in order to be read. And intelligibly – in order to be understood. But these (self-evident?) answers pose another problem, and that is how to produce persuasion and pleasure and clarity, without reproducing the illusion of plainness which makes everything so obvious that there is no room for debate. It is the sheer unsurprising obviousness of its propositions that has perpetuated the humanist legitimation of existing modes of domination. Feminism needs surprises, in order to denaturalise that obviousness. It is the magisterial, closed mode of address of so-called good writing that deflects criticism and forestalls debate. Feminism depends on criticism and debate. And above all, feminism is committed to the *continuation* of surprise and criticism and debate, because the project of feminist politics is precisely not to introduce new forms of subordination which replicate the old, merely transferring to women the power that previously belonged to men.

This problem of writing is one that I take very much to heart, having been consistently accused (and not without justification) of producing classic realist texts, raising questions only to resolve them in closure. I find it hard not to – but I pose more unanswered questions now.

The best account of the problem that I have found – and the best proposal of a solution that I know – is Mary Jacobus's essay, 'The Difference of View'. That essay is no longer new, but it still seems to me unsurpassed in its identification of the theoretical and practical issues. It argues that feminism cannot afford to reproduce patriarchal forms and conventions. At the same time, it continues, to repudiate them in their entirety is to reject all that is readily intelligible and therefore persuasive: it is, in other words, to risk madness. Jacobus proposes that instead we should inhabit the familiar forms, but inhabit them differently; we should reproduce conventional structures, but reproduce them other-wise, inserting an unexpected alterity which destabilises the soothing, reassuring obviousness and closure of rational argument conducted in the plain style.[10] Feminists, in other words, might do well to reject all efforts to emulate eighteenth-century gentlemen. Or rather, they might demonstrate that it is easy enough to write like an eighteenth-century gentleman, but it is more challenging to introduce sporadic disruptions into the easy flow of what passes for good sense.

This is harder to do, in my opinion, than to theorise. It means, I believe, occasionally transgressing at critical moments the norms of good style, introducing sudden changes of tone in order to highlight a point and, above all, being content to leave a question in place where an answer might be expected. And at this moment in this essay it means not (at all costs) closing off the issue of feminist writing, since I have no comprehensive programme to offer.

VI

Supremely, of course, materialist feminism is self-conscious about its own politics, aware of itself as a political intervention. And it follows that materialist feminist criticism is equally aware of the political questions we need repeatedly to address, even if we are less sure of the answers from one moment to another. To what extent, for instance, is it in itself a political act to analyse the gender relations presented in a literary text? And if it *was* a political act in the 1970s, when feminist readings were a scandal, an explicit defiance of existing institutional practices, is it so still, when the academy is proud to list the numbers of courses in feminist criticism, women's writing or literature and gender? Are there other things that we should do now? Or is it enough to do the same things but, having learnt from our predecessors, try to do them better?

In my view, feminist criticism cannot afford to stand still, to get arrested. Barbara Johnson in the introduction to her second book, *A World of Difference*, formulates a series of questions that now concern her. These might easily be appropriated as a useful check-list for materialist feminist criticism:

> While *The Critical Difference* seemed to say, 'Here is a text; let me read it'; the present volume adds: 'Why am I reading *this* text? What kind of act was the writing of it? What question about it does it itself *not* raise? What am I participating in when I read it?'[11]

The context of Johnson's acknowledged change of focus is perhaps individual, but the questions she adds in the present seem to me to point very sharply to the concerns of materialist feminist criticism. They invoke the politics of reading practices as well as the politics of writing, and they imply an attention to the politics of the institution in which our reading takes place. Materialist feminist criticism might fruitfully reiterate and reformulate those questions at intervals. At any specific moment we might ask ourselves how and why we are performing this particular reading. What difference (to cite the title of an important feminist anthology) does it make?

VII

But there is a danger in all this. (There is so often a danger.) Luckily, materialist feminism recognises the inevitability of contradiction – and does not panic. The danger, as I see it, is this: classification promotes reification. The adoption of a label, however valuable the move appears, always incurs the possibility of fixing meaning and deflecting the process of change. Commitments become dogmas; positions are institutionalised; potential allies are excluded. Feminism's newest category could rapidly become a force for conservatism.

Of course, any radical movement, eager to make alignments, develop analyses and define areas of debate, needs to make distinctions, to identify declared positions which facilitate discussion as well as action. Feminists, like socialists, therefore subdivide into groups with specific commitments based on specific analyses. And from the debates which arise within and between these groups, it becomes possible to delineate a range of ways forward, both theoretical and practical. The traditional categories of feminism – liberal, radical and socialist – or, more recently, French and Anglo-American – have self-evidently had their uses, both analytical and political.

But feminism can learn much from the failures of socialism, as well as from its strengths. And one of the most exemplary of its failures has been the history of internecine struggles between left groups which are held by their opponents to have betrayed the true cause, or travestied the essence of socialism itself. The differences that labels identify are easily cemented as oppositions. From the point of view of feminism, it begins to seem increasingly probable that the traditional categories have eventually come to exclude as many women as they enlist. Certainly socialist feminism has not proved very attractive in the United States. And as Rachel Bowlby has suggested, the notion of French thought as homogeneous, a conviction crucial to the preservation of the antithesis between Anglo-American and French feminisms, is itself an Anglo-American fantasy.[12] That antithesis tells us very little in a world inhabited by Alice Jardine (though *Gynesis* in one sense depends on it, and in another refutes it), by Rosalind Coward, Barbara Johnson, Teresa de Lauretis and Rachel Bowlby herself. Moreover, it runs the perpetual risk of effacing other differences, including non-western differences:

> Possibly, in crossing the ocean between two places whose identities are known and evaluated from the moment of take-off, the transatlantic feminist misses the chance of finding something else – a lost continent, for example – beneath the waters of the Atlantic glimpsed from the plane.[13]

I welcome the advent of materialist feminism, as I welcome theoretical specificity and political alignment. But I fear it too. Names can so easily obscure the need to re-examine and reconstruct our political commitments. Happily, feminists have consistently shown that they know when to discard a label once it has outlived its usefulness.

4

Toward a More Feminist Criticism

Adrienne Rich

I come to this task as a writer in need of criticism, as a student of literature who also sometimes writes criticism, as co-editor of a small lesbian-feminist journal, *Sinister Wisdom*, and as a member of the community of feminist and/or lesbian editors, printers, booksellers, publishers, archivists, and reviewers who met in Washington, DC, several weekends ago, defining ourselves as 'Women in Print'. It is especially out of that community that I wish to speak, and much of what I shall bring together here I have absorbed from and with other lesbian and feminist members of that community in the process of trying to address issues of survival. As the first call for that conference stated: *The survival of the women's movement, as of any revolutionary movement, depends directly on that of our communications network.* The need for more and better criticism as a part of that network was one theme in our discussions.

It strikes me that at present there are really two kinds of self-defined feminist criticism being done. One originates in the universities, usually in Women's Studies, and addresses that community primarily; it concentrates on works of the past which can most readily be included within an already existing canon or on contemporary works which are published by commercial presses. The other, though sometimes written by women with university degrees, is grounded in the larger feminist community with its increasing consciousness of diversity and the ensuing differences of tone, language, style. The first kind of criticism tends to be published in journals like *Signs, Women's Studies, Feminist Studies* as well as now and then in non-feminist literary and critical journals like *College English, Parnassus*, and professional quarterlies. The second tends to appear in magazines like *Conditions, Feminary, The Feminist Review, off our backs, Sinister Wisdom*, as well as in such journals as *First World, Radical Teacher, Freedomways, Southern Exposure*, etc. The trouble is that the first kind of criticism is not listening to the second – is in fact drawing back from the second. It is this schism that I want to examine here.

I'd like to begin by noting that there is a well-known split in Western literary culture between a literary 'establishment' which represents middle-class and traditional values, and an 'avant-garde' which has seen itself variously as challenging entrenched ideas and forms, flouting the rules, 'smashing the iamb', publishing 'little' magazines in opposition to the current establishment mode. Sometimes, but not always, the literary 'avant-garde' has been politically radical as well; sometimes (as with the Fugitive movement in the South, which rapidly became an establishment) it has reflected conservative to fascistic political attitudes within a 'modernist' or formally rebellious aesthetic. Feminist criticism began not as a school of literary criticism but as a politically motivated act of looking at literature, both by men and by women, in terms of *'sexual politics'* as Kate Millett named her landmark book in 1970. In her preface Millett wrote:

This essay, composed of equal parts of literary and cultural criticism, is something of an anomaly, a hybrid, possibly a new mutation altogether. I have operated on the premise that there is room for a criticism which takes into account the larger cultural context in which literature is conceived and produced. Criticism which originates from literary history is too limited in scope to do this; criticism which originates in aesthetic considerations, 'New Criticism', never wished to do so.[1]

Feminist criticism grew out of a Women's Liberation movement which took seriously the work of critiquing *all* of culture, from beauty pageants to university texts, in terms of its reflection of, and impact on, women's lives. In her 1977 essay 'Toward a Black Feminist Criticism', Barbara Smith reminds us all that

for books to be real and remembered they have to be talked about. For books to be understood they must be examined in such a way that the basic intentions of the writers are at least considered. ... Before the advent of specifically feminist criticism in this decade, books by white women ... were not clearly perceived as the cultural manifestation of an oppressed people. It took the surfacing of the second wave of the North American feminist movement to expose the fact that these works contain a stunningly accurate record of the impact of patriarchal values and practice upon the lives of women and more significantly that literature by white women provides essential insights into female experience.[2]

With this statement in mind, I would define a feminist literary criticism as a criticism which is consciously involved in a movement for women's liberation – indeed, a revolutionary movement. I would not define as feminist literary criticism simply the writing by a woman about other women's books without consciousness of the political context of women's writing; or by an author who perceives herself as merely participating in some female 'alternative reading' in a liberal supermarket of the intellect; or by one who accepts the parameters of whiteness, heterosexuality, and academic scholarship as furnishing an essentially complete view of things. I would like to invoke a definition of feminist criticism which implies continuous and conscious accountability to the lives of women – not only those women who read and write books or are working, however tenuously, in academic settings. For white feminists, who make up by far the largest group of academic feminists, this involves deliberately trying to unlearn the norm of universal whiteness, which is the norm of the culture of academia and of the dominant culture beyond; it also and equally means trying to unlearn the norm of universal heterosexuality. It means that we do not attribute to our work an inclusiveness it does not possess, that we don't rest satisfied with ritualistically tacking on a chapter or a paragraph or a footnote alluding to women of colour and/or lesbians. To challenge the universality of whiteness and heterosexuality implies as radical and astonishing a process as many of us went through over a decade ago in challenging patriarchal values and practice. It is, I believe, the next unavoidable step that feminist criticism must make – and it is already beginning.

In looking at literary criticism by white academic feminists, I am often surprised at the wealth of reading cited from the works of white male critics and at how often there goes along with this a tone of defensiveness, of needing to argue with these gentlemen, of being still somewhat enmeshed in dialogues which serve to isolate the feminist as a woman rather than connect her with a larger community of women. I can feel a kind of underlying strain, too, the strain of trying to explain oneself yet again when one needs to be moving on – the strain of trying bravely to carry the banner of feminism high in a hostile setting, trying to exchange collegial banter without perceptible 'bitterness', bringing into play a panoply of terms and methods learned in the classrooms of lit. crit., all the time using women writers – mostly white – as the 'texts' to be treated. I know this strain very well in myself, as a white and middle-class woman who lived for years as a heterosexual in academia. It is the strain of trying to have it both ways, be both pleasing and bold, the token straining not to act like a token. (I cannot help but recognise how much of this I've done myself or am still capable of doing.)

I want to ask the feminist critic of literature to inform herself not just with training in literary exegesis but in a concrete and grounded knowledge of the feminist movement – which means reading not only books by women, but feminist newspapers, periodicals, pamphlets, articles; studies on woman battering, welfare mothers, sexual and economic struggles in the workplace, compulsory sterilisation, incest, women in prison; resources from the feminist presses like the *Fight Back!* anthology on feminist resistance to male violence, published here in Minneapolis by Cleis Press; or *This Bridge Called My Back: Writings by Radical Women of Color*, edited by Cherríe Moraga and Gloria Anzaldúa and published by Persephone Press; or *Top Ranking: Racism and Classism in the Lesbian Community*, published by February 3 Press; or J. R. Roberts's *Black Lesbians: An Annotated Bibliography*, published by Naiad Press. I want to ask her to consider her work a potential resource also, a resource *for us*, for our movement; to see herself not as writing just for other critics and scholars, but to help make books both 'real and remembered', to stir ordinary women to read what they might otherwise miss or avoid, to help us all sort through which words, in Lillian Smith's phrase, chain us and which can set us free.

In a provocative recent piece of feminist criticism, which is grounded in this way, Jan Clausen suggests that the striking role of poetry and poets in the movement has led some women to attribute too much power to words and language, to elevate the poet rather than the organiser or practical strategist to the role of spokeswoman. 'Feminism desperately needs actions as well as words', she says.[3] I share Clausen's uneasiness about a movement infatuated with language to the neglect of action. I share it particularly because I am a poet who often finds herself assigned the role of spokeswoman. Some of us are increasingly concerned about the level of ritual assent accorded to our poetic language – 'assent without credence', as a friend once defined it, to my own relief; about the frustration of being listened to, written about, objectified, perhaps, but not heard – at least in any sense of hearing which might bear on action. Even to be able to express this in public is a measure of how harshly I have felt the experience of applause and accolade without discrimination or true on-going critical response. It's not that I believe in a direct line of response, from a poem to an action: I'm not convinced that such a connection would be desirable or that the poet necessarily knows what action is needed. In fact, it may be action that leads to poetry, the deed to the word, when the poet identifies with others like and unlike herself who are trying to transform an oppressive order. But I do believe that words *can* help us move or keep us paralysed, and that our choices of language and verbal tone have something – a great deal – to do with how we live our lives and whom we end up speaking with and hearing; and that we can deflect words, by trivialisation, of course, but also by ritualised respect, or we can let them enter our souls and mix with the juices of our minds.

And the critique of language needs to come not just from women who define themselves as writers but from women who will test the work against their experience – who, like Woolf's 'common reader', are interested in literature as a key to life, not an escape from it. I think that every feminist poet must long – I do – for real criticism of her work – not just descriptive, but analytical criticism which takes her language and images seriously enough to question them, as Susan Wood-Thompson questioned my use of images of blindness in a review in the southern lesbian-feminist journal *Feminary*. I also need to know when in my work I am merely doing well what I know well how to do and when I am avoiding certain expressive risks. And while I can count on friends for some of this, it would be better for all feminist writers if such principled criticism were to come also from strangers – it would broaden the field in which we are working.

But this kind of criticism implies a commitment not just to literature but to readers, and not just to women who are readers here and now but to widening the possibility of reading and writing for women to whom books have been closed. In her beautiful and thought-provoking essay 'Researching Alice Dunbar-Nelson', the Black critic Gloria T. Hull describes her search for a new way of writing as a feminist scholar, visualising the diverse kinds of readers she wants to address, from parents, brothers, lovers, to academic colleagues to other Black feminists, trying to create 'organic' articles 'rather than write sneaky, schizophrenic essays from under two or three different hats'.[4] In this particular essay, Hull describes her work with the manuscript collection preserved by Dunbar-Nelson's surviving niece, the dynamics of her relationship with the niece herself, and the meaning of this work and its discoveries for Hull personally and for the study of Black women writers in general. Toward the end of the essay she formulates some principles for a Black feminist critical methodology. I want to cite them here:

> (1) everything about the subject is important for a total understanding and analysis of her life and work; (2) the proper scholarly stance is engaged rather than 'objective'; (3) the personal (both the subject's and the critic's) *is* political; (4) description must be accompanied by analysis; (5) consciously maintaining the angle of vision of a person who is both Black and female is imperative; as is the necessity for a class-conscious, anticapitalist perspective; (6) being principled requires rigorous truthfulness and 'telling it all' [here Hull is alluding, among other things, to her discovery, in editing Dunbar-Nelson's diary, of her lesbian relationships]; (7) research/criticism is not an academic/intellectual game, but a pursuit with social meanings rooted in the 'real world'. I had always proceeded from the assumption that Dunbar-Nelson had much to say to us and, even more importantly, that dealing honestly with her could, in a more-than-metaphoric sense, 'save' some Black woman's life – as being able to write in this manner about her had, in a very concrete way, 'saved' my own.[5]

And so the question hangs before us: Can a truly feminist criticism be carried on within the university or for academic publications, and if so, how? What does it mean, for example, that my own work can be respectfully quoted and discussed in academic classrooms and in articles without acknowledging that it is the work of a lesbian, where lesbians are never mentioned? And what does it mean that, several years after Barbara Smith's 'Toward a Black Feminist Criticism' and Alice Walker's essay/meditation 'One Child of One's Own', and over a year after *Signs* published my essay 'Compulsory Heterosexuality and Lesbian Existence', the current issue of *Signs* can open with a lengthy article which makes strong claims for feminist thought as 'rethinking thinking itself' and discusses a number of recent books of academic feminist criticism, all white-centred and heterosexist, without the slightest comment on that fact?[6] How is it possible that a similarly ambitious article, published in *Feminist Studies*, can 'discuss a "feminist literary criticism" without reference to the work of women of colour and/ or identifiable lesbians'?[7] What does it mean about the very terms, the structures with which the critic tries to conceptualise her ideas, when she tries to build an exhaustive theory merely on one limited, white, heterosexual slice of experience and reading? What does it mean about how seriously the white academic feminist critic reads the work of an Alice Walker, a Barbara Smith, an Elly Bulkin, a Michele Russell, a Toni Cade Bambara? Does she read the journals in which she might find their criticism – such as *Conditions, First World, Freedomways, Radical Teacher, Sinister Wisdom;* or does she, as a literary critic, feel it more important to keep up with *Partisan Review, Critical Inquiry, Semiotics,* and the journals emanating from half a dozen English departments, thus imbibing not only their measure of what counts but their language? Why *is* the language of much academic feminist criticism so ultra-cool, so bright, so spruce and polished? Gloria T. Hull speaks of the kind of style she has consciously rejected as a Black feminist critic:

> Probably as an (over?) reaction to the condescending, witty but empty, British urbanity of tone which is the hallmark of traditional white male literary scholarship (and which I dislike intensely) I usually discuss Dunbar-Nelson with level high seriousness – and always with caring.[8]

Essential for the feminist critic who believes that her work is 'a pursuit with social meanings rooted in the "real world"' is a clear understanding of power: of how culture, as meted out in the university, works to empower some and disempower others; of how she herself may be writing out of a situation of unexamined privilege, whether of skin colour, heterosexuality, economic and educational background, or other. For example, if I write (as I have done) on fiction by Black women, it must be clear to me that my interpretation of that fiction is that of a white, middle-class, Jewish lesbian feminist – a complex view but not an authoritative one; that I have, being white, no special overview which allows me to speak with any authority

Gender

beyond trying to describe what the effect and impression of this literature
has been on me, and why I think it valuable for other white women. Even so,
I am probably going to be taken more seriously in some quarters than the
Black woman scholar whose combined experience and research give her far
more penetrating knowledge and awareness than mine. I will be taken more
seriously because I am white, because though a lesbian I am often wilfully
not perceived as such, and because the invisibility of the woman of colour
who is the scholar/critic *or* the poet *or* the novelist is part of the structure of
my privilege, even my credibility.

No one is suggesting that the woman with all or many of the privileges of
white skin, heterosexuality, class background is thereby disqualified from
writing and criticising. However, I believe she has a responsibility not to
read, think, write, and act as if all women had the same privileges, or to
assume that privilege confers some kind of special vision. She has a responsibility to be as clear as possible about the compromises she makes, about her
own fear and trembling as she sits down to write; to admit her limitations
when she picks up work by women who write from a very different culture
and sourcement, to admit to feelings of confusion and being out of her
depth. We need to support each other in rejecting the limitations of a
tradition – a manner of reading, of speaking, of writing, of criticising –
which was never really designed to include us at all.

From the perspective of that tradition, of the academy, of course, other
questions can be and are daily raised. *Aren't you trying to make literature
accountable to the winds of political change? Aren't politics and art always
disastrous bedfellows? Are feminist critics supposed to judge works by some
party line of political correctness, whatever the writer's personal intentions?*
But these questions are not as pure, as politically neutral, as they seem to be:
they spring from the dominant white male culture, a culture profoundly
hostile to the self-definition and self-love of people of colour, and/or poor
people, and/or white women, and/or lesbians and gay men. *Can art be
political and still be timeless? All* art is political in terms of who was allowed
to make it, what brought it into being, why and how it entered the canon,
and why we are still discussing it.

I believe that when we posit a movement of women, a movement both
conscious of our oppression as women and profoundly aware of differences
among us, a true Women's Liberation movement, we enter a realm more
complex than we have moved in before, so that the very questions about
literature become new questions. When the Black feminist critic Mary Helen
Washington, in her anthology of fiction by and about Black women, *Mid-
night Birds*, includes a single story by a Black lesbian (never identified as
such) and makes no reference to the existence of Black lesbians in her
foreword, she is limiting the questions she as critic can ask. When a white
feminist critic merely tacks on women of colour to her analysis as a separate

chapter or footnote, or erases their existence altogether, she is not simply omitting but distorting, and the organic fabric of her criticism is weakened by these distortions. When she deliberately tries to work from a point of view that is *not* white solipsist, she will feel her analysis changing; she is going to see differently and further, not just about the writings of women of colour but also about the writings of white women. The consciousness of racism and homophobia does not mean simply trying to excise racist language or homophobic stereotypes (though that is a necessary beginning); it does mean working to see the field with a fresh vision, to experience whiteness or heterosexuality as relative states and not as authoritative positions. But this can be upsetting: it makes us hear things we didn't use to hear, feel split between familiar and emergent parts of ourselves; it makes us question unexamined loyalties; it is not conducive to pleasant collegiality and banter; it makes us reread our own past writings with impatience; it changes the list of issues we thought it important to explore; and it has everything to do with what we find in literature.

During a couple of workshops at the Women in Print conference I felt that I was hearing a new kind of literature described, a literature desired and needed, yet still uncreated. Women of colour and white women talked of the possibility of learning, whether as authors of fiction or as reviewers, to look from the angle of women unlike ourselves. How much do our differences mitigate what we hold in common as women? We talked of how the critic or reviewer needs to develop a clear sense of her own political and cultural identity, and locate herself honestly in relation to the work she attempts to criticise. How the imaginative writer could learn to write with accountability of women who are not simply of her own caste or class or background, resisting stereotypes, trying to create whole persons – and how this may mean changing her life, not just her writing. We talked of the urge to create literary superwomen, whether dark-skinned or lesbian or both, to make up for years of invisibility or degrading portrayals in literature, and the need to reject feminist versions of 'socialist realism'. In one workshop, two blind white lesbians, one Puerto Rican lesbian, one Black lesbian, and one white working-class lesbian spoke of wanting to find themselves and women like them in literature – 'not always in the foreground either, but in the background too, as just part of the scene, if we can be treated seriously there', as one woman put it. We began to imagine a poetic language, a prose language, which was free of stereotypes – whether of dark or light, or of disability or age, or body image – which was beyond frozen, reductive, repetitive image making. We began to talk as if one task of the critic might be to keep such possibilities before us, both as readers and as writers.

When I was an undergraduate English major, there were a number of 'major critical texts' in the English language, written by English men and considered indispensable: Sidney's 'A Defense of Poetry'; Wordsworth's

'Preface to *Lyrical Ballads';* Coleridge's introduction to *Biographia Liter-
aria;* Eliot's 'Tradition and the Individual Talent'; Empson's *Seven Types of
Ambiguity;* and numerous others. And that list has lengthened in the last
thirty years. I began to realise, when I started to write this talk, that the
present wave of United States feminism has, in a little over ten years,
produced some equally indispensable critical texts – which are by extension
cultural criticism. If *Sexual Politics*, through its ambitious synthesis and high
visibility, opened the way, Barbara Smith's 'Toward a Black Feminist Criticism' was the antithetical necessary next step, acknowledging what had been
done and driving a critique into the hearts of both white feminist and Black
literary criticism. I think, then, of writings – and here I am by no means
chronological – such as Mab Segrest's essay 'Southern Women Writing:
Toward a Literature of Wholeness';[9] of the essays by Jan Clausen and
Gloria T. Hull I have quoted here; of Elly Bulkin's introductions to *Lesbian
Fiction* and *Lesbian Poetry*.[10] I think of Alice Walker's 'In Search of Our
Mothers' Gardens' and 'One Child of One's Own'; of Gloria Anzaldúa's
'Speaking in Tongues: A Letter to Third World Women Writers';[11] of Irena
Klepfisz's remarkable story 'The Journal of Rachel Robotnik', which *is*
lesbian-feminist literary theory in a new form.[12] I would hope that feminist
literary critics within the academy feel a responsibility to the questions raised
by critics who are also activists in the movement. I wish that academic
feminist critics would search out journals like *Azalea, Conditions, Feminary,
Sinister Wisdom* and see them for what they are – very tough and subversive
historical entities, not all of a piece or pursuing a single 'correct line', but
calling into question most of the activity of the dominant lit. crit. and the
culture it reflects, and absolutely needed in the classroom. I hope that
feminist criticism can renounce the temptation to be graceful, pleasing, and
respectable and strive instead to be strong-minded, rash, and dangerous. I
hope that feminist critics in the universities can take their own work seriously as a political force, as part of the network of communications for the
survival of our movement. I wish for all of us – writers, reviewers, editors,
scholars, organisers, booksellers, printers, publishers, students, and teachers
– to share in the power of each others' work.

5

Under Western Eyes: Feminist Scholarship and Colonial Discourses

Chandra Talpade Mohanty

Any discussion of the intellectual and political construction of 'third world feminisms' must address itself to two simultaneous projects: the internal critique of hegemonic 'Western' feminisms, and the formulation of autonomous, geographically, historically, and culturally grounded feminist concerns and strategies. The first project is one of deconstructing and dismantling; the second, one of building and constructing. While these projects appear to be contradictory, the one working negatively and the other positively, unless these two tasks are addressed simultaneously, 'third world' feminisms run the risk of marginalisation or ghettoisation from both mainstream (right and left) and Western feminist discourses.

It is to the first project that I address myself. What I wish to analyse is specifically the production of the 'third world woman' as a singular monolithic subject in some recent (Western) feminist texts. The definition of colonisation I wish to invoke here is a predominantly *discursive* one, focusing on a certain mode of appropriation and codification of 'scholarship' and 'knowledge' about women in the third world by particular analytic categories employed in specific writings on the subject which take as their referent feminist interests as they have been articulated in the US and Western Europe. If one of the tasks of formulating and understanding the locus of 'third world feminisms' is delineating the way in which it resists and *works against* what I am referring to as 'Western feminist discourse', an analysis of the discursive construction of 'third world women' in Western feminism is an important first step.

Clearly Western feminist discourse and political practice is neither singular nor homogeneous in its goals, interests, or analyses. However, it is possible to trace a coherence of *effects* resulting from the implicit assumption of 'the West' (in all its complexities and contradictions) as the primary referent in theory and praxis. My reference to 'Western feminism' is by no means intended to imply that it is a monolith. Rather, I am attempting to draw attention to the similar effects of various textual strategies used by writers which codify Others as non-Western and hence themselves as (implicitly) Western. It is in this sense that I use the term *Western feminist*. Similar arguments can be made in terms of middle-class urban African or Asian scholars producing scholarship on or about their rural or working-class sisters which assumes their own middle-class cultures as the norm, and codifies working-class histories and cultures as Other. Thus, while this essay focuses specifically on what I refer to as 'Western feminist' discourse on women in the third world, the critiques I offer also pertain to third world scholars writing about their own cultures, which employ identical analytic strategies.

It ought to be of some political significance, at least, that the term *colonisation* has come to denote a variety of phenomena in recent feminist and left writings in general. From its analytic value as a category or exploitative economic exchange in both traditional and contemporary Marxisms[1] to its use by feminist women of colour in the US to describe the appropriation of their experiences and struggles by hegemonic white women's movements,[2] colonisation has been used to characterise everything from the most evident economic and political hierarchies to the production of a particular cultural discourse about what is called the 'third world'.[3] However sophisticated or problematical its use as an explanatory construct, colonisation almost invariably implies a relation of structural domination, and a suppression – often violent – of the heterogeneity of the subject(s) in question.

My concern about such writings derives from my own implication and investment in contemporary debates in feminist theory, and the urgent political necessity (especially in the age of Reagan/Bush) of forming strategic coalitions across class, race, and national boundaries. The analytic principles discussed below serve to distort Western feminist political practices, and limit the possibility of coalitions among (usually white) Western feminists and working-class feminists and feminists of colour around the world. These limitations are evident in the construction of the (implicitly consensual) priority of issues around which apparently *all* women are expected to organise. The necessary and integral connection between feminist scholarship and feminist political practice and organising determines the significance and status of Western feminist writings on women in the third world, for feminist scholarship, like most other kinds of scholarship, is not the mere production of knowledge about a certain subject. It is a directly political and discursive *practice* in that it is purposeful and ideological. It is best seen as a mode of intervention into particular hegemonic discourses (for example, traditional anthropology, sociology, literary criticism, etc.); it is a political praxis which counters and resists the totalising imperative of age-old 'legitimate' and 'scientific' bodies of knowledge. Thus, feminist scholarly practices (whether reading, writing, critical, or textual) are inscribed in relations of power – relations which they counter, resist, or even perhaps implicitly support. There can, of course, be no apolitical scholarship.

The relationship between 'Woman' – a cultural and ideological composite Other constructed through diverse representational discourses (scientific, literary, juridical, linguistic, cinematic, etc.) – and 'women' – real, material subjects of their collective histories – is one of the central questions the practice of feminist scholarship seeks to address. This connection between women as historical subjects and the re-presentation of Woman produced by hegemonic discourses is not a relation of direct identity, or a relation of correspondence or simple implication.[4] It is an arbitrary relation set up by particular cultures. I would like to suggest that the feminist writings I analyse here discursively colonise the material and historical heterogeneities of the lives of women in the third world, thereby producing/re-presenting a composite, singular 'third world woman' – an image which appears arbitrarily constructed, but nevertheless carries with it the authorising signature of Western humanist discourse.[5]

I argue that assumptions of privilege and ethnocentric universality, on the one hand, and inadequate self-consciousness about the effect of Western scholarship on the 'third world' in the context of a world system dominated by the West, on the other, characterise a sizeable extent of Western feminist work on women in the third world. An analysis of 'sexual difference' in the form of a cross-culturally singular, monolithic notion of patriarchy or male dominance leads to the construction of a similarly reductive and homogeneous notion of what I call the 'third world difference' – that stable, ahistorical something that apparently oppresses most if not all the women in these countries. And it is in the production of this 'third world difference' that Western feminisms appropriate and 'colonise' the constitutive complexities which characterise the lives of women in these countries. It is in this process of discursive homogenisation and systematisation of the oppression of women in the third world that power is exercised in much of recent Western feminist discourse, and this power needs to be defined and named.

In the context of the West's hegemonic position today, of what Anouar Abdel-Malek calls a struggle for 'control over the orientation, regulation and decision of the process of world development on the basis of the advanced sector's monopoly of scientific knowledge and ideal creativity',[6] Western feminist scholarship on the third world must be seen and examined precisely in terms of its inscription in these particular relations of power and struggle. There is, it should be evident, no universal patriarchal framework which this scholarship attempts to counter and resist – unless one posits an international male conspiracy or a monolithic, ahistorical power structure. There is, however, a particular world balance of power within which any analysis of culture, ideology, and socio-economic conditions necessarily has to be situated. Abdel-Malek is useful here, again, in reminding us about the inherence of politics in the discourses of 'culture':

> Contemporary imperialism is, in a real sense, a hegemonic imperialism, exercising to a maximum degree a rationalised violence taken to a higher level than ever before – through fire and sword, but also through the attempt to control hearts and minds. For its content is defined by the combined action of the military-industrial complex and the hegemonic cultural centres of the West, all of them founded on the advanced levels of development attained by monopoly and finance capital, and supported by the benefits of both the scientific and technological revolution and the second industrial revolution itself.[7]

Western feminist scholarship cannot avoid the challenge of situating itself and examining its role in such a global economic and political framework. To do any less would be to ignore the complex interconnections between first and third world economies and the profound effect of this on the lives of women in all countries. I do not question the descriptive and informative value of most Western feminist writings on women in the third world. I also do not question the existence of excellent work which does not fall into the analytic traps with which I am concerned. In fact I deal with an example of such work later on. In the context of an overwhelming silence about the experiences of women in these countries, as well as the need to forge international links between women's political struggles, such work is both pathbreaking and absolutely essential. However, it is both to the *explanatory potential* of particular analytic strategies employed by such writing, and to their *political effect* in the context of the hegemony of Western scholarship that I want to draw attention here. While feminist writing in the US is still marginalised (except from the point of view of women of colour addressing privileged white women), Western feminist writing on women in the third world must be considered in the context of the global hegemony of Western scholarship   i.e., the production, publication, distribution, and consumption of information and ideas. Marginal or not, this writing has political effects and implications beyond the immediate feminist or disciplinary audience. One such significant effect of the dominant 'representations' of Western feminism is its conflation with imperialism in the eyes of particular third world women.[8] Hence the urgent need to examine the *political* implications of our *analytic* strategies and principles.

My critique is directed at three basic analytic principles which are present in (Western) feminist discourse on women in the third world. Since I focus primarily on the Zed Press Women in the Third World series, my comments on Western feminist discourse are circumscribed by my analysis of the texts in this series.[9] This is a way of focusing my critique. However, even though I am dealing with feminists who identify themselves as culturally or geographically from the 'West', as mentioned earlier, what I say about these presuppositions or implicit principles holds for anyone who uses these methods, whether third world women in the West, or third world women in the third world writing on these issues and publishing in the West. Thus, I am not making a culturalist argument about ethnocentrism; rather, I am trying to uncover how ethnocentric universalism is produced in certain analyses. As a matter of fact, my argument holds for any discourse that sets up its own authorial subjects as the implicit referent, i.e., the yardstick by which to encode and represent cultural Others. It is in this move that power is exercised in discourse.

The first analytic presupposition I focus on is involved in the strategic location of the category 'women' *vis-à-vis* the context of analysis. The assumption of women as an already constituted, coherent group with identical interests and desires, regardless of class, ethnic or racial location, or contradictions, implies a notion of gender or sexual difference or even patriarchy which can be applied universally and cross-culturally. (The context of analysis can be anything from kinship structures and the organisation of labour to media representations.) The second analytical presupposition is evident on the methodological level, in the uncritical way 'proof' of universality and cross-cultural validity is provided. The third is a more specifically political presupposition underlying the methodologies and the analytic strategies, i.e., the model of power and struggle they imply and suggest. I argue that as a result of the two modes – or, rather, frames – of analysis described above, a homogeneous notion of the oppression of women as a group is assumed, which, in turn, produces the image of an 'average third world woman'. This average third world woman leads an essentially truncated life based on her feminine gender (read: sexually constrained) and her being 'third world' (read: ignorant, poor, uneducated, tradition-bound, domestic, family-oriented, victimised, etc.). This, I suggest, is in contrast to the (implicit) self-representation of Western women as educated, as modern, as having control over their own bodies and sexualities, and the freedom to make their own decisions.

The distinction between Western feminist re-presentation of women in the third world and Western feminist self-presentation is a distinction of the same order as that made by some Marxists between the 'maintenance' function of the housewife and the real 'productive' role of wage labour, or the characterisation by developmentalists of the third world as being engaged in the lesser production of 'raw materials' in contrast to the 'real' productive activity of the first world. These distinctions are made on the basis of the privileging of a particular group as the norm or referent. Men involved in wage labour, first world producers, and, I suggest, Western feminists who sometimes cast third world women in terms of 'ourselves undressed',[10] all construct themselves as the normative referent in such a binary analytic.

'WOMEN' AS CATEGORY OF ANALYSIS, OR: WE ARE ALL SISTERS IN STRUGGLE

By women as a category of analysis, I am referring to the crucial assumption that all of us of the same gender, across classes and cultures, are somehow socially constituted as a homogeneous group identified prior to the process of analysis. This is an assumption which characterises much feminist discourse. The homogeneity of women as a group is produced not on the basis of biological essentials but rather on the basis of secondary sociological and anthropological universals. Thus, for instance, in any given piece of feminist analysis, women are characterised as a singular group on the basis of a shared oppression. What binds women together is a sociological notion of the 'sameness' of their oppression. It is at this point that an elision takes place between 'women' as a discursively constructed group and 'women' as material subjects of their own history.[11] Thus, the discursively consensual homogeneity of 'women' as a group is mistaken for the historically specific material reality of groups of women. This results in an assumption of women as an always already constituted group, one which has been labelled 'powerless', 'exploited', 'sexually harassed', etc., by feminist scientific, economic, legal, and sociological discourses. (Notice that this is quite similar to sexist discourse labelling women weak, emotional, having math anxiety, etc.) This focus is not on uncovering the material and ideological specificities that constitute a particular group of women as 'powerless' in a particular context. It is, rather, on finding a variety of cases of 'powerless' groups of women to prove the general point that women as a group are powerless.

In this section I focus on specific ways in which 'women' as a category of analysis is used in Western feminist discourse on women in the third world. Each of these examples illustrates the construction of 'third world women' as a homogeneous 'powerless' group often located as implicit *victims* of particular socio-economic systems. I have chosen to deal with a variety of writers – from Fran Hosken, who writes primarily about female genital mutilation, to writers from the Women in International Development school, who write about the effect of development policies on third world women for both Western and third world audiences. The similarity of assumptions about 'third world women' in all these texts forms the basis of my discussion. This is not to equate all the texts that I analyse, nor is it to equalise their strengths and weaknesses. The authors I deal with write with varying degrees of care and complexity; however, the *effect* of their representation of third world women is a coherent one. In these texts women are defined as victims of male violence (Fran Hosken); victims of the colonial process (Maria Cutrufelli); victims of the Arab familial system (Juliette Minces); victims of the economic development process (Beverley Lindsay and the [liberal] WID School); and finally, victims of *the* Islamic code (Patricia Jeffery). This mode of defining women primarily in terms of their *object status* (the way in which they are affected or not affected by certain institutions and systems) is what characterises this particular form of the use of 'women' as a category of analysis. In the context of Western women writing/studying women in the third world, such objectification (however benevolently motivated) needs to be both named and challenged. As Valerie Amos and Pratibha Parmar argue quite eloquently, 'Feminist theories which examine our cultural practices as "feudal residues" or label us "traditional", also portray us as politically immature women who need to be versed and schooled in the ethos of Western feminism. They need to be continually challenged . . .'.[12]

WOMEN AS VICTIMS OF MALE VIOLENCE

Fran Hosken, in writing about the relationship between human rights and female genital mutilation in Africa and the Middle East, bases her whole discussion/condemnation of genital mutilation on one privileged premise: that the goal of this practice is 'to mutilate the sexual pleasure and satisfaction of woman'.[13] This, in turn, leads her to claim that woman's sexuality is controlled, as is her reproductive potential. According to Hosken, 'male sexual politics' in Africa and around the world 'share the same political goal: to assure female dependence and subservience by any and all means'.[14] Physical violence against women (rape, sexual assault, excision, infibulation, etc.) is thus carried out 'with an astonishing consensus among men in the world'.[15] Here, women are defined consistently as the *victims* of male control – the 'sexually oppressed'.[16] Although it is true that the potential of male violence against women circumscribes and elucidates their social position to a certain extent, defining women as archetypal victims freezes them into 'objects-who-defend-themselves', men into 'subjects-who-perpetrate-violence', and (every) society into powerless (read: women) and powerful (read: men) groups of people. Male violence must be theorised and interpreted *within* specific societies, in order both to understand it better and to effectively organise to change it.[17] Sisterhood cannot be assumed on the basis of gender; it must be forged in concrete historical and political practice and analysis.

WOMEN AS UNIVERSAL DEPENDENTS

Beverly Lindsay's conclusion to the book *Comparative Perspectives of Third World Women: The Impact of Race, Sex and Class* states: 'dependency relationships, based upon race, sex and class are being perpetuated through social, educational, and economic institutions. These are the linkages among Third World Women.'[18] Here, as in other places, Lindsay implies that third world women constitute an identifiable group purely on the basis of shared dependencies. If shared dependencies were all that was needed to bind us together as a group, third world women would always be seen as an apolitical group with no subject status. Instead, if anything, it is the *common context* of political struggle against class, race, gender, and imperialist hierarchies that may constitute third world women as a strategic group at this historical juncture. Lindsay also states that linguistic and cultural differences exist between Vietnamese and black American women, but 'both groups are victims, of race, sex, and class'. Again black and Vietnamese women are characterised by their victim status.

Similarly, examine statements such as 'My analysis will start by stating that all African women are politically and economically dependent',[19] 'Nevertheless, either overtly or covertly, prostitution is still the main if not the only source of work for African women'.[20] *All* African women are dependent. Prostitution is the only work option for African women as a *group*. Both statements are illustrative of generalisations sprinkled liberally through a recent Zed Press publication, *Women of Africa: Roots of Oppression*, by Maria Rosa Cutrufelli, who is described on the cover as an Italian writer, sociologist, Marxist, and feminist. In the 1980s, is it possible to imagine writing a book entitled *Women of Europe: Roots of Oppression*? I am not objecting to the use of universal groupings for descriptive purposes. Women from the continent of Africa can be descriptively characterised as 'Women of Africa'. It is when 'women of Africa' becomes a homogeneous sociological grouping characterised by common dependencies or powerlessness (or even strengths) that problems arise – we say too little and too much at the same time.

This is because descriptive gender differences are transformed into the division between men and women. Women are constituted as a group via dependency relationships *vis-à-vis* men, who are implicitly held responsible for these relationships. When 'women of Africa' as a group (versus 'men of Africa' as a group?) are seen as a group precisely because they are generally dependent and oppressed, the analysis of specific historical differences becomes impossible, because reality is always apparently structured by divisions – two mutually exclusive and jointly exhaustive groups, the victims and the oppressors. Here the sociological is substituted for the biological, in order, however, to create the same – a unity of women. Thus, it is not the descriptive potential of gender difference but the privileged positioning and explanatory potential of gender difference as the *origin* of oppression that I question. In using 'women of Africa' (as an already constituted group of oppressed peoples) as a category of analysis, Cutrufelli denies any historical specificity to the location of women as subordinate, powerful, marginal, central, or otherwise, *vis-à-vis* particular social and power networks. Women are taken as a unified 'powerless' group prior to the analysis in question. Thus, it is then merely a matter of specifying the context *after the fact*. 'Women' are now placed in the context of the family, or in the workplace, or within religious networks, almost as if these systems existed outside the relations of women with other women, and women with men.

The problem with this analytic strategy, let me repeat, is that it assumes men and women are already constituted as sexual-political subjects prior to their entry into the arena of social relations. Only if we subscribe to this assumption is it possible to undertake analysis which looks at the 'effects' of kinship structures, colonialism, organisation of labour, etc., on women, who are defined in advance as a group. The crucial point that is forgotten is that women are produced through these very relations as well as being implicated in forming these relations. As Michelle Rosaldo argues, 'Woman's place in human social life is not in any direct sense a product of the things she does (or even less, a function of what, biologically she is) but the meaning her activities acquire through concrete social interactions'.[21] That women mother in a variety of societies is not as significant as the value attached to mothering in these societies. The distinction between the act of mothering and the status attached to it is a very important one – one that needs to be stated and analysed contextually. [...]

WOMEN AND FAMILIAL SYSTEMS

Elizabeth Cowie [...] emphasises the specifically political nature of kinship structures which must be analysed as ideological practices which designate men and women as father, husband, wife, mother, sister, etc.[22] Thus, Cowie suggests, women as women are not *located* within the family. Rather, it is *in* the family, as an effect of kinship structures, that women as women are *constructed*, defined within and by the group. Thus, for instance, when Juliette Minces cites *the* patriarchal family as the basis for 'an almost identical vision of women' that Arab and Muslim societies have, she falls into this very trap.[23] Not only is it problematical to speak of a vision of women shared by Arab and Muslim societies (i.e., over twenty different countries) without addressing the particular historical, material, and ideological power structures that construct such images, but to speak of the patriarchal family or the tribal kinship structure as the origin of the socio-economic status of women is to again assume that women are sexual-political subjects prior to their entry into the family. So while on the one hand women attain value or status within the family, the assumption of a singular patriarchal kinship system (common to all Arab and Muslim socie-ties) is what apparently structures women as an oppressed group in these societies! This singular, coherent kinship system presumably influences another separate and given entity, 'women'. Thus, all women, regardless of class and cultural differences, are affected by this system. Not only are *all* Arab and Muslim women seen to constitute a homogeneous oppressed group, but there is no discussion of the specific *practices* within the family which constitute women as mothers, wives, sisters, etc. Arabs and Muslims, it appears, don't change at all. Their patriarchal family is carried over from the times of the prophet Mohammed. They exist, as it were, outside history.

WOMEN AND RELIGIOUS IDEOLOGIES

A further example of the use of 'women' as a category of analysis is found in cross-cultural analyses which subscribe to a certain economic reductionism in describing the relationship between the economy and factors such as politics and ideology. Here, in reducing the level of comparison to the economic relations between 'developed and developing' countries, any spe-cificity to the question of women is denied. Mina Modares, in a careful analysis of women and Shi'ism in Iran, focuses on this very problem when she criticises feminist writings which treat Islam as an ideology separate from and outside social relations and practices, rather than a discourse which includes rules for economic, social, and power relations within society.[24] Patricia Jeffery's otherwise informative work on Pirzada women in purdah considers Islamic ideology a partial explanation for the status of women in that it provides a justification for the purdah.[25] Here, Islamic ideology is reduced to a set of ideas whose internalisation by Pirzada women contributes to the stability of the system. However, the primary explanation for purdah is located in the control that Pirzada men have over economic resources, and the personal security purdah gives to Pirzada women.

By taking a specific version of Islam as *the* Islam, Jeffery attributes a singularity and coherence to it. Modares notes, '"Islamic Theology" then becomes imposed on a separate and given entity called "women". A further unification is reached: Women (meaning *all women*), regardless of their differing positions within societies, come to be affected or not affected by Islam. These conceptions provide the right ingredients for an unproblematic possibility of a cross-cultural study of women'.[26] Marnia Lazreg makes a similar argument when she addresses the reductionism inherent in scholar-ship on women in the Middle East and North Africa:

A ritual is established whereby the writer appeals to religions as *the* cause of gender inequality just as it is made the source of underdevelopment in much of modernisation theory. In an uncanny way, feminist discourse on women from the Middle East and North Africa mirrors that of theologians' own interpretation of women in Islam. ...

The overall effect of this paradigm is to deprive women of self-presence, of being. Because women are subsumed under religion presented in fundamental terms, they are inevitably seen as evolving in nonhistorical time. They virtually have no history. Any analysis of change is therefore foreclosed.[27]

While Jeffery's analysis does not quite succumb to this kind of unitary notion of religion (Islam), it does collapse all ideological specificities into economic relations, and universalises on the basis of this comparison.

WOMEN AND THE DEVELOPMENT PROCESS

The best examples of universalisation on the basis of economic reductionism can be found in the liberal 'Women in Development' literature. Proponents of this school seek to examine the effect of development on third world women, sometimes from self-designated feminist perspectives. At the very least, there is an evident interest in and commitment to improving the lives of women in 'developing' countries. Scholars such as Irene Tinker and Michelle Bo Bramsen, Ester Boserup and Perdita Huston have all written about the effect of development policies on women in the third world.[28] All three women assume 'development' is synonymous with 'economic development' or 'economic progress'. As in the case of Minces's patriarchal family, Hosken's male sexual control, and Cutrufelli's Western colonisation, development here becomes the all-time equaliser. Women are affected positively or negatively by economic development policies, and this is the basis for cross-cultural comparison.

For instance, Perdita Huston states that the purpose of her study is to describe the effect of the development process on the 'family unit and its individual members' in Egypt, Kenya, Sudan, Tunisia, Sri Lanka, and Mexico.[29] She states that the 'problems' and 'needs' expressed by rural and urban women in these countries all centre around education and training, work and wages, access to health and other services, political participation, and legal rights. Huston relates all these 'needs' to the lack of sensitive development policies which exclude women as a group or category. For her, the solution is simple: implement improved development policies which emphasise training for women fieldworkers, use women trainees, and women rural development officers, encourage women's cooperatives,

etc. Here again, women are assumed to be a coherent group or category
prior to their entry into 'the development process'. Huston assumes that all
third world women have similar problems and needs. Thus, they must have
similar interests and goals. However, the interests of urban, middle-class,
educated Egyptian housewives, to take only one instance, could surely not
be seen as being the same as those of their uneducated, poor maids. Development policies do not affect both groups of women in the same way.
Practices which characterise women's status and roles vary according to
class. Women are constituted as women through the complex interaction
between class, culture, religion, and other ideological institutions and frameworks. They are not 'women' – a coherent group – solely on the basis of a
particular economic system or policy. Such reductive cross-cultural compar-
isons result in the colonisation of the specifics of daily existence and the
complexities of political interests which women of different social classes and
cultures represent and mobilise.

Thus, it is revealing that for Perdita Huston, women in the third world
countries she writes about have 'needs' and 'problems', but few if any have
'choices' or the freedom to act. This is an interesting representation of
women in the third world, one which is significant in suggesting a latent
self-presentation of Western women which bears looking at. She writes,
'What surprised and moved me most as I listened to women in such very
different cultural settings was the striking commonality – whether they were
educated or illiterate, urban or rural – of their most basic values: the
importance they assign to family, dignity, and service to others.'[30] Would
Huston consider such values unusual for women in the West?

What is problematical about this kind of use of 'women' as a group, as a
stable category of analysis, is that it assumes an ahistorical, universal unity
between women based on a generalised notion of their subordination.
Instead of analytically *demonstrating* the production of women as socio-
economic political groups within particular local contexts, this analytical
move limits the definition of the female subject to gender identity, completely bypassing social class and ethnic identities. What characterises women
as a group is their gender (sociologically, not necessarily biologically,
defined) over and above everything else, indicating a monolithic notion
of sexual difference. Because women are thus constituted as a coherent
group, sexual difference becomes coterminous with female subordination,
and power is automatically defined in binary terms: people who have it
(read: men), and people who do not (read: women). Men exploit, women
are exploited. Such simplistic formulations are historically reductive; they
are also ineffectual in designing strategies to combat oppressions. All they do
is reinforce binary divisions between men and women.

What would an analysis which did not do this look like? Maria Mies's
work illustrates the strength of Western feminist work on women in the third

world which does not fall into the traps discussed above. Mies's study of the lace makers of Narsapur, India, attempts to carefully analyse a substantial household industry in which 'housewives' produce lace doilies for consumption in the world market.[31] Through a detailed analysis of the structure of the lace industry, production and reproduction relations, the sexual division of labour, profits and exploitation, and the overall consequences of defining women as 'non-working housewives' and their work as 'leisure-time activity', Mies demonstrates the levels of exploitation in this industry and the impact of this production system on the work and living conditions of the women involved in it. In addition, she is able to analyse the 'ideology of the housewife', the notion of a woman sitting in the house, as providing the necessary subjective and socio-cultural element for the creation and maintenance of a production system that contributes to the increasing pauperisation of women, and keeps them totally atomised and disorganised as workers. Mies's analysis shows the effect of a certain historically and culturally specific mode of patriarchal organisation, an organisation constructed on the basis of the definition of the lace makers as 'non-working housewives' at familial, local, regional, statewide, and international levels. The intricacies and the effects of particular power networks not only are emphasised, but they form the basis of Mies's analysis of how this particular group of women is situated at the centre of a hegemonic, exploitative world market.

This is a good example of what careful, politically focused, local analyses can accomplish. It illustrates how the category of women is constructed in a variety of political contexts that often exist simultaneously and overlaid on top of one another. There is no easy generalisation in the direction of 'women' in India, or 'women in the third world'; nor is there a reduction of the political construction of the exploitation of the lace makers to cultural explanations about the passivity or obedience that might characterise these women and their situation. Finally, this mode of local, political analysis which generates theoretical categories from within the situation and context being analysed, also suggests corresponding effective strategies for organising against the exploitation faced by the lace makers. Narsapur women are not mere victims of the production process, because they resist, challenge, and subvert the process at various junctures. Here is one instance of how Mies delineates the connections between the housewife ideology, the self-consciousness of the lace makers, and their interrelationships as contributing to the latent resistances she perceives among the women:

> The persistence of the housewife ideology, the self-perception of the lace makers as petty commodity producers rather than as workers, is not only upheld by the structure of the industry as such but also by the deliberate propagation and reinforcement of reactionary patriarchal norms and

institutions. Thus, most of the lace makers voiced the same opinion about the rules of *purdah* and seclusion in their communities which were also propagated by the lace exporters. In particular, the *Kapu* women said that they had never gone out of their houses, that women of their community could not do any other work than housework and lace work etc. but in spite of the fact that most of them still subscribed fully to the patriarchal norms of the *gosha* women, there were also contradictory elements in their consciousness. Thus, although they looked down with contempt upon women who were able to work outside the house – like the untouchable *Mala* and *Madiga* women or women of other lower castes, they could not ignore the fact that these women were earning more money precisely because they were *not* respectable housewives but workers. At one discussion, they even admitted that it would be better if they could also go out and do coolie work. And when they were asked whether they would be ready to come out of their houses and work in one place in some sort of a factory, they said they would do that. This shows that the *purdah* and housewife ideology, although still fully internalised, already had some cracks, because it has been confronted with several contradictory realities.[32]

It is only by understanding the *contradictions* inherent in women's location within various structures that effective political action and challenges can be devised. Mies's study goes a long way toward offering such analysis. While there are now an increasing number of Western feminist writings in this tradition,[33] there is also, unfortunately, a large block of writing which succumbs to the cultural reductionism discussed earlier.

METHODOLOGICAL UNIVERSALISMS, OR: WOMEN'S OPPRESSION IS A GLOBAL PHENOMENON

Western feminist writings on women in the third world subscribe to a variety of methodologies to demonstrate the universal cross-cultural operation of male dominance and female exploitation. I summarise and critique three such methods below, moving from the simplest to the most complex.

First, proof of universalism is provided through the use of an arithmetic method. The argument goes like this: the greater the number of women who wear the veil, the more universal is the sexual segregation and control of women.[34] Similarly, a large number of different, fragmented examples from a variety of countries also apparently add up to a universal fact. For instance, Muslim women in Saudi Arabia, Iran, Pakistan, India, and Egypt all wear some sort of a veil. Hence, this indicates that the sexual control of women is a universal fact in those countries in which the women are veiled.[35] Fran Hosken writes, 'Rape, forced prostitution, polygamy, genital mutilation, pornography, the beating of girls and women, purdah (segregation of women) are all violations of basic human rights'.[36] By equating purdah with rape, domestic violence, and forced prostitution, Hosken asserts its 'sexual control' function as the primary explanation for purdah, whatever the context. Institutions of purdah are thus denied any cultural and historical specificity, and contradictions and potentially subversive aspects are totally ruled out.

In both these examples, the problem is not in asserting that the practice of wearing a veil is widespread. This assertion can be made on the basis of numbers. It is a descriptive generalisation. However, it is the analytic leap from the practice of veiling to an assertion of its general significance in controlling women that must be questioned. While there may be a physical similarity in the veils worn by women in Saudi Arabia and Iran, the specific meaning attached to this practice varies according to the cultural and ideological context. In addition, the symbolic space occupied by the practice of purdah may be similar in certain contexts, but this does not automatically indicate that the practices themselves have identical significance in the social realm. For example, as is well known, Iranian middle-class women veiled themselves during the 1979 revolution to indicate solidarity with their veiled working-class sisters, while in contemporary Iran, mandatory Islamic laws dictate that all Iranian women wear veils. While in both these instances, similar reasons might be offered for the veil (opposition to the Shah and Western cultural colonisation in the first case, and the true Islamicisation of Iran in the second), the concrete *meanings* attached to Iranian women wearing the veil are clearly different in both historical contexts. In the first case, wearing the veil is both an oppositional and a revolutionary gesture on the part of Iranian middle-class women; in the second case, it is a coercive, institutional mandate.[37] It is on the basis of such context-specific differentiated analysis that effective political strategies can be generated. To assume that the mere practice of veiling women in a number of Muslim countries indicates the universal oppression of women through sexual segregation not only is analytically reductive, but also proves quite useless when it comes to the elaboration of oppositional political strategy.

Second, concepts such as reproduction, the sexual division of labour, the family, marriage, household, patriarchy, etc., are often used without their specification in local cultural and historical contexts. Feminists use these concepts in providing explanations for women's subordination, apparently assuming their universal applicability. For instance, how is it possible to refer to 'the' sexual division of labour when the *content* of this division changes radically from one environment to the next, and from one historical juncture to another? At its most abstract level, it is the fact of the differential assignation of tasks according to sex that is significant; however, this is quite different from the *meaning* or *value* that the content of this sexual division of labour assumes in different contexts. In most cases the assigning of tasks on the basis of sex has an ideological origin. There is no question that a claim such as 'women are concentrated in service-oriented occupations in a large number of countries around the world' is descriptively valid. Descriptively, then, perhaps the existence of a similar sexual division of labour (where women work in service occupations such as nursing, social work, etc., and men in other kinds of occupations) in a variety of different countries can be asserted. However, the concept of the 'sexual division of labour' is more than just a descriptive category. It indicates the differential *value* placed on 'men's work' versus 'women's work'.

Often the mere existence of a sexual division of labour is taken to be proof of the oppression of women in various societies. This results from a confusion between and collapsing together of the descriptive and explanatory potential of the concept of the sexual division of labour. Superficially similar situations may have radically different, historically specific explanations, and cannot be treated as identical. For instance, the rise of female-headed households in middle-class America might be construed as a sign of great independence and feminist progress, whereby women are considered to have *chosen* to be single parents, there are increasing numbers of lesbian mothers, etc. However, the recent increase in female-headed households in Latin America,[38] where women might be seen to have more decision-making power, is concentrated among the poorest strata, where life choices are the most constrained economically. A similar argument can be made for the rise of female-headed families among black and Chicana women in the US. The positive correlation between this and the level of poverty among women of colour and white working-class women in the US has now even acquired a name: the feminisation of poverty. Thus, while it is possible to state that there is a rise in female-headed households in the US and in Latin America, this rise cannot be discussed as a universal indicator of women's independence, nor can it be discussed as a universal indicator of women's impoverishment. The *meaning* of and *explanation* for the rise obviously vary according to the socio-historical context.

Similarly, the existence of a sexual division of labour in most contexts cannot be sufficient explanation for the universal subjugation of women in the work force. That the sexual division of labour does indicate a devaluation of women's work must be shown through analysis of particular local contexts. In addition, devaluation of *women* must also be shown through careful analysis. In other words, the 'sexual division of labour' and 'women' are not commensurate analytical categories. Concepts such as the sexual division of labour can be useful only if they are generated through local, contextual analyses.[39] If such concepts are assumed to be universally applicable, the resultant homogenisation of class, race, religious, and daily material practices of women in the third world can create a false sense of the commonality of oppressions, interests, and struggles between and among women globally. Beyond sisterhood there are still racism, colonialism, and imperialism!

Finally, some writers confuse the use of gender as a superordinate category of organising analysis with the universalistic proof and instantiation of this category. In other words, empirical studies of gender differences are confused with the analytical organisation of cross-cultural work. Beverly Brown's review of the book *Nature, Culture and Gender* best illustrates this point.[40] Brown suggests that nature:culture and female:male are superordinate categories which organised and locate lesser categories (such as wild/domestic and biology/technology) within their logic. These categories are universal in the sense that they organise the universe of a system of representations. This relation is totally independent of the universal substantiation of any particular category. Her critique hinges on the fact that rather than clarify the generalisability of nature:culture :: female:male as subordinate organisation categories, *Nature, Culture and Gender* construes the universality of this equation to lie at the level of empirical truth, which can be investigated through fieldwork. Thus, the usefulness of the nature:culture :: female:male paradigm as a universal mode of the organisation of representation within any particular socio-historical system is lost. Here, methodological universalism is assumed on the basis of the reduction of the nature:culture :: female:male analytic categories to a demand for empirical proof of its existence in different cultures. Discourses of representation are confused with material realities, and the distinction made earlier between 'Woman' and 'women' is lost. Feminist work which blurs this distinction (which is, interestingly enough, often present in certain Western feminists' self-representation) eventually ends up constructing monolithic images of 'third world women' by ignoring the complex and mobile relationships between their historical materiality on the level of specific oppressions and political choices, on the one hand, and their general discursive representations, on the other.

To summarise: I have discussed three methodological moves identifiable in feminist (and other academic) cross-cultural work which seeks to uncover a universality in women's subordinate position in society. The next and final section pulls together the previous sections, attempting to outline the political effects of the analytical strategies in the context of Western feminist writing on women in the third world. These arguments are not against generalisation as much as they are for careful, historically specific generalisations responsive to complex realities. Nor do these arguments deny the necessity of forming strategic political identities and affinities. Thus, while Indian women of different religions, castes, and classes might forge a political unity on the basis of organising against police brutality toward women,[41] an *analysis* of police brutality must be contextual. Strategic coalitions which construct oppositional political identities for themselves are based on generalisation and provisional unities, but the analysis of these group identities cannot be based on universalistic ahistorical categories. [...]

THE SUBJECT(S) OF POWER

[...] The setting up of the commonality of third world women's struggles across classes and cultures against a general notion of oppression (primarily the group in power – i.e., men) necessitates the assumption of what Michel Foucault calls the 'juridico-discursive' model of power, the principal features of which are 'a negative relation' (limit and lack), an 'insistence on the rule' (which forms a binary system), a 'cycle of prohibition', the 'logic of censorship', and a 'uniformity' of the apparatus functioning at different levels.[42] Feminist discourse on the third world which assumes a homogeneous category – or group – called women necessarily operates through the setting up of originary power divisions. Power relations are structured in terms of a unilateral and undifferentiated source of power and a cumulative reaction to power. Opposition is a generalised phenomenon created as a response to power – which, in turn, is possessed by certain groups of people.

The major problem with such a definition of power is that it locks all revolutionary struggles into binary structures – possessing power versus being powerless. Women are powerless, unified groups. If the struggle for a just society is seen in terms of the move from powerless to powerful for women as a *group*, and this is the implication in feminist discourse which structures sexual difference in terms of the division between the sexes, then the new society would be structurally identical to the existing organisation of power relations, constituting itself as a simple *inversion* of what exists. If relations of domination and exploitation are defined in terms of binary divisions – groups which dominate and groups which are dominated – surely the implication is that the accession to power of women as a group is sufficient to dismantle the existing organisation of relations? But women as a group are not in some sense essentially superior or infallible. The crux of the problem lies in that initial assumption of women as a homogeneous group or category ('the oppressed'), a familiar assumption in Western radical and liberal feminisms.[43]

What happens when this assumption of 'women as an oppressed group' is situated in the context of Western feminist writing about third world women? It is here that I locate the colonialist move. By contrasting the representation of women in the third world with what I referred to earlier as Western feminisms' self-presentation in the same context, we see how

Western feminists alone become the true 'subjects' of this counterhistory. Third world women, on the other hand, never rise above the debilitating generality of their 'object' status. [...]

Legal, economic, religious, and familial structures are treated as phenomena to be judged by Western standards. It is here that ethnocentric universality comes into play. When these structures are defined as 'underdeveloped' or 'developing' and women are placed within them, an implicit image of the 'average third world woman' is produced. This is the transformation of the (implicitly Western) 'oppressed woman' into the 'oppressed third world woman'. While the category of 'oppressed woman' is generated through an exclusive focus on gender difference, 'the oppressed third world women' category has an additional attribute – the 'third world difference!' The 'third world difference' includes a paternalistic attitude toward women in the third world.[44] Since discussions of the various themes I identified earlier (kinship, education, religion, etc.) are conducted in the context of the relative 'underdevelopment' of the third world (which is nothing less than unjustifiably confusing development with the separate path taken by the West in its development, as well as ignoring the directionality of the first-third world power relationship), third world women as a group or category are automatically and necessarily defined as religious (read 'not progressive'), family-oriented (read 'traditional'), legal minors (read 'they-are-still-not-conscious-of-their-rights'), illiterate (read 'ignorant'), domestic (read 'backward'), and sometimes revolutionary (read 'their-country-is-in-a-state-of-war; they-must-fight!') This is how the 'third world difference' is produced.

When the category of 'sexually oppressed women' is located within particular systems in the third world which are defined on a scale which is normed through Eurocentric assumptions, not only are third world women defined in a particular way prior to their entry into social relations, but since no connections are made between first and third world power shifts, the assumption is reinforced that the third world just has not evolved to the extent that the West has. This mode of feminist analysis, by homogenising and systematising the experiences of different groups of women in these countries, erases all marginal and resistant modes and experiences.[45] It is significant that none of the texts I reviewed in the Zed Press series focuses on lesbian politics or the politics of ethnic and religious marginal organisations in third world women's groups. Resistance can thus be defined only as cumulatively reactive, not as something inherent in the operation of power. If power, as Michel Foucault has argued recently, can really be understood only in the context of resistance,[46] this misconceptualisation is both analytically and strategically problematical. It limits theoretical analysis as well as reinforces Western cultural imperialism. For in the context of a first/third world balance of power, feminist analyses which perpetrate and sustain the hegemony of the idea of the superiority of the West produce a corresponding set of universal images of the 'third world woman', images such as the veiled woman, the powerful mother, the chaste virgin, the obedient wife, etc. These images exist in universal, ahistorical splendour, setting in motion a colonialist discourse which exercises a very specific power in defining, coding, and maintaining existing first/third world connections.

To conclude, then, let me suggest some disconcerting similarities between the typically authorising signature of such Western feminist writings on women in the third world, and the authorising signature of the project of humanism in general – humanism as a Western ideological and political project which involves the necessary recuperation of the 'East' and 'Woman' as Others. Many contemporary thinkers, including Foucault,[47] Derrida,[48] Kristeva (1980),[49] Deleuze and Guattari,[50] and Said,[51] have written at length about the underlying anthropomorphism and ethnocentrism which constitute a hegemonic humanistic problematic that repeatedly confirms and legitimates (Western) Man's centrality. Feminist theorists such as Luce Irigaray,[52] Sarah Kofman,[53] and Hélène Cixous[54] have also written about the recuperation and absence of woman/women within Western humanism. The focus of the work of all these thinkers can be stated simply as an uncovering of the political *interests* that underlie the binary logic of humanistic discourse and ideology whereby, as a valuable recent essay puts it, 'the first (majority) term (Identity, Universality, Culture, Disinterestedness, Truth, Sanity, Justice, etc.), which is, in fact, secondary and derivative (a construction), is privileged over and colonises the second (minority) term (difference, temporality, anarchy, error, interestedness, insanity, deviance, etc.), which is in fact, primary and originative'.[55] In other words, it is only insofar as 'Woman/Women' and 'the East' are defined as *others*, or as peripheral, that (Western) Man/Humanism can represent him/itself as the centre. It is not the centre that determines the periphery, but the periphery that, in its boundedness, determines the centre. Just as feminists such as Kristeva and Cixous deconstruct the latent anthropomorphism in Western discourse, I have suggested a parallel strategy in this essay in uncovering a latent ethnocentrism in particular feminist writings on women in the third world.[56]

As discussed earlier, a comparison between Western feminist self-presentation and Western feminist re-presentation of women in the third world yields significant results. Universal images of 'the third world woman' (the veiled woman, chaste virgin, etc.), images constructed from adding the 'third world difference' to 'sexual difference', are predicated upon (and hence obviously bring into sharper focus) assumptions about Western women as secular, liberated, and having control over their own lives. This is not to suggest that Western women *are* secular, liberated, and in control of their own lives. I am referring to a *discursive* self-presentation, not necessarily to material reality. If this were a material reality, there would be no need for political movements in the West. Similarly, only from the vantage point of the West is it possible to define the 'third world' as underdeveloped and economically dependent. Without the overdetermined discourse that creates the *third* world, there would be no (singular and privileged) first world. Without the 'third world woman', the particular self-presentation of Western women mentioned above would be problematical. I am suggesting, then, that the one enables and sustains the other. This is not to say that the signature of Western feminist writings on the third world has the same authority as the project of Western humanism. However, in the context of the hegemony of the Western scholarly establishment in the production and dissemination of texts, and in the context of the legitimating imperative of humanistic and scientific discourse, the definition of 'the third world woman' as a monolith might well tie into the larger economic and ideological praxis of 'disinterested' scientific inquiry and pluralism which are the surface manifestations of a latent economic cultural colonisation of the 'non-Western' world. It is time to move beyond the Marx who found it possible to say: They cannot represent themselves; they must be represented.

6
Look Back in Anger: Men in the Fifties
Lynne Segal

Fatherhood is not yet fashionable. Men are not present at the births of their children, if they can possibly help it. They do not shop, push prams, design the home. Marriage to the unmarried male is a trap, and sex the bait, which by stealth and cunning may yet be won.

(*Fay Weldon on the fifties*)[1]

'A new hero has risen among us', wrote Walter Allen in his influential review of Kingsley Amis's first novel, *Lucky Jim*, in January 1954.[2] The new hero is male, the 'intellectual tough' or 'tough intellectual'. He is rude, crude and clumsy, boasts his political apathy, his suspicion of all causes, and he is out to do nobody any good but himself. His heroism consists in the fact that he is honestly self-serving, fiercely critical of all he sees as phoney, pretentious or conformist – a passion which expresses itself most readily in a rejection of what he sees as womanly, or domestic. He exudes a bullying contempt for women.

Explaining the appeal of this young cynic tells us a good deal about the nature of men's lives in the fifties. It also provides a good starting point for reassessing contemporary debate on the changing nature of men and masculinity in the eighties. Back in 1958 the writer and critic Kenneth Allsop was already wondering how someone in 1984 might look back on the fifties: 'I think that he will see a sensitive, emotional, intelligent but wretchedly neurotic society, obedient to protocol beneath the exhibitionist "rebelling", and obsessively class-conscious.'[3] What *he* will not see are public forms of rebellion – exhibitionist or not – from women. It was a woman writer though, Storm Jameson (never of course ranked among the Angry Young Men), who perhaps most clearly expressed what was most refreshing in fifties literary protest. 'What we need now', she argued, 'may be just that insolent irresponsibility, the contempt for safety and comfort and riches, the passionate delight in freedom, the curiosity, the blind hunger for experience and new knowledge, of the mediaeval wandering scholar.'[4]

What was also needed but was largely absent then – for those wishing to shed some light on the existential angst of the new man of mid-century

72

Britain – was some greater understanding of the social and political reality surrounding everyday life in the period. At a conference held in 1987 on the new left of the fifties, Jean McCrindle, one of the handful of women who were part of that movement from its inception, expressed incredulity at the absence of women from the politics of the time: 'I just don't know why women were so absent, so silent – there was a pathological absence of women, silencing of women, in those days.'[5] Exploring the reasons behind the 'pathological silencing' of women in those days can tell us something of the nature of men's lives at the time.

Our most familiar images of the political climate following the defeat of the Labour Party in 1951 conjure up complacency, inertia, illusion. Economic problems were solved, class conflicts dissolved, household harmony restored – so both Labour and Tory politicians declared. By the early fifties, economic growth and Keynesian demand management had yielded full employment and ensured a steady rise in working-class standards of living. Further change, the conventional wisdom ran, was unnecessary. As central as the new myth of classlessness to this cross-party consensus was the myth of sexual equality. 'The feminine sex is a social problem', the eminent sociologist Alva Myrdal had announced a decade earlier.[6] But now women's problems too were solved. Gone for good, it was thought, was the toil and misery of the pre-war working-class housewife, raising too many unplanned, unwanted, underfed and unhealthy children, in dismal poverty and wretched housing. Child benefit, family planning and other forms of welfare provision for mothers and their children did cushion the post-war family from the levels of poverty and ill-health it had often previously experienced. Many women may have returned to the home after the war, with the birth rate soaring and attitudes towards working wives largely hostile – but so too had men. There were many new demands placed upon women as wives and mothers, but, it was felt, women could hardly complain when unlike former times they were no longer alone in their interests and preoccupations.

MAN ABOUT THE HOUSE

The man's place was also in the home. Men too, in popular consciousness, were being domesticated. They had returned from battlefield to bungalow with new expectations of the comforts and the pleasures of home. Both the popular and the academic writing of the fifties celebrate a new 'togetherness', domestic harmony and equality between the sexes. The sociological writing of the fifties, for example, applauds the profound changes underway in contemporary family life. The well known community studies of Young and Willmott on working-class families in the early fifties rapidly move on

from describing the stereotypical working-class husband of yesteryear –
mean with money, callous in sex, harsh to his children, neither helpful nor
affectionate towards 'the wife' – to affirming the end of the absentee husband and a new partnership in marriage: 'In place of the old comes a new
kind of companionship between man and women, reflecting the rise in status
of the young wife and children which is one of the great transformations of
our time.'[7] The influential work of John and Elizabeth Newson reached
similar conclusions: 'At a time when he has more money in his pocket, and
more leisure in which to spend it, than ever before, the head of the household
chooses to sit at his own fireside, a baby on his knee and a feeding-bottle in
his hand.'[8]

In some ways the domestication of men was real enough. In his *Anatomy
of Britain* (1961) Anthony Sampson wrote of the threat posed by domesticity
to professional men's clubs:

> At lunch time they seem confident enough: but it is in the evenings, when
> the wife and family beckon, that the loyalty of the clubman is tested: and it
> is then that the crumbling of clubs is revealed. A few defiant masculine
> clubs like White's, succeed in drinking and gambling till late in the night.
> But in most clubs, only a handful of bachelors, grass widowers and
> visitors inhabit the cavernous rooms. No doubt clubs will survive a long
> time, with their myths, their sites and the convenience: but the old mis-
> ogynist zeal, which built the Empire and kept wives in their place – that
> has gone.[9]

The box-office hits of the day and the new Hollywood heroes (in a world
now saturated with North American culture) also seemed to reflect a post-
war cult of domesticity strong enough to embrace men too. Tough guys were
on their way out. As North American film critic Peter Biskind recalls: 'By
the fifties, the tough, hard-boiled Hemingway male of the thirties and forties,
the man who hid his feelings, if he had any . . . who endured adversity alone
with proud, stoical silence or wooden unconcern, had seen his best days.'[10]
The new male stars – tough but tender Rock Hudson, slight and sensitive
Montgomery Clift, mixed-up and moody James Dean – were a different
breed from Humphrey Bogart, James Cagney or Gary Cooper, increasingly
portrayed in fifties films as either neurotics or crazies. The new films generally put family before career. And the female stars, whether Marilyn
Monroe in *The Seven Year Itch*, Jane Powell in *Seven Brides for Seven
Brothers*, Debbie Reynolds in *The Tender Trap* or Elizabeth Taylor in
Giant, were busy civilising men, and teaching them that their real desires
were for matrimony and domesticity.

The new man of Hollywood, like *Homo Sociologicus* of the fifties, may
have been putting family first more often, but, as we shall see, his place

within it remained decidedly limited. Reviewing the sociological and psychological literature on the family of the fifties two decades later, Elizabeth Wilson suggests:

> To study this body of literature is above all to study how ideology operates by *excluding* whole areas of debate from the very consciousness of readers and authors alike... The sexual division of labour, because it was taken for granted, was an *absence* in these works... About this conflict [between women and men] there was also silence, for these books are about a myth – a myth of happiness.[11]

But there are ways of seeing through the myth to observe something of what men were actually doing in the home in the fifties, and the conflicts and tensions of family life at the time. 'Man About the House' is a chapter heading from an interesting handbook published in 1958, *The Man's Book*. Aimed at middle-class men – the ones deserting Sampson's clubland – it indicates what they might have been up to in the home: hammers, saws, smoothing tools, gripping tools, boring and drilling tools, scissors, nails, screws and glues are successively illustrated and explained. The book contains not a single reference to children, housework, or any activity traditionally regarded as 'women's work'.[12] Significantly, the topic 'fathers' is rarely listed in the index of fifties books on the family; and when it does appear it is not in connection with childcare.

It is clear from the data on English attitudes in 1950 collected by the anthropologist Geoffrey Gorer that the idea of quite separate roles for husband and wife was completely dominant. Asked which qualities they most desired in husbands, women replied: 'understanding' (helping in the home was mentioned by less than 5 per cent). What husbands most wanted from their wives was good housekeeping (sharing the husband's interests was mentioned by only 8 per cent). Some wives did comment upon their husbands' unwillingness to participate in any housework or childcare. A 'typical twenty-eight year old working-class wife', for example, complained of husbands who were 'afraid of being thought a cissy; mine hates people to know he helps at all in the house; won't push pram'.[13] Gorer reports that it is the younger married wives 'who are the loneliest members of English society, without even the faint friendliness of pub or cafe'.[14] Taking the sexual division of labour for granted, Gorer does not enquire into the nature or extent of men's participation in housework or childcare – except to ponder whether father or mother is the most appropriate person to punish a very naughty child.

[...]

MATERNITY RULES

Women, it seems, knew something about the limitations of men's new domesticity. As Betty Thorne, the wife of a Sheffield steel worker, wrote forcefully to *The Manchester Guardian* in 1960, describing life on her street, 'The husband is an ornament or a nuisance alternately.'[15]

The general social concern with adequate mothering, and the assumed biological imperative dictating women's exclusive responsibility for it, had contradictory effects on women. Ideologically, at least, mothering was accorded new value and importance. Housework or 'homemaking' was portrayed not as a drudgery, but as a 'craft': the 'creative' work of efficient domestic consumption. Shopping was no longer to be seen as labour, but more as a type of leisure: a symbol of the 'good times' now accompanying and sustaining the golden years of economic growth in Britain. But women also faced new anxieties and accusations – as incompetent carers and selfish slatterns – were they to complain too loudly of the isolation, boredom and strain accompanying their work in the home.

Complain, of course, some of them did. In a sudden public outburst of resentment in the *Guardian* 'Women's Page' in 1959 one women ('J. B. H.') confessed: 'I love both my sons devotedly, but I suffer the most excruciating boredom in their company'. Another confided:

> I have five children and I found those baby years about which my child-loving friends wax lyrical, full of the most appalling boredom and weariness. It did not get better. It got worse with each one and it is just as bad with my grandchildren.[16]

But for these women, there was no alternative – not even one to ponder on – as the discontented 'JBH' was sharply reminded by another mother of the day: 'Once a woman confesses boredom with any aspect of her God-given role of wife and mother it is a very short step to finding the whole thing intolerable, and to do so J. B. H. must have forgotten the millions of weary, bored women, on whom civilisation was built and depends for its continuance, and whom she has to thank for her position.'[17] (A short step, indeed, but one which it would take women another ten years to make! In the early 1970s a significant number of young mothers were to decide that their position was, precisely, intolerable.)

Meanwhile, the well-nigh obsessive focus on the importance of the mother–child bond in the psychology of the day provoked a backlash: the growth of a youthful rebellion against the oppressiveness of those dutiful mothers attempting to act out the advice so freely heaped upon them. An early warning had appeared in the United States, when *Catcher in the Rye* became a bestseller in 1951. For J.D. Salinger, parents, but in particular mothers, exist to torment and warp the young.[18] Predictably, 'domesticity' came to symbolise 'conformity' in the fifties: the extreme domestication of women – represented as more 'feminine' both in blissful maternity and in the 'New Look' seductive fashions of the fifties – paralleled the mild domestication of men, represented as more home-based (if not more house-trained). Since class differences were now considered surmountable through education and welfare provision, men who felt at odds with their time – bored and dissatisfied – were to turn their anger against the ideals of hearth and home. They turned against women, especially against the 'powerful' mother in the home (powerful because she alone took real responsibility there), displacing onto her all the hatred and resentment they felt towards 'the Establishment'.

ANGRY YOUNG MEN

Many young men of the late 1950s identified strongly with the tough, amoral, anarchic working-class heroes of Alan Sillitoe in *Saturday Night and Sunday Morning* or *The Loneliness of the Long Distance Runner* – men fighting for a sense of freedom and fun against the dreary grey jobs and marriages awaiting them. 'What I want is a good time. All the rest is propaganda,' the Sillitoe hero declares, in rejection of 'the doubled-faced society that really takes no account of him.'[19] In these bestselling books (later made into films) women are never to be trusted. They are part of the system trying to trap, tame and emasculate men. 'Women are all the same', Arthur Seaton announces in *Saturday Night and Sunday Morning*, 'whores, shrews, fools', enticing the suckers into 'the hell that older men call marriage.'[20] While male protagonists see themselves as opposing all authority – 'fighting every day until I die ... fighting with mothers and wives, landlords and gaffers, coppers, army, government'[21] – in reality the battle is with mothers and wives alone. There is no reflection on women's lot in Sillitoe's celebration of an aggressive, misogynistic masculinity: 'There was something about the whole situation which made him want to hurt her' ... 'all you could do was end up by giving them a smack in the chop'.[22] As Nigel Gray subsequently pointed out in his study of post-war working-class fiction, 'Arthur is against all authority – except the authority of men over women. He fights the authorities with his mouth when they are out of earshot – that's cunning, and saves his muscle for women'.[23]

Sillitoe's individualistic angry young man shares the cynical, self-seeking character and quest of other contemporary heroes, whether created by John Wain, John Osborne, John Braine, Stan Barstow, David Storey or J. P. Donleavy. (The flippant and facetious Kingsley Amis hero – rather like Waterhouse's *Billy Liar* – is less physically aggressive, but no less contemptuous of all he sees as effeminate, sensitive or refined.) By the close of the fifties, similar new working-class idols – Tommy Steele, Marty Wilde and Billy Fury – had appeared on the pop charts to drown out the sugary, suave sentimentality of Frank Sinatra: the yearning for *Love and Marriage* with which the decade had opened had yielded to the new teenage dream *Rock with the Caveman*. It is John Osborne's play *Look Back in Anger*, however, which has been hailed as most representative 'in every nuance' of the context of the mid-fifties.[24] At the time, leading theatre critic Kenneth Tynan welcomed its 'anarchy', its 'instinctive leftishness' and its 'automatic rejection of "official" attitudes'.[25] Writer and critic David Lodge has written of the impact Jimmy Porter, Osborne's young hero, had on his Royal Court audience in 1956: 'I... remember well the delight and exhilaration its anti-establishment rhetoric afforded me, and the exactness with which it matched my own mood at that juncture in my life.'[26] (Lodge was then a military conscript on weekend leave, and conscription, as we shall see, played a not insignificant role in constructing the masculine mood of the moment.)

Osborne himself was always exceptionally, almost pathologically, hostile to women – witness his great admiration for Tennessee Williams: 'In Baby Doll, Williams has hit off the American Girl-Woman of the last hundred years – spoilt, ignorant, callous, resentful... Make no mistake about it – this Baby Doll kid is a killer. She would eat a couple of guys and spit them out before breakfast... The female must come toppling down to where she should be – on her back. The American male must get his revenge some-time.'[27] His revenge is rape. Jimmy Porter speaks for his creator in expressing his fear of his middle-class wife Allison, whom he systematically torments and abuses. He compares her to a gorging python devouring men, and draining them of all vitality: 'She'll go on sleeping and devouring until there's nothing left of me... Why do we let these women bleed us to death?... No, there's nothing left for it, me boy, but to let yourself be butchered by the women.'[28]

Life is dull, these rebels roar; life is unheroic – there are no great causes left for men to fight in the 'Brave-New-nothing-very-much-thank-you' fifties world.[29] A stifling domesticity has killed the spirit and ripped out the guts of men, and who is there to blame but women? Who indeed, if, like Osborne and most of the other 'Angries', you are a rebel without a cause and believe that class struggle is obsolete and Marx a fraud? Even Colin MacInnes had bought the fifties myth of classlessness. Though less cynically apolitical than most of his literary poets, in *Absolute Beginners* (1959) MacInnes created yet another scornful, anti-social cult male hero who touched the pulse of con-temporary British youth: 'Do try to understand that, clobbo! I'm just not interested in the whole class crap that seems to needle you and all the tax-payers – needle you all, whichever side of the tracks you live on, or suppose you do.'[30] Class hostility, however, was not extinct; rather, in writings like these it is repressed and twisted into new forms of sexual hostility.

In retrospect it is clear that the scorn which the Angry Young Men hurled at 'the Establishment' was a class resentment, but one devoid of any collective class consciousness. As many have since commented, these new writers were mostly university graduate ex-grammar school boys, from lower middle- or working-class backgrounds, climbing quickly – but for them not quickly enough – up the class ladder. They faced a Britain as class conscious as ever – at least, that is, in its upper echelons, where power, authority and prestige still resided, and with it contempt and ridicule for the grant-aided student ('They are scum', as Somerset Maugham blandly pronounced).[31] Life was frustrating for the working-class grammar school boy, as Hoggart – himself from that background – had declared: 'He both wants to go back and yet thinks he has gone beyond his class, feels himself weighted with knowledge of his own and their situation, which hereafter forbids him the simpler pleasures of his father and mother. And this is only one of his temptations to self-dramatisation.'[32]

Another temptation was his desire for, yet fear of, middle- and upper-class women. Beware 'the perils of hypergamy', Geoffrey Gorer warned in 1957, referring to the process of men marrying upwards, he goes on: 'NOW I'M PRACTICALLY SURE OF IT. *Lucky Jim, Look Back in Anger* and all that lot roused my suspicions; the clincher has come with John Braine's *Room at the Top*, which tells much the same story all over again, brilliantly and bitterly. The curse which is ruining, in fantasy if not their own lives, these brilliant young men of working-class origin and welfare-state opportunity is what anthropologists have dubbed hypergamy. It is a new pattern in English life, and apparently a very distressing one.'[33] Displaying the patronising and, inevitable, sexist perspective of the academic elite of his day, Gorer was nevertheless probably right to speculate that these educated sons of the working class felt in especial danger of losing their virility. Having abstained from the money and pleasures available earlier on to their less studious peers, and now perhaps attracted to women they were less sure of being able to dominate, they asserted a particularly pugnacious manliness and heterosexual aggressiveness. One of the main targets of mockery for Amis, Wain or Osborne, in deriding their upper class antagonists, is their effeminacy, as in Amis's constant homophobic references: 'standing rigid with popping eyes ... they had a look of being Gide or Lytton Strachey'.[34]

HOMOPHOBIA AND THE FEAR OF UNMANLINESS

Homophobia, coupled with new forms of sexual insecurity and fear of women, was not, however, confined to Angry Young Men like Amis, Braine and Osborne – en route via the political apathy and scepticism of the fifties, to a true-blue conservatism. Such sentiments were the spirit of the times. As

others have noticed, there has always been a close link between misogyny
and homophobia in our culture.[35] As we shall see many times throughout
this book, although the persecution of homosexuals is most commonly the
act of men against a minority of other men, it is also the forced repression of
the 'feminine' in all men. It is a way of keeping men separated off from
women, and keeping women subordinate to men. Craig Owen, for example,
has argued that 'homophobia is not primarily an instrument for oppressing a
sexual minority; it is, rather, a powerful tool for regulating the entire
spectrum of male relations.'[36] The fifties was not only a time when the
symbol of the Happy Housewife embraced all women, when Hollywood
could portray the career woman, rather than the seductress, as *femme fatale*
(as in the celebrated *All About Eve*), it was also a time of intense persecution
of homosexual desire.

The social study *English Life and Leisure*, conducted in 1951 by B. Seebohm Rowntree and G.R. Lavers, with the intention of influencing and
improving the cultural and spiritual state of the country, attests to the
anxieties of the period. After referring to a general awareness of the wide-
spread existence of homosexuality, they add: 'It is only necessary to see a few
of the unfortunate persons who have become addicted to it to realise how
demoralising and degenerating an influence it is.'[37] Moreover, they warn,
'sexual excesses are both a symptom of national weakness and a powerful
secondary cause of it.'[38] This was a decade when, as Jonathan Dollimore has
reminded us in his study of the fiction of the fifties, senior Law Lord Patrick
Devlin explicitly associated 'immorality' with treason, demanding the suppression of 'vice' as inherently subversive.[39] Associations of this kind were
consolidated in 1951 with the defection of British diplomats Burgess and
Maclean to the Soviet Union, and the concurrent McCarthy witch-hunt
against Communists and homosexuals in the United States. There was a
dramatic increase in police activity against male homosexuality in both
Britain and North America, culminating in Britain in the anti-homosexual
drive instigated by the authorities in the early 1950s, in which young detectives were employed as *agents provocateurs*.[40] [...] persecution of homosexuals continued up to and beyond the close of the decade (the
homosexual MP Montgomery Hyde, for example, was forced by his consti-
tuency association to stand down once his sexual orientation had been
revealed).

Amidst this onslaught of persecution, imprisonment and punitive forms of
'treatment' such as aversion therapy, homosexuals themselves came to view
their own desire, in the words of Colin MacInnes, as 'a crippled state of
being'[41] or, like Quentin Crisp, as 'a fatal flaw in masculinity'[42] or, like Mary
Renault in her novels, as an affliction to be endured and overcome.[43]
Perhaps the most moving portrayal of the internalised self-hatred of the
male homosexual, unable to conform to the masculine ideal of heterosexu-

ality, is provided by the Black American writer, James Baldwin.[44] As with the rage of the Angry Young Man, the plight of the male homosexual in the fifties tells us much about the contemporary anxieties over manhood – especially in the area of sex. Colin MacInnes, as his biographer Tony Gould illustrates, is as aware as any heterosexual stud of the importance of being manly, delivering this message in one of his unpublished novels: 'What you must do, son, is become a fucker, and not become a fucked. It's simple as that. Boys or girls, up the pussy or the arse, whichever you prefer, but you've got to remember there's a cock between your legs and you're a *man.*'[45]

The post-war contrasts between wartime memories and civilian life, and the maintenance of military conscription marking men's entrance into adulthood, were both significant aspects of the tension over 'manhood' in the 1950s. Trevor Royle opens his book on military conscription between 1945 and 1963, *The Best Years of Their Lives*, by observing that National Service cast a long shadow over boys in the 1950s: 'it was simply a part of the fabric of everyday life.'[46] The writings of David Lodge, Alan Sillitoe and others testify to the casual brutality and crude insensitivity generated by the futile monotony of conscript life; while in *All Bull* B.S. Johnson pronounces it 'tedious, belittling, coarsening, brutalising, unjust and possibly psychologically very harmful'.[47] The daily tedium of army life was relieved only by the swearing, drinking and boasting bravado of male bonding. At the same time, however, intensified male friendship and comradeship were real and lasting joys of National Service. Those, like Colin MacInnes, who remember military life with pleasure recall 'the unexpected egalitarianism, the unlikely friendships, the blissful irresponsibility'.[48] Army training relies upon intensifying the opposition between male and female, with 'women' used as a term of abuse for incompetent performance, thereby cementing the prevalent cultural links between virility, sexuality and aggressiveness. Such practices serve not only to discipline men, but to raise 'masculine' morale in the face of a more typically 'feminine' reality – the enforced servility and conformity characteristic of army life. 'Effeminacy', as Royle observes, was 'the ultimate soldier's crime' and 'to some people, carrying a gun was like having a permanent hard-on'.[49]

One 'problem' for some of these young male conscripts, therefore, was that they were unlikely to realise their sexualised fantasies of military glory (even if such realisation would have served merely to bring home to them the horrors of war). These were men who were not actually killing anyone, although they were nonetheless taught to kill as the appropriate training for men. Some, like 'Jimmy Porter', were to claim to regret that they had little prospect of ever confronting and defeating an actual enemy. This was a time, it is also relevant to note, of heightened hostilities between East and West, with Western chauvinism kept continually on the boil by US propaganda about the Red Menace, and brand new fears of the Bomb and nuclear extinction. Trained for military action, fed on a Cold War diet of espionage and treason, these men were the first generation to live in a post-imperial Britain and observe the old Empire dismantled – 'given away'. One dramatic exception was the Suez crises in 1956. Ray Gosling, a railway signalman at the time, recalls:

> I can remember the feeling that ran down the line as they 'stood behind Eden', the man who was to show them and the world that the Old Bulldog could bite as well as bark . . . that they were still at the heart of 'the greatest Empire of all time'. They would send a gunboat and show the wogs how the lion still roared. There was not one man who at the time spoke against Eden, yet one could feel in the comments made their knowledge that the Empire was dead; pre-war Britain would never return, Eden would fail.[50]

And he did. (He failed, it is worth noting, primarily because President Eisenhower reminded Britain that their special relationship with the United States involved a subaltern role for Britain.)

The links between army life, masculinity and violence, however, are always more ambiguous than they might at first appear. Actual violence and fighting did not necessarily accompany the near obligatory smoking, swearing, drinking, aggressive sexual boasting and phallic symbolism of military equipment, which permeated the all-male culture of young conscripts. Recollecting his period of National Service in the late fifties, the sociologist David Morgan remembers little actual violence. There was talk of fights, but the reality was more 'an overt disdain for anything that might appear soft or wet' – more 'a taboo on tenderness' than a celebration of violence.[51] In particular, at least in terms of public discussion, there was little room for tenderness in accounts of sexuality. The army did help forge and consolidate certain dominant patterns of masculinity, yet Morgan is cautious in drawing the links: 'It was not that, simply, boys learnt to swear, drink, desire women, favour toughness, rely on their mates and so on . . . It was more a matter of learning to identify masculinity and being a male with these traits and pieces of behaviour.'[52]

These same traits and pieces of behaviour also predominated in the staple literary diet of the fifties. As Ken Worpole reports, the most popular books in Britain in the 1950s, selling in their millions to boys and men – and significant numbers of women as well – were about the experiences of male combatants in the Second World War.[53] Though unquestionably one of the most faint-hearted pupils at my all-girls school in fifties Australia, I can remember feeling obliged to read *The Wooden Horse* by Eric Williams. Like *Colditz Story* and others of the genre, it typifies the male adventure story linking masculinity and rugged individualism: men (usually RAF officers) fight for their freedom against the enormous odds of wartime imprisonment. These books were also a powerful influence in the promotion of apparently 'apolitical', but actually intensely conservative, politics and values. Strange as it may seem, although in keeping with the elimination of any political analysis of recent history, not one of these wartime bestsellers, as Worpole notes, ever mention the word 'fascism': the enemy is 'German'.[54] The hero is a man untrammelled by the everyday ties and responsibilities of sexual relationships and family.

In short, there were at least two opposed faces of masculinity in the fifties. There was the new family man, content with house and garden. And there was the old wartime hero, who put 'freedom' before family and loved ones. In the home, men had new responsibilities as husbands, though not yet as fathers. (The marriage guidance literature of the day, for example, was now stressing that men should be able to satisfy their wives sexually.) Men were still seen as necessarily the sexual instigators and educators of women, and one result was the growing visibility of impotence [. . .] A literature was developing on the dilemmas of contemporary masculinity, much of it expressing anxieties over male delinquency and educational failure. The rising divorce rates and suppressed reality of family discord similarly stirred up professional anxiety about the popularly celebrated harmonious roles of men and women. Addressing many of these social anxieties, the US sociologist Helen Hacker published a paper in 1957 on 'The New Burdens of Masculinity' in which she outlined the conflicts in 'the masculine role'. Men were expected to be more patient, understanding and gentle in their dealings with others, and yet 'with regard to women they must still be sturdy oaks'.[55] Hacker also characterised what she saw as the increased incidence of homosexuality as an index of men's flight from the new burdens of masculinity.

Whatever the real or imagined burdens on men created by the Janus-face of masculinity, new levels of antagonism in the old 'sex war' are evident in the ubiquitous misogynistic humour of the fifties. If, as Freud has argued, the function of joking is the reduction of anxiety, then male anxiety was running very deep at the time. *The Man's Book* of 1958 referred neither to women nor to children since, as the preface facetiously inquires, 'What really useful advice could one give about women in a twenty-volume encyclopaedia?' It continued by explaining that their final section on humour – 'Wit's End' – was designed to give the last word to men: 'And that in itself makes, as they say, a nice change'.[56] If there was one thing men had in common at the time, as I remember well from my own father's humour, it was the jokey pleasures of insulting women. There are 46 jokes in 'Wit's End', every one of them insulting to women, many expressing violent or destructive fantasies: 'Here lies my wife: here let her lie. / Now she's at rest. And so am I'; 'No man regards his wife with pleasure, save twice: in her bridal bed, and in her grave'; 'A gentleman is a man who never strikes a woman without provocation'; 'But Eve from scenes of bliss / Transported him for life / The more I think of this / The more I beat my wife'. Etc. etc., *ad nauseam*.[57]

We might suggest, and many feminists would, that this pervasive anti-woman humour was simply a weapon used by men to discipline women – a type of propaganda for male dominance and a warning to women of the consequences of challenging it ... later ... I will be dealing with the difficult question of the relationship between fantasy and actual behaviour. But, whatever the connections we make, there are signs of very high levels of confusion and conflict over male identity in the popular culture of the time. In the late fifties the cartoons of Jules Feiffer began to appear in the American radical paper *The Village Voice*, and were soon to be syndicated worldwide. They portrayed baffled and tortured men confronted by neurotic women in a sad, sick world of non-communication. 'Men Really Don't Like Women' Feiffer confided in an article in *Look* magazine which is pessimistically perceptive about relations between the sexes:

> The American woman is a victim. Her trouble is she is doing comparatively well as a victim. Her problem is not taken seriously. Woman is a second-class victim. And what is her problem? We all know it is man ... Man has always seen woman as his enemy. But he needs her.[58]

WOMEN AND THE LEFT IN THE FIFTIES

Amidst this taunting and teasing of women by men in the fifties, a few of the 'victims' were writing or speaking publicly and prominently; but those who were, perceived the world in ways which complemented, rather than contradicted, male perceptions. Doris Lessing's ambitious novel *The Golden Notebook* was published in 1962, but is set in the atmosphere of the despair and disillusion experienced by so many on the communist left in the late fifties: 'we have to admit that the great dream has faded and the truth is something else.'[59] It documents its heroine's quest for authenticity and fulfilment, not via the Angries' anarchic (and privately authoritarian) anti-authoritarianism, but through the earlier, more earnest and romantic Lawrentian view of sex as 'the quick of self': Anna Wolf can express herself fully and genuinely only through the love of a '*real* man'.

Doris Lessing shared the fifties anxieties over manhood, and an England 'full of men who are little boys and homosexuals and half-homosexuals'.[60] She does, however, passionately portray the sufferings of women as mothers and lovers, trying to cope with the selfishness, dishonesty and aggressive insecurity of men, as well as the anxieties, embarrassment and self-disgust many women felt about their own bodies. She is aware of the boredom and depression of women trapped in the home – 'the disease of our time', she called it.[61] Yet for Lessing, as for the wider world of the fifties, there is no alternative. We cannot blame men: 'If I were a man I'd be the same,' she writes.[62] On the contrary, women need to bolster men up, 'for the truth is, women have this deep instinctive need to build a man up as a man... I suppose this is because real men become fewer and fewer and we are frightened, trying to create men.'[63]

Those women who could articulate women's sufferings saw them as inevitable. Margaret Drabble, for example, reflected in her first novel in 1963: 'What happens otherwise is worse than what happens normally, the embroidery and the children and the sagging mind. I felt all women were doomed... born to defend and depend instead of to attack.'[64] And ironically, if unsurprisingly, when the assault on the stifling nature of family life in the fifties did finally surface in the writings of R. D. Laing and David Cooper in the sixties, it took the form of an attack on women. It denounced the pathological possessiveness of all those housebound mothers who had had little option but to live through the lives of their children. It condemned mothers who could not leave their children alone; who were denying them autonomy and driving them mad: 'A young man has only to look a little cross with his manipulative, incestuously demanding mother to end up on a detention order as "dangerous to others",'[65] David Cooper accused in 1964. R. D. Laing and his fellow anti-psychiatrists spread the verdict of maternal guilt.

The left in the fifties was as silent as everybody else on relations between the sexes, accepting unquestioningly the belief that women's problems were solved. The same was true even of the younger, renovating new left born in 1956 out of the twin crises of Suez and Hungary. As the new left grew rapidly with the rise of the Campaign for Nuclear Disarmament (CND), the first decisive break was made with the politics of the Cold War and the politics of Stalinism. Unlike the bureaucratic and economistic old left, its successor had an exciting, enriching interest in contemporary culture. Yet as Stuart Hall, one of its founding members, recalls: 'We were totally unconscious of questions of gender, totally entombed on that issue – even though we were beginning to think about personal life, even though we realised the boundaries of politics had to be ruptured to bring in those aspects of life seen as important to people.'[66] Another co-founder, Raphael Samuel, has also spoken of the left's anti-feminism:

We were worse than the Labour Party, who did at least have one-third women members. Like Colin MacInnes we romanticised the working-class male hero as the hope for the future. There was some truth in this, but also a blindness.[67]

Jean McCrindle has written of searching for books 'that would make sense
to me as a woman...There wasn't an awful lot of encouragement from
looking at women's actual lives in the 1950s.'[68] Fear and confusion accompanied women's sexual involvement with men outside marriage, with no
accessible contraception for single women, no legal abortion, and a crushing
stigma attached to unmarried mothers or 'fallen women'. Inside or outside
marriage, Jean McCrindle recalls, there was little open discussion of sexual
problems, and 'feminism' was utterly scorned as 'bourgeois': 'You were a
comrade and wanted to be treated exactly as men were.'[69] '*The Golden
Notebook*', she continues, 'describes very brilliantly the kind of women
who stayed active in the party and they were often bitter, hard, and certainly
didn't identify with the quiet wives sitting in the corner making tea while
"the comrades" discussed politics.'[70]

   What we can learn from the silence about women on the left goes beyond
the ineluctable sexism of the men (however obnoxious they may or may not
have been in their relations with women). In what little they did write women
were as silent as men about any alternative solutions to the strains placed
upon them, whether isolated in the home or, increasingly, going out to work
but expected to give complete priority to their families. Discontent was
unspoken, unshared: every woman felt she carried her burdens, her fears,
boredoms, guilts and anxieties, alone. What was needed was a whole new
way – a collective way – of looking at the problem of marriage, childbearing,
sexuality and employment. But such thinking was just not available to either
women or men at the time, and the consequences, as Jean McCrindle
suggests, were relationships 'heavy with boredom and frustration for
women, and with guilt for many men.'[71] The solutions, or attempts at
them, were [...] to inform the sexual politics of the sixties, seventies and
eighties, when both men and women began in earnest to rebel against
conventional respectability, and to go searching for other routes beyond
'the battle of the sexes' and the 'trap' of domesticity.

   On the evidence of this flashback to the fifties, it is clear that the relationship of men to home and family has undergone irreversible change over the
last three decades. Though domesticity acquired a new salience for men as
well as women in the fifties, questions of men's relationship to childcare,
housework, violence in the home, were not yet on the conceptual, let alone
the political, agenda. Today they have become an essential, if politically
often still token, part of it. Nowhere is this change clearer than in the
literature on fatherhood in the 1980s. [...] however, the extent and meaning
of the change is, as always, contradictory.

7
Mr Nice (and Mr Nasty)
Jonathan Rutherford

The Mr Nice and Mr Nasty of the title are the two archetypal responses of white men to racial difference. This... brings me to contemporary Britain and to the ways in which white middle-class men's masculinities are shaped by English ethnicity and the legacy of empire. In particular I want to focus on white men's relationship to black men, a relationship which is a potent source of white racial antagonism and fear and which is closely connected to men's uncertainties about their gender roles and identities.

In 1994, the film production company 'Working Title' launched its low budget film, *Four Weddings and a Funeral*. Despite the lack of critical acclaim, it was a popular success in the US and Britain, and a vehicle for a new, unlikely, English hero. The film transformed Hugh Grant from a nice, middle-class boy into an ambassador of English manliness. His swept back hair, his good looks and his image of harmless, bumbling, repressed ex-public school boy had a remarkable resemblance to that other doyen of mythologised homoerotic boyishness, Rupert Brooke. Grant was well aware of the Edwardian origins of his own particular appeal.

> They love me in Japan. But unfortunately I don't want their love. I want their money. I was cooking up schemes to try and get it. I thought I might write some sensitive poetry because they all think I'm sensitive and poetic [and publish it] with a nice big picture of me perhaps dressed as Rupert Brooke on the front.[1]

Unlike the muscle-bound action heroes of Hollywood who had dominated poplar cinema in the 1980s, Grant's appeal lay in his understated masculinity; his slender body, his Bermuda shorts and unathletic legs. Despite, or perhaps because of, his ineptitude in love, women were sympathetic to him. As he mumbled and fumbled beneath the cool and appraising gaze of his co-star, Andie MacDowell, English manliness found its renaissance in a compliant, self-deprecating boyishness. *Four Weddings and a Funeral* is all about a man too nice to be manly.

Grant plays Charles, who along with his upper-middle-class circle of friends, is a frequent attender of posh weddings. Saturday mornings appear as an endless ritual of oversleeping and late arrivals at weddings located in pastoral landscapes and wealthy London venues. The weddings symbolise the cultural reproduction of an English, *haute bourgeois* way of life. Whether in Somerset, London or the Highlands of Scotland, the rituals of conjugation are associated with the symbols and landscapes of the British Union: sexual reproduction and patrimony are closely entwined with a sense of place and nation. The problem for Charles is that he has never attended his own wedding; his personal crisis is his inability to connect with the right women and find true love. Charles, as the saying goes in the film, is a serial monogamist who cannot make the commitment of marriage and so cannot inherit his place in a patrilineal culture. The film's celebration of marriage and its associated culture of grand houses, gardens and pastoral scenery is an attempt to recover a one nation Toryism; an image of England as muddled, romantic and at ease with itself. Through Charles' emotional incompetence and eventual success in love, it seeks to allay the sexual insecurities of an English middle-class masculinity, offering the prospect of success in the pursuit of that elusive quality, manliness. Being nice and sensitive will pay the dividend of a woman and patrimony.

Hugh Grant epitomises a masculinity which has adopted the social tactics of niceness, compliance and liberal tolerance in response to the rising aspirations and assertiveness of women. Both in his public persona and in his fictional character of Charles, his hesitant speech and self-effacement appear to leave him incapable of asserting himself. But this foppish play-acting is designed to preserve his narcissism. In *Four Weddings*, Charles' pursuit of true love is a quest for his masculine and heterosexual prowess in marriage. However, confirmation of his manliness has been continually thwarted by a heterosexual world where true love appears to be lacking. In the end, of course, he commits himself to leading lady Carrie. Weddings, masculinity, heterosexual union and the English way of life, all appear to be confirmed as they kiss beneath an umbrella and the credits roll. But the film leaves behind a frisson of instability in this representation of male heterosexual love. In spite of its preoccupation with marriage, it is the relationship of Charles' two gay friends, Gareth and Matthew, which embodies true love. Both men are assimilated into the heterosexual culture of weddings and appear at first to be tokens of the film's liberalism. In spite of the ideal they symbolise, their relationship exists outside the symbolic and legal structures of patrimony. In this respect they offer neither a threat nor a viable alternative to the happy ending. But the significance of their relationship in the film destabilises its conventional narrative of romance. Their love for one another reflects the unresolved sexual insecurities of heterosexual men and their ambivalence toward women.

Gareth's demise from a heart attack precipitates the funeral of the film's title. Unlike the idyllic surrounds of the weddings, it takes place in an industrial area, close to his working-class, childhood home. While the various heterosexual unions are in symbolic locations of nationhood and its continuity, homosexuality is located 'outside'. The funeral is markedly different from the exclusive upper-class ambience of the weddings: the camera lingers on young gay men and one young black man, as well as older white working-class men and women. This representation of difference defines homosexual love as tolerated but extraneous to 'England'. It cannot be allowed representation or public recognition in a wedding. Instead it is expressed in terms of a profound sense of loss. After the funeral, Charles walks with Tom, the film's dimwit aristocrat, who admits that the only true love in his life was a dog he once owned. Charles doubts he will ever find love at all. Both acknowledge Gareth and Matthew as role models of men who can love. This is Charles' dilemma. What he desires to emulate is the antithesis of the English heterosexual manliness he aspires to. He gives expression to that recurring difficulty of upper and middle-class, heterosexual Englishmen – loving women. Women are necessary to confirm a man's masculinity and to continue the patrilineal culture of the nation. But the film's representation of homosexual love as something lost suggests that Charles must renounce the homoerotic origins of his desire. He succeeds in securing a woman through the efficacy of sensitivity and niceness. But the doubt remains that what he was loving was more his own desire (for himself, for other men) than a woman.

The significance of *Four Weddings and a Funeral* is not its celebration of Englishness, but what it reveals about the loose threads in the fabric of English male heterosexuality and ethnicity. Its insistent celebration of the niceness and compliance of its hero and his culture of weddings only serves to highlight the contemporary crisis in the relationship of middle-class masculinities to marriage, home and family. During the 1990s there has been an increasing willingness amongst liberal middle-class men to reject the benign masculinity associated with the New Man and reassert their personal and political interests against those of women.

BEHIND THE PAINTED SMILE

In the post-feminist era of the 1990s, there has been a growing disaffection amongst middle-class men with the ideal of sexual equality. The massive expansion of part-time jobs for women and the pattern of women divorcing men, have created a new wave of doubt and uncertainty in men's private lives. Organisations like 'Families need Fathers', campaigning against the divorce laws and for men's right to custody of their children, had already carved out a political space for a men's anti-feminist politics during the 1980s. Middle-class men began to experience a relative loss in their social prestige and economic status. An era of economic insecurity has been precipitated by globalisation, technology driven job losses and economic recession. Careers are being superseded by short-term contracts, freelancing, part-time work and piecework at home. For growing numbers in full-time employment, conditions of work are too insecure and idiosyncratic to be called jobs. Throughout the golden age of post-war consumer capitalism, full-time, tenured employment underpinned the middle-class nuclear family and its twenty-five year mortgage. By the year 2000 it will have become a minority form of work.[2] In apparent contradiction to this trend, negative equity and falling salaries have propelled men into working longer hours. The impact of this new work order on a generation of thirty and forty something men, who inherited their father's expectations of a career for life, threatens to undermine their role of head of household. At the same time it is destroying work as the principal source of their masculine self-esteem and personal integrity.

The decline in male jobs has been accompanied by changing masculine sensibilities, as increasing numbers of men invest more time in domestic life and their children. However, this turn to the home has served to heighten male insecurity as women's increased independence has led to their greater willingness to leave men. By 1993, two and a half times more divorces were granted to women than to men.[3] It is a state of affairs which led David Thomas to declare in his book *Not Guilty: In Defence of the Modern Man*: 'The fact is, people are in pain. And right now, the ones who wear trousers and stand up to piss don't seem to count for much when it comes to being healed' (p.7). But this notion that men are the new victims has little grounding in social and economic reality. In August 1993, The National Child Development Study, which had been following the lives of 11,500 men and women born in one week in March 1958, presented a report to the annual British Association meeting in Keele. It argued that, 'Marital breakdowns are creating a new underclass of women who are trapped in a downward economic spiral.' It added: 'There are few signs that men had metamorphosed into the caring and labour-sharing breed that the media was trumpeting in the early 1990s.'[4] In December 1993 the market research group Mintel published *Women 2000*, a survey of 1500 men and women.[5] It came to similar conclusions. Only one man in a hundred, it claimed, did his 'fair share of the housework'. While two men in ten said they took an equal share in the cooking, only one in ten women thought they did. Over half of the women interviewed had full-time jobs, but they were paid, on average, 29 per cent less than men in comparable jobs and were significantly less likely to have a company pension. Only 20 per cent of the working women claimed their male partners equally shared any single domestic task. Mintel's consumer manager Angela Hughes told the *Guardian*: 'Men seem to set out with good intentions to share the domestic chores but the catalyst appears to be the arrival of children. At this stage, the man appears to abdicate responsibility for his share, regardless of whether his partner is working.'[6] The surveys indicate that the downturn in men's fortunes is unrelated to any tangible increase in female equality. Men may be doing badly, but women are still worse off.

The most publicised anti-feminist diatribe was publised in 1992 by a journalist, Neil Lyndon. His book, *No More Sex War: The Failures of Feminism*, argued that the women's liberation movement had been 'fundamentally false in logic, thoroughly false in history and poisonous in effect'.[7] Lyndon's career as a spokesman for a male backlash against feminism began with an article in the *Sunday Times Magazine* in 1991. 'It is hard to think,' he declared, 'of one example of systemic and institutionalised discrimination against women in Britain today.' He argued that the liberation of women in the past twenty-five years had been a consequence of the new technologies of contraception and the right to abortion. Feminism had merely served to entrench gender stereotypes and promote antagonism and sex war between men and women. The effect of this revolution on his own life can be gauged by an article written by his wife, Deirdre Lyndon, which appeared in the *Daily Mail* on 21 September 1992 (reprinted in the *Guardian*, the following day). Her opening sentence – 'This is the book that killed my marriage' – summed up the consequence of what had become her husband's obsessive loathing of feminism: 'I kept urging Neil to temper his arguments... "It's not feminists you're attacking," I would say. "Surely it's only militant feminists?" But it became clear that it was indeed all feminists and that, to some extent, the war was indeed being waged on women.' Lyndon moved out of the family home and began a relationship with another woman who had been acting as his part-time secretary. In trying to understand her husband's 'politics of hatred', Deirdre Lyndon suggested he had moved out because 'he needed to shred all the strands of domesticity to write this book'. She added: 'In some ways I think Neil wants to strip women of motherhood.'

Deirdre Lyndon had put her finger on the primary target of anti-feminist rhetoric. Men's confusion over their role in society and feelings of impotence have encouraged the search for a scapegoat in mothers and motherhood. For Lyndon, society's neglect of the needs of men is epitomised in men's exclusion from their own homes and children: 'If our society is a patriarchy, why does it allow no statutory right to paternity leave?'[8] For anti-feminists, the problem men face, and the predicament of society and culture, is the declining authority of the father and the subsequent prevalence of female-led one-parent families. [...]

LIBERAL MEN AND SEXUAL CONSERVATIVES

Both Lyndon and Thomas are middle-class men whose lives have been shaped by the cultural freedoms and social permissiveness ushered in by the 1960s. [...]

Neil Lyndon traces the cause of his angry reaction to feminism back to his student days in the 1960s: 'I think that modern feminism was rooted in the totalitarian attitudes of the late Sixties when, in its search for a "class enemy", the New Left in America and the rest of the West appropriated the axioms of Black Power about white "honky" culture and applied them to sexual politics.'[9] In his book he locates the origins of the new social movements in the New Left of the 1960s. He argues that the biggest problem faced by the white middle-class student radicals was to identify a class enemy and a revolutionary agent of change. Black Power provided the answer. With the 'bludgeon and cleavers of totalitarianism', it persuaded white students that black people were the revolutionary agents and that white people were the enemy. According to Lyndon, the 'nincompoop generation', eager to prove themselves guilty, happily swallowed this logic. Unable to explain this act of political masochism, he speculates that it assuaged young whites' feelings of exclusion and powerlessness and made a confusing world comprehensible on a personal level. Personal psychology was more manageable than the complex realities of geopolitics, and it provided white students with something concrete to do: they could work on themselves and their relationships to exorcise their racism. Lyndon refutes the idea that feminism invented the term 'the personal is political'. He claims that this 'particular spark of unreason' originated with the Black Panthers. Adopted by the wider white political movement, it ensured the 'instantaneous collapse of liberal principle' and provided the central tenet of the offspring of Black Power and Marxism: feminism.

Lyndon's book has been dismissed as the rantings of an embittered maverick. However, his wild overestimation of the influence of Black Power on the lives of young middle-class whites and his analysis of the new social movements – anti-rational and socially destructive – shares the New Right perspective which began with Enoch Powell and his 1970 speech 'The Enemy Within'. Powell described the enemies of society as multifaceted and potentially everywhere. But he was quite clear on their social origin: they began with the influx of 'Negroes' into the northern states of America, which flung them into the 'furnace of anarchy' and created 'Black Power'. Powell described 'race', as the common factor linking the operations of 'the enemy' on several fronts.[10] 'Race' was the signifier of difference or 'otherness', subsuming the social antagonisms of the youth revolt, women's protest and class conflict under its rubric. Powell was emphatic: 'Race' would 'play a major, perhaps a decisive part in the battle of Britain.'[11] Powell's 'enemy within', originating in the culture and politics of African Americans, signified blackness as a threat to white English ethnicity and its way of life. Lyndon has appropriated Powell's argument to legitimise his casting feminism beyond the boundaries of respectable white society. In effect, Lyndon constructs feminism as a metaphorical form of 'blackness'. His anti-feminism redirects Powell's discourse of 'race' to signify an attack on white patrimony; on his own paternal role and manliness. And he has not been alone in doing this. The themes of race, the undermining of fatherhood and the family, and the racial and gendered treachery of the liberal intelligentsia have been the key preoccupations of new right social discourse since the 1980s.

In their introduction to *Family Portraits*, a collection of right-wing essays on the family, Digby Anderson and Graham Dawson identified 'brands of feminism which are deeply hostile to the family, most especially to the role of fathers.'[12] Patricia Morgan's contribution develops this theme. Her essay, 'Feminist Attempts to Sack Father: A case of unfair dismissal', prefigures Lyndon's anti-feminism and echoes the language of Robert Bly, albeit in a different political register. She begins: 'If there is a "war over the family", then one of its principal battle fronts is whether homes need fathers' (p.38). In recent years, she claims, 'fathers have faced not only the dismissal, but a positive denigration of their role. Informed by Marxism feminism and a more thorough-going collectivism, a strong lobby now exists to disestablish men's ties to the family' (p.39). She argues that the absence of fathers and exclusive feminine nurture condemn young males to a life of violent crime and underachievement at school. Her political crusade is to defend 'the home', its 'cultural heritage and the "middle class values" which it, and thus the family, is felt to harbour and transmit' (p.61). To defend the home, it is necessary to defend the father. He is the principal socialiser and educator of these values and consequently the prime target of the feminist detractors of the family:

What we can predict with certainty is that any rise in the number of boys without close ties to males with socially acceptable standards of behaviour is the very thing which is virtually guaranteed to generate a brutalised and violent masculine style ... Sexual identification is best facilitated in relationships where the father is affectionate, nurturant and extensively participates in child-rearing. (p.53)

Morgan dismisses the statistics which reveal the paucity of men's involvement in household chores: 'the range of household tasks a father undertakes does not necessarily reflect his involvement with the children ... it becomes quite inappropriate to measure any parental contribution to child-rearing in terms of practical caretaking' (p.54). What the father provides is his stabilising role of breadwinner and his ability to maintain and furnish the home; these activities construct the psychological and material parameters of family life and foster a 'more coherent, constructive and responsible world view which itself tends toward higher aspirations, good performance and low criminality' (p.55). The father might not be concretely present for his children, but his formal attachment to the household serves as a transcendental signifier of good order and stability.

Morgan uses her idealised model of paternal participation as a yardstick to judge lower-working-class and black British families whom she sees as sources of social dislocation and disruption. She draws on a study of different ethnic groups in a Midlands town, which revealed a 41 per cent level of paternal absenteeism in families of West Indian origin, as opposed to 7.5 per cent in white families.[13] She is unwilling to explore the cultural, economic and historical reasons for this differential level of female-run households. Instead she infers that black families in which the father is absent are a primary source of the 'proliferation, diversification and accentuation of violence as an individual and group phenomenon' (p.58). A society without fathers, she argues, would degenerate into a state of 'rootlessness – where there are no heritage or ties and people have no place or past, but simply wander about the face of the earth . . . a world without responsibilities in which relationships are thin and transitory' (p.60). Her eloquent paranoia about the destruction of a patrilineal society is both racial and gendered in character. For Morgan, the ideological function of the father is to enforce social discipline and to represent the moral, ethical and social foundations of culture; its symbolic law. It is an opinion she has reiterated in her 1955 booklet *Farewell to the Family*: 'Fatherhood, that "creation of society", exemplifies the rule-making and rule-following without which no culture is possible.'[14]

The perception of a causal relation between absent fathers, social disorder and the ties of national-racial identity articulated by the New Right in the 1980s, reflected the chronic uncertainties about the meanings of English ethnic identity. Paternal authority reaches beyond the realm of gender to embrace the social order as a whole; the Law of the Father is seen to protect the racial continuity and homogeneity of the family and of the nation. Anxieties aroused by the imagined failure of white patrimony create a desire for the reassertion of the symbolic function of the White Father, to guard against miscegenation and to propagate a white ethnic patrilineality. This Law of the Father is expressed by politicians and political commentators in that ubiquitous and ambiguous phrase, family values. As long as it remains predominant, white men can aspire to the dream of a patriarchal authority. But masculinity is an identity built on illusions: white men can never satisfy the demands of the idealised Father, and because a patriarchal authority is an impossibility white men project their own shameful, patrimonial failure into a racialised contempt for black patrimony. White masculinity teeters between an abstracted superiority over the black man, and a sense of its own failed manliness. To achieve some degree of stability in its identity, white ethnicity and white masculinity projects its dilemmas onto black people. The fatherless black family becomes a symbol of social breakdown, and the most potent source of white fear and desire, the young black man is fantasised as a sexually dangerous threat to the white familial order.

RACIAL DIFFERENCE, MASCULINITY AND ABSENT FATHERS

In the early 1990s this self-perpetuating racial economy of stereotypes and fantasies adhered itself to the black hyper-masculinity of gangsta rap. Rappers like Snoop Doggy Dogg, Dr Dre and the late Tupac Shakur echo the anger of young, poor African American men who have been structured out of the mainstream economy and made reliant on drugs and gangs for financial and personal survival. Self-defined as the CNN of the ghetto, gangsta rap 'reflected the nihilism of the gun culture of the black ghetto and its language of violence, male heterosexual prowess, misogyny and hopelessness'. Snoop Doggy Dogg, on trial as an accessory to murder in October 1955, exemplified this trend by releasing a song about his forthcoming trial and using the killing of 20-year-old Philip Woldemariam to promote his street credibility. As Paul Gilroy has put it, 'an amplified and exaggerated masculinity has become the boastful centrepiece of a culture of compensation that self-consciously salves the misery of the disempowered and subordinated'.[15] The gangsta rappers who have celebrated the AK 47, black-on-black murder and drive-by shootings, and employed an abusive sexual language of 'ho's and 'bitches' have personified the white stereotype of a sexually violent and dangerous black masculinity. An image – eagerly commodified by corporate America – which tended to overshadow the pleasure and excitement of the music itself.

By the mid 1990s rap's popularity transcended divisions of class, race and gender. Its element of machismo and misogyny attracted the emulation of white teenage boys who appropriated the signifiers of black, hyper-masculinity as symbols of social prestige. White boys adopted significations of blackness to enhance their masculinity: it might be a turn of phrase or swing of the body, reversing their baseball caps or wearing their jeans on their hips. The popular teen band of the early 1990s, East 17, was a prominent example of this appropriation. Their use of rap iconography defined their difference – their bad boy, working-class street image – from the more feminised, soulful masculinities of their then rivals, Take That. Les Back, in a study of working-class, white boys' adoption of black popular culture, confirms its preoccupation with masculine prowess: 'For young white men, the imaging of black masculinity in heterosexual codes of "hardness" and "hypersexuality" is one of the core elements which attracts them to black masculine style.'[16] Amongst middle-class boys too, identification with black hyper-masculinity has been a way of rebelling against their mothers and the 'soft' masculinities bestowed on them. Representations of the black male body in rap culture exemplified forms of body management and display which offered an antidote to their feelings of lack. For white boys, masquerading blackness is part of a (short-lived) adolescent revolt, a means of asserting themselves against parental authority and stabilising an uncertain masculine identity. For black boys, the impact of rap stereotypes can trap them in the representational economy of the dominant white society, which reproduces and reinforces restricted and unrepresentative images of black masculinity.

[...]

MR NICE (AND MR NASTY)

The black cultural critic and writer bell hooks has argued for caution in the controversy surrounding violence and misogyny in rap which, she believes, has become an 'elaborate form of scapegoating'. Similarly, other black cultural critics have attempted to establish a critical stance against rap's homophobia and treatment of women, without at the same time letting themselves be positioned alongside white conservatives and racists.[17] Because gangsta rap has been so popular amongst the children of the white middle class it became for a while, a litmus test of white liberal attitudes towards black people. White liberals remained guarded in their opinions. The fear of becoming embroiled in a racist discourse or being challenged by black critics for covert racism ensured that white liberalism maintained its strategy of resolving its guilty feelings about black people by being nice. It is a response which submerges the white interlocutor in a welter of platitudes which leave the polarised dichotomy of 'race' relatively untouched. In effect it imposes a cultural silence around issues of racial difference.

[...]

At the Labour Party conference in Brighton in 1995, Tony Blair spoke of the British as 'Decent People. Good people. Patrotic people ... these are "our people" ... It is a new Britain. One Britain: the people united by shared values and shared aims.' His populist language of one nation represented a cultural homogeneity which denied the plurality of ethnic identities which make up British culture. It is a rhetoric which evades the racial antagonisms which exist between ethnic groups and downplays the continuing racial discrimination against ethnic minorities. His communitarian principles of individual responsibility towards, and cultural deferral to, an ill-defined notion of community, has much in common with the social conservative tactics of 'colour blindness' and no special favours for any ethnic group. Blair's emphasis on a national collectivity denies racial diversity and is symptomatic of the liberal retreat from race.

[...]

In *Black Skin White Masks*, Fanon explores how the racial alterity of Self and Other has been constructed and how it has affected him as a black man. In the process, he offers white masculinity a language of self-reflection.[18]

His analysis draws upon the work of Jean-Paul Sartre. In *Being and Nothingness*, Sartre argues that the existence of other people can be defined as the Other; the self which is not one's own self.[19] The Other is 'indispensable...to my consciousness as self-consciousness' (p.235). An individual can only be for him or her self through another; but at the same time; 'it is only in so far as each man is opposed to the Other that he is absolutely for himself' (p.236). The Other is simultaneously the origin of self-consciousness and the source of its destruction. To be looked at, or recognised by, the Other, is to become an object of his world, an event which undermines the self-consciousness of one's own world. Sartre's philosophical structure of Self and Other relies on Hegel's dialectic of recognition, which structures alterity as a relationship of domination and struggle – only through the domination of the Other can an individual achieve an identity (for self-knowledge, self-preservation and self-mastery). Following this logic, Sartre's relation to the Other mimics the binarism of 'race'. Like Hegel's epistemology it offers a powerful descriptive insight into what it is like to live within the binarism of 'race', but it cannot provide a language to deconstruct its binarism and establish the basis of a dialogue between Self and Other. [20] Fanon attempts that dialogue.

Fanon tempers Sartre's duality of Self and Other by introducing a psychoanalytic model of human relations. In his essay, 'Fact of Blackness', he describes a confrontation between himself, a small white boy and the boy's mother. Whether it was a real life event or invented, the confrontation serves a metaphorical function as the imaginary scene of racial difference; a triangular, homosocial relationship which fixes him in the discourse of 'race'. [21] Fanon is caught in the look of the small boy: 'Mama, see the Negro! I'm frightened' (p.112). This misrecognition defines his blackness.

> My body was given back to me sprawled out, distorted, recoloured, clad in mourning in that white winter day. The Negro is an animal, the Negro is bad, the Negro is mean, the Negro is ugly; look, a nigger, it's cold, the nigger is shivering, the nigger is shivering because he is cold, the little boy is trembling because he is afraid of the nigger, the nigger is shivering with cold, that cold that goes through your bones, the handsome little boy is trembling because he thinks that the nigger is quivering with rage, the little white boy throws himself into his mother's arms: Mama, the nigger's going to eat me up. (pp.113–14)

It is a misrecognition which also defines the boy's whiteness and in this respect the scene serves as a metaphor for white men's relationship to their black Other. Fanon's triangle of man, mother and son is a representation of Freud's primal scene and introduces the gendered, oedipal nature of this

confrontation. In his case study of the 'Wolf Man', Freud analysed a young
man's nightmare about being eaten by wolves, which he argued was the
condensation and displacement of his childish terror at the sight of his
parents copulating.[22] The young man conceived the act as an aggressive
assertion of his father's sexual power over his mother. The boy's fear of his
father – being eaten by the wolves – represents the threat of castration which
will annihilate his attachment to his mother. However, while the young
man's dream signifies his desire to escape the oedipal tyranny of his father,
it also represents his desire both to succumb to and have his father's sexual
power.

> It semms, therefore, as though he had identified himself with his castrated
> mother during the dream, and was now fighting against the fact. 'If you
> want to be sexually satisfied by Father', we may perhaps represent him as
> saying to himself, 'you must allow yourself to be castrated like Mother;
> but I won't have that.' In short, a clear protest on the part of his
> masculinity.[23]

Despite Freud's depiction of the boy's masculine protest, his analysis reveals
the son's identification with the father as ambiguous and never fully secured:
should he be like his father or to retain an identification with his mother.[24]
Freud's small boy stands before his father in much the same way as Fanon's
small white boy stands before his black Other; incapacitated by the uncertainty of his own identity and shamed by his incompleteness. It is the childhood legacy of adult men. As Sartre writes: 'I am ashamed of myself as I
appear to the Other ... Shame is by nature recognition. I recognise that I am
as the other sees me ... Thus shame is the shame of oneself before the
Other ... But at the same time I need the Other in order to realise fully all
the structures of my being' (p.222).

Fanon, like Freud, heralds the arrival of Otherness in the form of a
frightening male figure. Confronted with this black father figure, he places
the boy in a feminised position, seeking an identification with the mother.
This identification contains the vestiges of his pre-oedipal relationship; his
immature ego is undifferentiated from the maternal object and his meaning
resides in the mind and body of his mother. In this pre-oedipal state, the
struggle for recognition and mastery over the Other is absent, but so too, is
self and identity. In the moment he throws himself into his mother's arms, he
turns his back on the Law of the Father and with it his gendered subjectivity.
In oedipal terms, the boy's identification with his mother reverses the male
trajectory through the oedipus complex; he becomes his father's daughter.
Even as the black man trembles in his own fear, the white boy learns that the
site of racial difference is the potential undoing of his own masculine
identity.

This imaginary scene of racial difference confronts the white man with the limits of his masculinity. To secure his place in the patrimony and diminish the threat of the black Other, he must destroy the paternal function of black masculinity which threatens him with castration. To defend himself he has two archetypal strategies. The first is to defend his own internal boundaries, to reassert his masculine independence from his mother and aggressively align himself with the existing polarities of 'race' and the heterosexual gender order. This way lies racial paronoia and the struggle for domination: the black man is the threatening Other who covets 'his' mother/woman. His domination over the black Other is an integral part of his desire, to inherit the patriarchal mantle of the white father figure; to repress his mother love, subordinate women and pursue the illusion of an undivided masculine plenitude. But he can never fully achieve patriarchy's idealised symmetry of gendered antinomies. Behind his militant reaction, his own fear of the Other ignites his repressed wish for union with his mother. Humiliated by the Other's recognition of his lack, he redoubles his hostility towards the black man. The self-perpetuating cycle of fear, shame and hatred escalates until the obvious solution presents itself – castrate the black man metaphorically, and if necessary literally. Once unmanned, the black father can no longer sit in judgement over the white man's infantile choice of castration in that primal confrontation with the Father/Other. With the destruction of the black father, black men in the white man's imaginary are reduced to his own level of permanent adolescence. But the fantasy of castration eroticises the black man, his mutilated body signifies its willingness to be penetrated. Each confrontation with his black Other ignites the white man's repressed homoerotic desire. His racial paranoia is fuelled by his homophobia and spirals into an ever increasing brutality as he attempts to subjugate and destroy his unmanly and illicit desires. 'Race' becomes a sexual war in which the body of the black man functions as the involuntary screen onto which the white man projects his oedipal dilemmas.

Against this backdrop of racial hatred, and its historic practices of lynching and sexual mutilation, is counterposed a second strategy, one which is associated with a white liberal politics of race. This second strategy is designed to evade the troubling and potentially dangerous confrontation with Otherness; to negate it, to reduce difference to sameness, to love the Other in an attempt to place him outside the sphere of mastery. The black man is de-structured as an Other and refashioned as the same as the white man. What unites them in the mind of the white man is a shared enemy, the White Father. It is the fantasy of the rebellious white son in search of potential allies – a brotherhood of the dispossessed. But the white man's open embrace, his social tactic of niceness and of compliance with the Other, repeatedly pushes him into a masochistic position. As Sartre wrote:

'Masochism is characterised as a species of vertigo . . . before the abyss of the Other's subjectivity.'[25] In spite of his apparent good intentions and pleasant words, this white man is even more afraid of his black Other than his paranoid brother. While the latter struggles to defend his ego boundaries by whatever means necessary, the nice man is unable to lock anyone out. He feels constantly under threat of invasion. To retain the integrity of his boundaries in the face of his own eagerness to give them up, he hones a language of evasion, abstracting black men into an amorphous victimhood. He can champion victims, but he cannot conceive of the black man's own separately defined integrity and manliness. His niceness is essentially a narcissistic attack on the Other, designed to disarm difference and render the Other pliable and benign. Because he fears black men as he fears his own father, he fosters fantasies about black women brutalised by black men and neglected by black fathers. Like his own mother, they need his protection and care.

[. . .]

The purpose of this essay has been to explore a third way to respond to racial difference: one in which white, middle-class Englishmen stop pretending to be the considerate host and recognise the relations of power and subordination such a role is built upon. In the white liberal politics of race such a recognition has often been followed by a state of contrition and self-effacement; a denial of identity and self-interest which all too often culminates in an angry if covert backlash. Disowning white English ethnicity has done little towards understanding our intimate, emotional connections to it. A third way has to avoid self-deception and recognise that the archetypes of Mr Nice and Mr Nasty are both elements of our racialised subjectivities. It means acknowledging the contradictory, often confused nature of our feelings about, and reaction to, black and Asian British people. The white liberal politics of race has celebrated the shared humanity of ethnic groups and avoided engaging with the incommensurabilities of racial difference. Consequently it has failed to develop a language which can speak of racial antagonisms, conflicts of interest and cultural values, personal anxieties and fears. Faced with these, language withers into racial sterotypes and prejudice. The celebratory language of multi-culturalism has tended to reproduce Asian and black British people as Other simply because it never took white English ethnicity as a problematic. Similarly white anti-racism in its disavowal of whiteness and English ethnicity ignored or denigrated white peoples' emotional attachments to their ethnicity. Neither strategy provided the space to analyse whiteness and English ethnicity and make it a subject of debate. We need that critical self-reflection because the alternative is to continue to resurrect the old imperial dream of English manliness, and to hinder still further the protracted process of decolonising and deracialising the the

the same collective self-deception as the film, *Four Weddings and a Funeral.* It will put white England back to sleep with Mr Nice and allow the long dream to continue...

8

Are You a Man or a Mouse?

Homi K. Bhabha

For my father

To speak of masculinity in general, sui generis, must be avoided at all costs. It is as a discourse of self-generation, reproduced over the generations in patrilineal perpetuity, that masculinity seeks to make a name for itself. 'He', that ubiquitous male member, is the masculinist signature writ large – the pronoun of the invisible man; the subject of the surveillant, sexual order; the object of humanity personified. It must be our aim not to deny or disavow masculinity, but to disturb its manifest destiny – to draw attention to it as a prosthetic reality – a 'prefixing' of the rules of gender and sexuality; an appendix or addition, that willy-nilly, supplements and suspends a 'lack-in-being'.

This is the collective project of those who contributed to a dossier on masculinity in a recent issue of *Artforum*.[1] For instance, writer and poet Wayne Koestenbaum says. 'I have swallowed the word "masculine" – even my shadow talks too loudly', and then he acts out/performs the prosthetic nature of masculinity that I have proposed, 'Yet I don't know what "it" is. I dropped it – will you pick it up?'[2] Masculinity, then, is the 'taking up' of an enunciative position, the making up of a psychic complex, the assumption of a social gender, the supplementation of a historic sexuality, the apparatus of a cultural difference.

Film-maker Todd Hayne and historian of literature Herbert Sussman, in the same *Artforum* dossier, take up Koestenbaum's challenge and rush to pick 'it' up, only to find that the 'it', or 'he' – masculine identity – initiates a mobility, a movement of meanings and beings that function powerfully through an uncanny invisibility. 'To what else can you attribute that unique sense of naturalness, the standard against which the world of differences is compulsively measured?' Haynes asks.[3] And Sussman's response insists that the compulsive measure of masculinity is a 'problematic in which the governing terms are contradiction, conflict, and anxiety'.[4]

Each of these attempts at naming masculinity becomes a compulsive probing of the condition itself. Attempts at defining the 'subject' of masculinity unfailingly reveal what I have called its prosthetic process. My own masculinity is strangely separating from me, turning into my shadow, the place of my filiation and my fading. My attempt to conceptualise its conditionality becomes a compulsion to question it; my analytic sense that masculinity normalises and naturalises difference turns into a kind of neurotic 'acting out' of its power and its powerlessness. It is this oscillation that has enabled the feminist and gay revision of masculinity – the turning back, the re-turning, of the male gaze – to confront what historian Peter Middleton describes as the 'blocked reflexivity' that marks masculine self-identification, masked by an appeal to universalism and rationality.[5]

It is this oscillation, initiated at the heart of masculinity – its ambivalent identification – that turns its address from an innate invisibility, a normal condition, to a compulsive interrogation. 'Are you a man or a mouse?' I can still hear my attorney father repeatedly confronting me in Bombay, his barristerish bravura seeking a kind of exclusive, excluding, bonding. 'Do I have to choose?' I remember thinking, in anxious awkwardness, caught impossibly, ambivalently, in between 'two different creeds and two different outlooks on life'.[6] Gnawed by doubt and indecision, I felt terribly ratty about all of this. Much later, I realised that my question to my father should have been the Lacanian one, '*Qui Vuoi*: What do you want of me? Why do you keep asking me if I'm the mouse-man when you are rather like Freud's Rat Man?'

And, ironically, it was in that depressing Freudian bestiary, the case of the Rat Man, which dwells on the obsessive nature of one kind of 'blocked masculine reflexivity', that I found a response to my own problematic of the oscillatory and ambivalent moods of manhood. 'Who do you love most, Daddy or Mummy?' is another version of my father's question, which, Freud writes, 'accompanies the child throughout its life', whatever may be the relative intensity of its feelings toward the two sexes, or whatever may be the sexual aim upon which it finally becomes fixed. But, normally, this opposition soon loses the character of a hard-and-fast contradiction, of an inexorable 'either-or'. Room is found for satisfying the '*unequal demands* of both sides'.[7]

Holding on to this anxiety about the domestic scenario of rattish father-love, its compulsion and doubt, I want to displace it onto another kind of anxious love – *amor patriae* – the naturalist, phallic identification with the service of the nation. Now, this link that I am suggesting between nationalism and masculinism is clearly seen in the work of Johann Fichte, often credited with being the father of modern national sentiment. It is rarely remarked of his *Addresses to the German Nation* (1807–1808) that its central metaphor for rational, national identification is the scopic regime.[8] It is the world of perception – the eye of the mind – that fosters a naturalist, national pedagogy which defines the *Menschenfreundlichkeit* of the German nation: 'Naturalness [*and manliness*] on the German side,' he writes, 'arbitrariness and artificiality [*and effeminacy*] on the foreign side, are the fundamental differences.'[9]

The arbiter of this nationalist/naturalist ethic is the bearer of a peculiar, visible invisibility (some call it the phallus) – the familial patriarch. The position must be understood as an enunciative site – rather than an identity – whose identificatory axes can be gendered in a range of strategic ways. The instinct for respect – central to the civic responsibility for the *service* of nation-building – comes from the Father's sternness, which is an effect of his 'peripheral' position in the family: 'This is the natural love of the child for the father, not as the guardian of his sensuous well-being, but as the mirror from which his own self-worth or worthlessness is reflected for him.'[10]

But amidst the metaphysics of the 'directness of national perception', the Father's image is a form of identificatory indirection or elision – what we may call 'phallic' peripherality. For it is the absence of the Father – rather than the mother, who appears 'more directly as benefactor' – that constitutes the principle of national self-identification and the *service* of the nation. The national subject is then founded on the trace of the father's absent presence in the present of the mirror, whereas the mother's immanent 'over'-presentness is supplemental – marked by the overbearing shadow of the Father but more clearly held in the line of vision.

This gendering of the nation's familial, domestic metaphor makes its masculinism and its naturalism neurotic. The temporality of the national 'affect', represented in the parents' *fort/da* game, turns *amor patriae* into a much more anxious love. Explicitly so when we recall that, in a psycho-analytic sense, anxiety is a 'sign' of a danger implicit in/on the threshold of identity, *in between* its claims to coherence and its fears of dissolution, 'between identity and non-identity, internal and external'.[11] This anxious boundary that is also a displacement – the peripheral – has a specific relevance to national identification when we realise, after Freud, that what distinguishes fear from anxiety is the danger of a loss of perception (a *Wahrnehmungsverlust*) attached to familiar (and familial) images, situations, and representations.[12] The indeterminacy of anxiety produces, as with my reading of the Fichtean mirror, 'a traumatic divergence of representation and signification' at the very core of the gendering cathexes that stabilise the 'I'.[13] As if to emphasise further my articulation of anxiety's 'present' and the desire for a national past as a peripherality that borders and bothers the national discourse, Lacan suggests that the structure of anxiety 'seems to be that of a twisted border'.[14] This structure – a twisted border – has an immediate relevance to our speculations on the national past and its challenge to the naturalism and progressivism of the matrical myth of modern progress. For, as Lacan suggests, that spatial 'twisting' is part of a profound temporal disjunction at the heart of anxiety:

[Anxiety] challenges me, questioning me at the very root of my own desire... as cause of this desire and not as object. And it is because this entails *a relation of antecedence*, a temporal relation, that I can do nothing to break this hold rather than enter into it. *It is this temporal relation that is anxiety.*[15]

What happens when the phallic structure of *amor patriae* turns into an anxious ambivalence? What kind of atavism emerges in the political sphere when that 'relation of antecedence' which is traditionally associated with patriarchal precedence is challenged at the very root of its desire? Can democracy turn demonic in the service of the nation through observing the imperatives of phallic respect? Surprisingly, in a recent issue of *Time* magazine, Michael Kinsley reflects on such topics in an essay called 'Is Democracy Losing its Romance?' After a *tour d'horizon* of the postcommunist world, during which he concludes that 'democracy, far from suppressing [nationalist hatred], actually gives vent to [it]', Kinsley turns a homeward glance. In the United States today, he suggests, there has emerged a populism with an antidemocratic flavour, which 'hungers for a strong leader on a white horse. Thus Ross Perot, America's would-be Fujimori.' Then he continues:

As the current movie *The Remains of the Day* reminds us, there was a time not long ago, the 1930s, when openly expressed doubts about the wisdom of democracy as a system of government were positively fashionable, even in established democratic societies. These days everybody at least pays lip service to the democratic ideal. Will that change?[16]

Is it possible to read Kazuo Ishiguro's *The Remains of the Day*, centred on the very British bathos of the butler Stevens, a 'gentleman's gentleman', as a parable of the masculinist ritual of 'service' to the nation, with the domestic sphere as a substitute for the public sphere? In the British context, 'service' has a double cultural genealogy. It represents an implication in the class structure where domestic service normalises class difference by extravagantly 'acting it out' as an affiliative practice, perfectly exemplified in the metonymic mimicry of the idiomatic naming of the butler as a 'gentleman's gentleman': 'A butler's duty is to provide good service', Stevens meditates, 'by concentrating on what is within our realm... by devoting our attention to providing the best possible service to those great gentlemen in whose hands the destiny of civilisation truly lies.'[17]

But, in the very same English context, at the same historical moment, 'service' has an imperial and international connotation: the service to the ideal of Empire, conducted through knowledges and practices of cultural discrimination and domination. For instance, in a 1923 essay entitled 'The

Character of a Fine Gentleman', published in the protofascist journal *The English Review*, H. C. Irwin extols the virtues of 'Dutifulness (*pietas*) and reverence for all that deserves veneration', and then proposes three classes of gentleman: the 'English gentleman', his 'transatlantic cousins', and '*Anglo-Indian worthies*'.[18]

The brilliance of Ishiguro's exposition of the ideology of service lies in his linking the national and the international, the indigenous and the colonial, by focusing on the anti-Semitism of the interwar period. He thus mediates race and cultural difference through a form of difference – Jewishness – that confuses the boundaries of class and race and represents the '*insider's outsiderness*'. Jewishness stands for a form of historical and racial *in-betweenness* that again resonates with the Benjaminian view of history as a view from the 'outside, on the basis of a specific recognition from within'.[19]

If 'domestic service' in the figure of the butler is that 'unchosen' moment that naturalises class difference by ritualising it, then the narrative's attention to Jewishness and anti-Semitism raises the issue of gender and race, and, in my view, places these questions in a colonial frame. It is while Stevens is polishing the silver – the mark of the good servant – that the narrative deviates to recall the dismissal of two Jewish housemaids at the insistence of the fascist Lord Darlington. The gleam of the silver becomes that Fichtean national mirror where the master's paternal authority is both affirmed and, in this case, tarnished by the housekeeper Miss Kenton's pressing of the charge of anti-Semitism against both Darlington and Stevens. This is the ambivalent moment in the narrative, when the 'memory' of anti-Semitism and the interwar 'English' Nazi connection turns the naturalism and nationalism of the silver service into the 'anxiety' of the past – what Lacan has described as the temporal antecedence of the anxious moment.

The preservation of social precedence, embodied in the butler's service, is undone in the temporal antecedence that the presence of the Jew unleashes in the narrative present and the national memory. The English silver – the mark of the gentleman – becomes engraved with the image of Judas Iscariot, the sign of racial alterity and social inadmissibility. But the anti-Semitic historical past initiates, as anxiety is wont to do, a double frame of discrimination and domination that produces a temporal montage where Jew and colonised native, anti-Semitism and anticolonial racism, are intimately linked. For the British fascists, such as Ishiguro's Lord Darlington, argued for the Nazi cause on the grounds that Hitler's success was intimately bound up with the preservation of the British Empire. E. W. D. Tennant, who was undoubtedly amongst the most prominent of Lord Darlington's guests, and had certainly basked in the glow of Stevens' glinting silver, had this to say in 1933, in an article entitled 'Herr Hitler and his Policy', published in *The English Review*:

The evidence that I saw supports the idea that the burning of the Reichstag and the consequent seizing of the Karl Liebknecht house was an act of providence. The Karl Liebknecht house was set up as a printing works where Communist propaganda was prepared for distribution all over the world. There were thousands of pamphlets in many languages including thousands for distribution among the natives of India and South Africa. *Much information of the highest interest to the British Empire and particularly in regard to India and the Anti-Imperial league is available.*[20]

If 'phallic respect' leads periodically to the resurgence of the fascination with fascism – 'a strong leader on a white horse' – then I want to end up with an instance of feminist 'disrespect' for the hagiography of political father figures, however politically radical they are in intent. My emphasis on the 'doubly' gendered national identification, visible as an oscillation that 'loses the character of a hard-and-fast contradiction, of an inexorable either-or', enables an understanding of subaltern agency as the power to reinscribe and relocate the given symbols of authority and victimage.

One way of concretely envisaging such a practice is through the work of artist Adrian Piper. Her series entitled *'Pretend'* deploys the dynamic of the fetishistic gaze to replay the scenario of disavowal across the portraits of black men (including Martin Luther King, Jr), each of them bearing a piece of the text: 'Pretend not to know what you know.' The unmarked icon at the end of the series shows three apes in the familiar see-no-evil, hear-no-evil, speak-no-evil triptych. Piper substitutes for the mother figure of the Freudian fetishistic scenario the black father figure of the Civil Rights Movement. The mother's overdetermined 'lack' is replaced by the ineradicable *visibility and presence* of the black skin to which Fanon drew our attention; the signifier of sexuality, with its splitting, haunts the male icon of radical victimage that seeks to constitute itself in a continuist political/prophetic tradition of patriarchal activism.

The spectator's identification with the apes incites, even excites, two forms of disavowal and its undoing: it cuts both ways, Janus-faced, across sexual and racial difference and subjection. The viewer cannot but occupy an ambivalent, even incommensurable identification with the visible 'black' history of racial victimage and the struggle against it. There is, at the same time, a refusal to 'pretend', and a resistance to the disavowal, within black, patriarchal, 'race' politics, of the agency of women, gay, and lesbian activists.

Social splittings of form and context are at the core of Piper's work, according to one critic.[21] And in *Pretend*, I think, she is warning us that 'what we see is not what we need to get or desire', either in a political or sexual sense. By placing the viewer in a split position – an intermediacy between the ambivalent, phantasmatic scene of sexuality and the more binary, heterosexist tradition of a style of race politics – Piper makes us aware of the complex, perhaps contradictory relation between historical needs, political desires, and the destiny, even density, of our gendered selves.

9

How to Build a Man

Anne Fausto-Sterling

How does one become a man? Although poets, novelists, and playwrights long past answered with discussions of morality and honour, these days scholars deliberate the same question using a metaphor – that of social construction. In the current intellectual fashion, men are made, not born. We construct masculinity through social discourse, that array of happenings that covers everything from music videos, poetry, and rap lyrics to sports, beer commercials, and psychotherapy. But underlying all of this clever carpentry is the sneaking suspicion that one must start with a blueprint – or, to stretch the metaphor yet a bit more, that buildings must have foundations. Within the soul of even the most die-hard constructionist lurks a doubt. It is called the body.

In contrast, biological and medical scientists feel quite certain about their world. For them, the body tells the truth. (Never mind that postmodern scholarship has questioned the very meaning of the word 'truth'.) My task in this essay is to consider the truths that biologists extract from bodies, human and otherwise, to examine scientific accounts – some might even say constructions – of masculinity. To do this, I will treat the scientific/medical literature as yet another set of texts open to scholarly analysis and interpretation.

What are little boys made of? While the nursery rhyme suggests 'snips and snails, and puppy-dogs tails', during the past seventy years, medical scientists have built a rather more concrete and certainly less fanciful account. Perhaps the single most influential voice during this period has been that of psychologist John Money. Since at least the 1920s, embryologists have understood that during foetal development a single embryonic primordium – the indifferent foetal gonad – can give rise to either an ovary or a testis. In a similar fashion, both male and female external genitalia arise from a single set of structures. Only the internal sex organs – uteri, fallopian tubes, prostates, sperm transport ducts – arise during embryonic development from separate sets of structures. In the 1950s, Money extended these embryological understandings into the realm of psychological development. As he saw it, all humans start on the same road, but the path rapidly begins to fork. Potential males take a series of turns in one direction, potential females in another. In real time, the road begins at fertilisation and ends during late adolescence. If all goes as it should, then there are two, and only two, possible destinations – male and female.

But, of course, all does not always go as it should. Money identified the various forks in the road by studying individuals who took one or more wrong turns. From them, he derived a map of the normal. This is, in fact, one of the very interesting things about biological investigators. They use the infrequent to illuminate the common. The former they call abnormal, the latter normal. Often, as is the case for Money and others in the medical world, the abnormal requires management. In the examples I will discuss, management means conversion to the normal. Thus, we have a profound irony. Biologists and physicians use natural biological variation to define normality. Armed with this description, they set out to eliminate the natural variation that gave them their definitions in the first place.

How does all this apply to the construction of masculinity? Money lists ten road signs directing a person along the path to male or female. In most cases these indicators are clear, but, as in any large city these days, sometimes graffiti makes them hard to read and the traveller ends up taking a wrong turn. The first sign is *chromosomal sex*, the presence of an X or a Y chromosome. The second is *gonadal sex*: when there is no graffiti, the Y or the X instructs the foetal gonad to develop into a testis or an ovary. *Foetal hormonal sex* marks the third fork: the embryonic testis must make hormones which influence events to come – particularly the fourth (*internal morphologic sex*), fifth (*external morphologic sex*), and sixth (*brain sex*) branches in the road. All of these, but especially the external morphologic sex at birth, illuminate the road sign for step number seven, *sex of assignment and rearing*. Finally, to become either a true male or a true female in John Money's world, one must produce the right hormones at puberty (pubertal hormonal sex), acquire and express a consistent *gender identity and role*, and, to complete the picture, be able to reproduce in the appropriate fashion (*procreative sex*).[1]

Many medical texts reproduce this neat little scheme, and suggest that it is a literal account of the scientific truth, but they neglect to point out how, at each step, scientists have woven into the fabric their own deeply social understandings of what it means to be male or female. Let me illustrate this for several of the branches in the road. Why is it that usually XX babies grow up to be female while XYs become male? Geneticists say that it is because of a specific Y chromosome gene, often abbreviated SDY (for 'Sex-Determining Gene' on the Y). Biologists also refer to the SDY as the Master Sex-Determining Gene and say that in its *presence* a male is formed. Females, on the other hand, are said to be the default sex. In the *absence* of the master gene, they just naturally happen. The story of the SDY begins an account of maleness that continues throughout development. A male embryo must activate its master gene and seize its developmental pathway from the underlying female ground plan.

When the SDY gene starts working, it turns the indifferent gonad into a functional testis. One of the first things the testis does is to induce hormone synthesis. It is these molecules that take control of subsequent developmental steps. The first hormone to hit the decks (MIS, or Mullerian Inhibiting Substance) suppresses the development of the internal female organs, which lie in wait ready to unveil their feminine presence. The next, foetal testosterone, manfully pushes other embryonic primordia to develop both the internal and external trappings of physical masculinity. Again, medical texts offer the presence/absence hypothesis. Maleness requires the presence of special hormones; in their absence, femaleness just happens.[2]

Up to this point, two themes emerge. First, masculinity is an active presence which forces itself onto a feminine foundation. Money sometimes calls this 'The Adam Principle – adding something to make a male'. Second, the male is in constant danger. At any point male development can be derailed: a failure to activate SDY, and the gonad becomes an ovary; a failure to make MIS, and the foetus can end up with fallopian tubes and a uterus superimposed on an otherwise male body; a failure to make foetal testosterone, and, despite the presence of a testis, the embryo develops the external trappings of a baby girl. One fascinating contradiction in the scientific literature illustrates my point. Most texts write that femaleness results from the absence of male hormones, yet at the same time scientists worry about how male foetuses protect themselves from being femininised by the sea of maternal (female) hormones in which they grow.[3] This fear suggests, of course, that female hormones play an active role, after all; but most scientists do not pick up on that bit of logic. Instead, they hunt for special proteins the male embryo makes in order to protect itself from maternally induced feminisation. (It seems that mother is to blame even before birth.)

Consider now the birth of a boy-child. He is perfect: Y chromosomes, testes descended into their sweet little scrotal sacs, a beautifully formed penis. He is perfect – except that the penis is very tiny. What happens next? Some medical texts refer to a situation such as this as a social emergency, others see it as a surgical one. The parents want to tell everyone about the birth of their baby boy; the physicians fear he cannot continue developing along the road to masculinity. They decide that creating a female is best. Females are imperfect by nature, and if this child cannot be a perfect or near-perfect male, then being an imperfect female is the best choice. What do the criteria physicians use to make such choices tell us about the construction of masculinity?

Medical managers use the following rule of thumb:

Genetic females should always be raised as females, preserving reproductive potential, regardless of how severely the patients are virilised. In the
genetic male, however, the gender of assignment is based on the infant's
anatomy, predominantly the size of the phallus.[4]

Only a few reports on penile size at birth exist in the scientific literature,
and it seems that birth size in and of itself is not a particularly good indicator
of size and function at puberty. The average phallus at birth measures 3.5 cm
(1 to 1.5 inches) long. A baby boy born with a penis measuring only 0.9
inches raises some eyebrows, but medical practitioners do not permit one
born with a penis less than 0.6 inches long to remain as a male.[5] Despite the
fact that the intact organ promises to provide orgasmic pleasure to the future
adult it is surgically removed (along with the testes) and replaced by a much
smaller clitoris which may or may not retain orgasmic function. When
surgeons turn 'Sammy' into 'Samantha', they also build her a vagina. Her
primary sexual activity is to be the recipient of a penis during heterosexual
intercourse. As one surgeon recently commented, 'It's easier to poke a hole
than build a pole'.

All this surgical activity goes on to ensure a congruous and certain sex of
assignment and sex of rearing. During childhood, the medical literature
insists, boys must have a phallus large enough to permit them to pee standing up, thus allowing them to 'feel normal' when they play in little boys'
peeing contests. In adulthood, the penis must become large enough for
vaginal penetration during sexual intercourse. By and large, physicians use
the standard of reproductive potential for making females and phallus size
for making males, although Suzanne J. Kessler reports one case of a physi-
cian choosing to reassign as male a potentially reproductive genetic female
infant rather than remove a well-formed penis.[6]

At birth, then, masculinity becomes a social phenomenon. For proper
masculine socialisation to occur, the little boy must have a sufficiently large
penis. There must be no doubt in the boy's mind, in the minds of his parents
and other adult relatives, or in the minds of his male peers about the
legitimacy of his male identification. In childhood, all that is required is
that he be able to pee in a standing position. In adulthood, he must engage in
vaginal heterosexual intercourse. The discourse of sexual pleasure, even for
males, is totally absent from this medical literature. In fact, male infants who
receive extensive penile surgery often end up with badly scarred and thus
physically insensitive members. While no surgeon finds this outcome desirable, in assigning sex to an intersexual infant, sexual pleasure clearly takes a
backseat to ensuring heterosexual conventions. Penetration in the absence of
pleasure takes precedence over pleasure in the absence of penetration.

In the world of John Money and other managers of intersexuality, men are
made not born. Proper socialisation becomes more important than genetics.

Hence, Money and his followers have a simple solution to accidents as terrible as penile amputation following infant circumcision: raise the boy as a girl. If both the parents and the child remain confident of his newfound female identity, all will be well. But what counts as good mental health for boys and girls? Here, Money and his coworkers focus primarily on female development, which becomes the mirror from which we can reflect the truth about males. Money has published extensively on XX infants born with masculinised genitalia. Usually such children are raised as girls, receiving surgery and hormonal treatments to femininise their genitalia and to ensure a feminine puberty. He notes that frequently such children have a harder time than usual achieving clarity about their femininity. Some signs of trouble are these: in the toddler years, engaging in rough-and-tumble play, and hitting more than other little girls do; in the adolescent years, thinking more about having a career and fantasising less about marriage than other little girls do; and, as an adolescent and young adult, having lesbian relationships.

The homologue to these developmental variations can be found in Richard Green's description of the 'Sissy Boy Syndrome'. Green studied little boys who develop 'feminine' interests – playing with dolls, wanting to dress in girls' clothing, not engaging in enough rough-and-tumble play. These boys, he argued, are at high risk for becoming homosexuals. Money's and Green's ideas work together to present a picture of normality. And, surprise, surprise, there is no room in the scheme for a normal homosexual. Money makes a remarkable claim. Genetics and even hormones count less in making a man or a woman than does socialisation. In sustaining that claim, his strongest evidence, his trump card, is that the child born a male but raised a female becomes a heterosexual female. In their accounts of the power of socialisation, Money and his coworkers define heterosexual in terms of the sex of rearing. Thus, a child raised as a female (even if biologically male) who prefers male lovers is psychologically heterosexual, although genetically she is not.

Again, we can parse out the construction of masculinity. To begin with, normally developing little boys must be active and willing to push one another around; maleness and aggression go together. Eventually, little boys become socialised into appropriate adult behaviour, which includes heterosexual fantasy and activity. Adolescent boys do not dream of marriage, but of careers and a professional future. A healthy adolescent girl, in contrast, must fantasise about falling in love, marrying, and raising children. Only a masculinised girl dreams of a professional future. Of course, we know already that for men the true mark of heterosexuality involves vaginal penetration with the penis. Other activities, even if they are with a woman, do not really count.

This might be the end of the story, except for one thing. Accounts of normal development drawn from the study of intersexuals contain internal inconsistencies. How *does* Money explain the higher percentage than normal of lesbianism, or the more frequent aggressive behaviour among masculinised children raised as girls? One could imagine elaborating on the socialisation theme: parents aware of the uncertain sex of their children subconsciously socialise them in some intermediary fashion. Shockingly for a psychologist, however, Money denies the possibility of subconsciously driven behaviour. Instead, he and the many others who interpret the development of intersexual children resort to hormonal explanations. If an XX girl, born with a penis, surgically 'corrected' shortly after birth, and raised as a girl, subsequently becomes a lesbian, Money and others do not look to faulty socialisation. Instead, they explain this failure to become heterosexual by appealing to hormones present in the foetal environment. Excess foetal testosterone caused the masculinisation of the genitalia; similarly, foetal testosterone must have altered the developing brain, readying it to view females as appropriate sexual objects. Here, then, we have the last bit of the picture painted by biologists. By implication, normal males become sexually attracted to females because testosterone affects their brain during embryonic development. Socialisation reinforces this inclination.

Biologists, then, write texts about human development. These documents, which take the form of research papers, textbooks, review articles, and popular books, grow from interpretations of scientific data. Often written in neutral, abstract language, the texts have the ring of authority. Because they represent scientific findings, one might imagine that they contain no preconceptions, no culturally instigated belief systems. But this turns out not to be the case. Although based in evidence, scientific writing can be seen as a particular kind of cultural interpretation – the enculturated scientist interprets nature. In the process, he or she also uses that interpretation to reinforce old or build new sets of social beliefs. Thus, scientific work contributes to the construction of masculinity, and masculine constructs are among the building blocks for particular kinds of scientific knowledge. One of the jobs of the science critic is to illuminate this interaction. Once this is done, it becomes possible to discuss change.

10

Femininity and its Discontents

Jacqueline Rose

Is psychoanalysis a 'new orthodoxy' for feminism? Or does it rather represent the surfacing of something difficult and exceptional but important for feminism, which is on the verge (once again) of being lost? I will argue that the second is the case, and that the present discarding of psychoanalysis in favour of forms of analysis felt as more material in their substance and immediately political in their effects is a *return* to positions whose sensed inadequacy for feminism produced a gap in which psychoanalysis could – fleetingly – find a place.[1] What psychoanalysis offered up in that moment was by no means wholly satisfactory and it left many problems unanswered or inadequately addressed, but the questions which it raised for feminism are crucial and cannot, I believe, be approached in the same way, or even posed, from anywhere else. To ask what are the political implications of psychoanalysis for feminism seems to me, therefore, to pose the problem the wrong way round. Psychoanalysis is already political for feminism – political in the more obvious sense that it came into the arena of discussion in response to the internal needs of feminist debate, and political again in the wider sense that the repudiation of psychoanalysis by feminism can be seen as linking up with the repeated marginalisation of psychoanalysis within our general culture, a culture whose oppressiveness for women is recognised by us all.

Before going into this in more detail, a separate but related point needs to be made, and that is the peculiarity of the psychoanalytic object with which feminism engages. Thus to ask for effects from psychoanalysis in the arena of political practice is already to assume that psychoanalytic practice is a-political.[2] Recent feminist debate has tended to concentrate on theory (Freud's theory of femininity, whether or not psychoanalysis can provide an account of women's subordination). This was as true of Juliet Mitchell's defence of Freud[3] as it has been of many of the more recent replies. The result has been that psychoanalysis has been pulled away from its own practice. Here the challenge to psychoanalysis by feminists has come from alternative forms of therapy (feminist therapy and co-counselling). But it is worth noting that the way psychoanalysis is engaged with in much recent criticism already divests it of its practical effects at this level, or rather takes this question as settled in advance (the passing reference to the chauvinism of

the psychoanalytic institution, the assumption that psychoanalysis depoliti-
cises the woman analysand). In this context, therefore, the common theory/
practice dichotomy has a very specific meaning in that psychoanalysis can
only be held accountable to 'practice' if it is assumed not to be one, or if the
form of its practice is taken to have no purchase on political life. This
assumes, for example, that there is no politics of the psychoanalytic institution itself, something to which I will return.

Both these points – the wider history of how psychoanalysis has been
placed or discarded by our dominant culture, and the detaching of psychoanalysis from its practical and institutional base – are related, in as much as
they bring into focus the decisions and selections which have already been
made about psychoanalysis before the debate even begins. Some of these
decisions, I would want to argue, are simply wrong – such as the broad
accusation of chauvinism levelled against the psychoanalytic institution as a
whole. In this country at least, the significant impetus after Freud passed to
two women – Anna Freud and Melanie Klein. Psychoanalysis in fact continues to be one of the few of our cultural institutions which does not
professionally discriminate against women, and in which they could even
be said to predominate. This is not of course to imply that the presence of
women inside an institution is necessarily feminist, but women have historically held positions of influence inside psychoanalysis which they have been
mostly denied in other institutions where their perceived role as 'carers' has
relegated them to a subordinate position (e.g. nursing); and it is the case that
the first criticisms of Freud made by Melanie Klein can be seen to have
strong affinities with later feminist repudiation of his theories.

For those who are hesitating over what appears as the present 'impasse'
between feminism and psychoanalysis, the more important point, however,
is to stress the way that psychoanalysis is being presented for debate – that is,
the decisions which have already been made before we are asked to decide.
Much will depend, I suspect, on whether one sees psychoanalysis as a new
form of hegemony on the part of the feminist intelligentsia, or whether it is
seen as a theory and practice which has constantly been relegated to the
outside of dominant institutions and mainstream radical debate alike – an
'outside' with which feminism, in its challenge to both these traditions, has
its own important forms of allegiance.

COMPONENTS OF THE CULTURE

In England, the relationship between the institution of psychoanalysis and its
more general reception has always been complex, if not fraught. Thus in 1968,
Perry Anderson could argue that major therapeutic and theoretical advances
inside the psychoanalytic institution (chiefly in the work of Melanie Klein)

had gone hand in hand with, and possibly even been the cause of, the isolation of psychoanalysis from the general culture, the slowness of its dissemination (until the Pelican Freud started to appear in 1974, you effectively had to join a club to read *The Standard Edition* of Freud's work), and the failure of psycho-analysis to effect a decisive break with traditions of empiricist philosophy, reactionary ethics, and an elevation of literary 'values', which he saw as the predominant features of our cultural life.[4] Whether or not one accepts the general 'sweep' of his argument, two points from that earlier polemic seem relevant here.

Firstly, the link between empiricist traditions of thought and the resistance to the psychoanalytic concept of the unconscious. Thus psychoanalysis, through its attention to symptoms, slips of the tongue and dreams (that is, to what *insists* on being spoken against what is *allowed* to be said) appears above all as a challenge to the self-evidence and banality of everyday life and language, which have also, importantly, constituted the specific targets of feminism. If we use the (fairly loose) definition which Anderson provided for empiricism as the unsystematic registration of things as they are and the refusal of forms of analysis which penetrate beneath the surface of observ-able social phenomena, the link to feminism can be made. For feminism has always challenged the observable 'givens' of women's presumed natural qualities and their present social position alike (expecially when the second is justified in terms of the first). How often has the 'cult of common sense', the notion of what is obviously the case or in the nature of things, been used in reactionary arguments against feminist attempts to demand social change? For Anderson in his article of 1968, this espousal of empiricist thinking provided one of the chief forms of resistance to Freud, so deeply committed is psychoanalysis to penetrating behind the surface and conscious manifestations of everyday experience.

Secondly, the relationship between this rejection of psychoanalysis and a *dearth* within British intellectual culture of a Marxism which could both theorise and criticise capitalism as a social totality. This second point received the strongest criticism from within British Marxism itself, but what matters here is the fact that both Marxism *and* psychoanalysis were identified as forms of radical enquiry which were unassimilable to bourgeois norms. In the recent feminist discussion, however – notably in the pages of *Feminist Review* – Marxism and psychoanalysis tend to be posited as antag-onistic; Marxism arrogating to itself the concept of political practice and social change, psychoanalysis being accused of inherent conservatism which rationalises and perpetuates the subordination of women under capitalism, or else fails to engage with that subordination at the level of material life.

In order to understand this, I think we have to go back to the earlier moment. For while the argument that Marxism was marginal or even alien to British thought was strongly repudiated, the equivalent observation about psychoanalysis seems to have been accepted and was more or less allowed to stand. This was perhaps largely because no-one on the Left rushed forward to claim a radicalism committed to psychoanalytic thought. *New Left Review* had itself been involved in psychoanalysis in the early 1960s, publishing a number of articles by Cooper and Laing,[5] and there is also a strong tradition, which goes back through Christopher Caudwell in the 1930s, of Marxist discussion of Freud. But the main controversy unleashed by Anderson's remarks centred around Marxism; in an earlier article Anderson himself had restricted his critique to the lack of Marxism and classical sociology in British culture, making no reference to psychoanalysis at all.[6] After 1968 *New Left Review* published Althusser's famous article on Lacan and one article by Lacan,[7] but for the most part the commitment to psychoanalysis was not sustained even by that section of the British Left which had originally argued for its importance.

Paradoxically, therefore, the idea that psychoanalysis was isolated or cut off from the general culture could be accepted to the extent that this very marginalisation was being *reproduced* in the response to the diagnosis itself. Thus the link between Marxism and Freudian psychoanalysis, as the twin poles of a failed radicalism at the heart of British culture, was broken. Freud was cast aside at the very moment when resistance to his thought had been identified as symptomatic of the restrictiveness of bourgeois culture. Juliet Mitchell was the exception. Her defence of Freud[8] needs to be seen as a redress of this omission, but also as a critique of the loss of the concept of the unconscious in the very forms of psychoanalysis (for example, Laing) sponsored by the British Left (the second problem as the cause of the first). In this context the case for psychoanalysis was part of a claim for the fundamentally anti-empiricist and radical nature of Freudian thought. That this claim was made via feminism (could perhaps *only* be made via feminism) says something about the ability of feminism to challenge the orthodoxies of both Left and Right.

Thus the now familiar duo of 'psychoanalysis and feminism' has an additional and crucial political meaning. Not just psychoanalysis *for* feminism or feminism *against* psychoanalysis, but Freudian psychoanalysis and feminism *together* as two forms of thought which relentlessly undermine the turgid resistance of common-sense language to all forms of conflict and political change. For me this specific sequence has been ironically or negatively confirmed (that is, it has been gone over again backwards) by the recent attempt by Michael Rustin to relate psychoanalysis to socialism through a combination of F. R. Leavis and Melanie Klein – the very figures whose standing had been taken as symptomatic of that earlier resistance to the most radical aspects of Freudian thought (Klein because of the confinement of her often challenging ideas to the psychoanalytic institution itself; Leavis because of the inappropriate centrality which he claimed for the ethics of literary form and taste).[9] I cannot go into the details of Rustin's argument here, but its ultimate conservatism for feminism is at least clear; the advancement of 'mothering', and by implication of the role of women as mothers, as the psychic basis on which socialism can be built (the idea that psychoanalysis can *engender* socialism seems to be merely the flip side of the argument which accuses psychoanalysis of producing social conformity).

This history may appear obscure to many feminists who have not necessarily followed the different stages of these debates. But the diversion through this cultural map is, I think, important in so far as it can illustrate the ramifications of feminist discussion over a wider political spectrum, and also show how this discussion – the terms of the argument, the specific oppositions proposed – have in turn been determined by that wider spectrum itself.

Thus it will have crucial effects, for instance, whether psychoanalysis is discussed as an addition or supplement to Marxism (in relation to which it is then found *wanting*), or whether emphasis is laid on the concept of the unconscious. For while it is indeed correct that psychoanalysis was introduced into feminism as a theory which could rectify the inability of Marxism to address questions of sexuality, and that this move was complementary to the demand within certain areas of Marxism for increasing attention to the ideological determinants of our social being, it is also true that undue concentration on this aspect of the theory has served to cut off the concept of the unconscious, or at least to displace it from the centre of the debate. (This is graphically illustrated in Michèle Barrett's book, *Women's Oppression Today*, in which the main discussion of psychoanalysis revolves around the concept of ideology, and that of the unconscious is left to a note appended at the end of the chapter.)[10]

FEMININITY AND ITS DISCONTENTS

One result of this emphasis is that psychoanalysis is accused of 'functionalism', that is, it is accepted as a theory of how women are psychically 'induced' into femininity by a patriarchal culture, and is then accused of perpetuating that process, either through a practice assumed to be *prescriptive* about women's role (this is what women *should* do), or because the very effectiveness of the account as a *description* (this is what is demanded of women, what they are *expected* to do) leaves no possibility of change.

It is this aspect of Juliet Mitchell's book which seems to have been taken up most strongly by feminists who have attempted to follow through the political implications of psychoanalysis as a critique of patriarchy.

Thus Gayle Rubin, following Mitchell, uses psychoanalysis for a general critique of a patriarchal culture which is predicated on the exchange of

women by men.[11] Nancy Chodorow shifts from Freud to later object relations theory to explain how women's childcaring role is perpetuated through
the earliest relationship between a mother and her child, which leads in her
case to a demand for a fundamental change in how childcare is organised
between women and men in our culture.[12] Although there are obvious
differences between these two readings of psychoanalysis, they nonetheless
share an emphasis on the social exchange of women, or the distribution of
roles for women, across cultures: 'Women's mothering is one of the few
universal and enduring elements of the sexual division of labour'.[13]

The force of psychoanalysis is therefore (as Janet Sayers points out)[14]
precisely that it gives an account of patriarchal culture as a trans-historical
and cross-cultural force. It therefore conforms to the feminist demand for a
theory which can explain women's subordination across specific cultures and
different historical moments. Summing this up crudely, we could say that
psychoanalysis adds sexuality to Marxism, where sexuality is felt to be
lacking, and extends beyond Marxism where the attention to specific historical instances, changes in modes of production etc., is felt to leave something
unexplained.

But all this happens at a cost, and that cost is the concept of the unconscious. What distinguishes psychoanalysis from sociological accounts of
gender (hence for me the fundamental impasse of Nancy Chodorow's
work) is that whereas for the latter, the internalisation of norms is assumed
roughly to work, the basic premise and indeed starting-point of psychoanalysis is that it does not. The unconscious constantly reveals the 'failure' of
identity. Because there is no continuity of psychic life, so there is no stability
of sexual identity, no position for women (or for men) which is ever simply
achieved. Nor does psychoanalysis see such 'failure' as a special-case inability or an individual deviancy from the norm. 'Failure' is not a moment to be
regretted in a process of adaptation, or development into normality, which
ideally takes its course (some of the earliest critics of Freud, such as Ernest
Jones, did, however, give an account of development in just these terms).
Instead 'failure' is something endlessly repeated and relived moment by
moment throughout our individual histories. It appears not only in the
symptom, but also in dreams, in slips of the tongue and in forms of sexual
pleasure which are pushed to the sidelines of the norm. Feminism's affinity
with psychoanalysis rests above all, I would argue, with this recognition that
there is a resistance to identity at the very heart of psychic life. Viewed in this
way, psychoanalysis is no longer best understood as an account of how
women are fitted into place (even this, note, is the charitable reading of
Freud). Instead psychoanalysis becomes one of the few places in our culture
where it is recognised as more than a fact of individual pathology that most
women do not painlessly slip into their roles as women, if indeed they do at
all. Freud himself recognised this increasingly in his work. In the articles

which run from 1924 to 1931,[15] he moves from that famous, or rather infamous, description of the little girl struck with her 'inferiority' or 'injury' in the face of the anatomy of the little boy and wisely accepting her fate ('injury' as the *fact* of being feminine), to an account which quite explicitly describes the process of becoming 'feminine' as an 'injury' or 'catastrophe' for the complexity of her earlier psychic and sexual life ('injury' as its *price*).

Elizabeth Wilson and Janet Sayers are, therefore, in a sense correct to criticise psychoanalysis when it is taken as a general theory of patriarchy or of general identity, that is, as a theory which explains how women wholly internalise the very mode of being which is feminism's specific target of attack; but they have missed out half the (psychoanalytic) story. In fact the argument seems to be circular. Psychoanalysis is drawn in the direction of a general theory of culture or a sociological account of gender because these seem to lay greater emphasis on the pressures of the 'outside' world, but it is this very pulling away from the psychoanalytic stress on the 'internal' complexity and difficulty of psychic life which produces the functionalism which is then criticised.

The argument about whether Freud is being 'prescriptive' or 'descriptive' about women (with its associated stress on the motives and morals of Freud himself) is fated to the extent that it is locked into this model. Many of us will be familiar with Freud's famous pronouncement that a woman who does not succeed in transforming activity to passivity, clitoris to vagina, mother for father, will fall ill. Yet psychoanalysis testifies to the fact that psychic illness or distress is in no sense the prerogative of women who 'fail' in this task. One of my students recently made the obvious but important point that we would be foolish to deduce from the external trappings of normality or conformity in a woman that all is in fact well. And Freud himself always stressed the psychic cost of the civilising process for all (we can presumably include women in that 'all' even if at times he did not seem to do so).

All these aspects of Freud's work are subject to varying interpretation by analysts themselves. The first criticism of Freud's 'phallocentrism' came from inside psychoanalysis, from analysts such as Melanie Klein, Ernest Jones and Karen Horney who felt, contrary to Freud, that 'femininity' was a quality with its own impetus, subject to checks and internal conflict, but tending ultimately to fulfilment. For Jones, the little girl was 'typically receptive and acquisitive' from the outset; for Horney, there was from the beginning a 'wholly womanly' attachment to the father.[16] For these analysts, this development might come to grief, but for the most part a gradual strengthening of the child's ego and her increasing adaptation to reality, should guarantee its course. Aspects of the little girl's psychic life which were resistant to this process (the famous 'active' or 'masculine' drives) were defensive. The importance of concepts such as the 'phallic phase' in Freud's description of infantile sexuality is not, therefore, that such concepts can be taken as the point of insertion of patriarchy (assimilation to the norm). Rather their importance lies in the way that they indicate, through their very artificiality, that something was being *forced*, and in the concept of psychic life with which they were accompanied. In Freud's work they went hand in hand with an increasing awareness of the difficulty, not to say impossibility, of the path to normality for the girl, and an increasing stress on the fundamental divisions, or splitting, of psychic life. It was those who challenged these concepts in the 1920s and 30s who introduced the more normative stress on a sequence of development, and coherent ego, back into the account.

I think we go wrong again, therefore, if we conduct the debate about whether Freud's account was developmental or not entirely in terms of his own writing. Certainly the idea of development is present at moments in his work. But it was not present *enough* for many of his contemporaries, who took up the issue and reinstated the idea of development precisely in relation to the sexual progress of the girl (her passage into womanhood).

'Psychoanalysis' is not, therefore, a single entity. Institutional divisions within psychoanalysis have turned on the very questions about the phallo-centrism of analysts, the meaning of femininity, the sequence of psychic development and its norms, which have been the concern of feminists. The accusations came from analysts themselves. In the earlier debates, however, the reproach against Freud produced an account of femininity which was more, rather than less, normative than his own.

The politics of Lacanian psychoanalysis begin here. From the 1930s, Lacan saw his intervention as a return to the concepts of psychic division, splitting of the ego, and an endless (he called it 'insistent') pressure of the unconscious against any individual's pretension to a smooth and coherent psychic and sexual identity. Lacan's specific target was 'ego-psychology' in America, and what he saw as the dilution of psychoanalysis into a tool of social adaptation and control (hence the central emphasis on the concepts of the ego and identification which are often overlooked in discussions of his ideas). For Lacan, psychoanalysis does not offer an account of a developing ego which is 'not *necessarily* coherent',[17] but of an ego which is 'necessarily *not* coherent', that is, which is always and persistently divided against itself.

Lacan could therefore be picked up by a Marxist like Althusser not because he offered a theory of adaptation to reality or of the individual's insertion into culture (Althusser added a note to the English translation of his paper on Lacan criticising it for having implied such a reading),[18] but because the force of the unconscious in Lacan's interpretation of Freud was felt to undermine the mystifications of a bourgeois culture proclaiming its identity, and that of its subjects, to the world. The political use of Lacan's theory therefore stemmed from its assault on what English Marxists would call bourgeois 'individualism'. What the theory offered was a divided subject out of 'synch' with bourgeois myth. Feminists could legitimately object that the notion of psychic fragmentation was of little immediate political advantage to women struggling for the first time to find a voice, and trying to bring together the dissociated components of their life into a political programme. But this is a very different criticism of the political implications of psychoanalysis than the one which accuses it of forcing women into bland conformity with their expected role.

PSYCHOANALYSIS AND HISTORY. THE HISTORY OF PSYCHOANALYSIS

What, therefore, is the political purchase of the concept of the unconscious on women's lived experience? And what can it say to the specific histories of which we form a part?

One of the objections which is often made against psychoanalysis is that it has no sense of history, and an inadequate grasp of its relationship to the concrete institutions which frame and determine our lives. For even if we allow for a moment the radical force of the psychoanalytic insight, the exclusiveness or limited availability of that insight tends to be turned, not against the culture or state which mostly resists its general (and publicly funded) dissemination,[19] but against psychoanalysis itself. The 'privatisation' of psychoanalysis comes to mean that it only refers to the individual as private, and the concentration on the individual as private is then seen as reinforcing a theory which places itself above history and change.

Again I think that this question is posed back to front, and that we need to ask, not what psychoanalysis has to say about history, but rather what is the history of psychoanalysis, that is, what was the intervention of psychoanalysis into the institutions which, at the time of its emergence, were controlling women's lives? And what was the place of the unconscious, historically, in that? Paradoxically, the claim that psychoanalysis is a-historical dehistoricises it. If we go back to the beginnings of psychoanalysis, it is clear that the concept of the unconscious was radical at exactly that level of social 'reality' with which it is so often assumed to have nothing whatsoever to do.

Recent work by feminist historians is of particular importance in this context. Judith Walkowitz, in her study of the Contagious Diseases Acts of the 1860s, shows how state policy on public hygiene and the state's increasing control over casual labour, relied on a category of women as diseased (the suspected prostitute subjected to forcible examination and internment in response to the spread of venereal disease in the port towns).[20] Carol Dyhouse has described how debates about educational opportunity for women constantly returned to the evidence of the female body (either the energy expended in their development towards sexual reproduction meant that women could not be educated, or education and the overtaxing of the brain would damage their reproductive capacity).[21] In the birth control controversy, the Malthusian idea of controlling the reproduction, and by implication the sexuality, of the working class served to counter the idea that poverty could be reduced by the redistribution of wealth.[22] Recurrently in the second half of the nineteenth century, in the period immediately prior to Freud, female sexuality became the focus of a panic about the effects of industrialisation on the cohesion of the social body and its ability to reproduce itself comfortably. The importance of all this work (Judith Walkowitz makes this quite explicit) is that 'attitudes' towards women cannot be consigned to the sphere of ideology, assumed to have no purchase on material life, so deeply implicated was the concept of female sexuality in the legislative advancement of the state.[23]

Central to all of this was the idea that the woman was wholly responsible for the social well-being of the nation (questions of social division transmuted directly into the moral and sexual responsibility of subjects), or where she failed in this task, that she was disordered or diseased. The hysteric was either the overeducated woman, or else the woman indulging in non-procreative or uncontrolled sexuality (conjugal onanism), or again the woman in the lock hospitals which, since the eighteenth century, had been receiving categories refused by the general hospitals ('infectious diseases, "fever", children, maternity cases, mental disorders, as well as venereal diseases').[24] It was these hospitals which, at the time of the Contagious Diseases Acts, became the place of confinement for the diseased prostitute in a new form of collaborative relationship with the state.

This is where psychoanalysis begins. Although the situation was not identical in France, there are important links. Freud's earliest work was under Charcot at the Salpêtrière Clinic in Paris, a hospital for women: 'five thousand neurotic indigents, epileptics, and insane patients, many of whom of were deemed incurable'.[25] The 'dregs' of society comprised the inmates of the Salpêtrière (psychoanalysis does not start in the Viennese parlour). Freud was working under Charcot whose first contribution to the study of hysteria was to move it out of the category of sexual malingering and into that of a specific and accredited neurological disease. The problem with Charcot's work is that while he was constructing the symptomatology of the disease (turning it into a respected object of the medical institution), he was reinforcing it as a special category of behaviour, visible to the eye, and the result of a degenerate hereditary disposition.

Freud's intervention here was two-fold. Firstly, he questioned the visible evidence of the disease – the idea that you could know a hysteric by looking at her body, that is, by reading off the symptoms of nervous disability or susceptibility to trauma. Secondly (and this second move depended on the first), he rejected the idea that hysteria was an 'independent' clinical entity, by using what he uncovered in the treatment of the hysterical patient as the basis of his account of the unconscious and its universal presence in adult life.

The 'universalism' of Freud was not, therefore, an attempt to remove the subject from history; it stemmed from his challenge to the category of hysteria as a principle of classification for certain socially isolated and confined individuals, and his shifting of this category into the centre of everybody's psychic experience: 'Her hysteria can therefore be described as an acquired one, and it presupposed nothing more than the possession of what is probably a very wide-spread proclivity – the proclivity to acquire hysteria.'[26] The reason why the two moves are interdependent is because it was only by penetrating behind the visible symptoms of disorder and asking what it was that the symptom was trying to *say*, that Freud could uncover those unconscious desires and motives which he went on to expose in the slips, dreams and jokes of individuals paraded as normal. Thus the challenge to the entity 'hysteria', that is, to hysteria *as* an entity available for quite specific forms of social control, relied on the concept of the unconscious. 'I have attempted', wrote Freud, 'to meet the problem of hysterical attacks along a line other than *descriptive*.'[27] Hence Freud's challenge to the visible, to the empirically self-evident, to the 'blindness of the seeing eye'.[28] (Compare this with Charcot's photographs offered as the evidence of the disease.) It is perhaps this early and now mostly forgotten moment which can give us the strongest sense of the force of the unconscious as a concept against a fully social classification relying on empirical evidence as its rationale.

The challenge of psychoanalysis to empiricist forms of reasoning was therefore the very axis on which the fully historical intervention of psychoanalysis into late nineteenth-century medicine turned. The theories of sexuality came after this first intervention (in *Studies on Hysteria*, Freud's remarks on sexuality are mostly given in awkward footnotes suggesting the importance of sexual abstinence for women as a causal factor in the aetiology of hysteria). But when Freud did start to investigate the complexity of sexual life in response to what he uncovered in hysterical patients, his first step was a similar questioning of social definitions, this time of sexual perversion as 'innate' or 'degenerate', that is, as the special property of a malfunctioning type.[29] In fact, if we take dreams and slips of the tongue (both considered before Freud to result from lowered mental capacity), sexuality and hysteria, the same movement operates each time. A discredited, pathological, or irrational form of behaviour is given its psychic value by psychoanalysis. What this meant for the hysterical woman is that instead of just being looked at or examined, she was allowed to *speak*.

Some of the criticisms which are made by feminists of Freudian psychoanalysis, especially when it is filtered through the work of Lacan, can perhaps be answered with reference to this moment. Most often the emphasis is laid either on Lacan's statement that 'the unconscious is structured like a language', or on his concentration on mental representation and the ideational contents of the mind. The feeling seems to be that the stress on ideas and language cuts psychoanalysis off from the materiality of being, whether that materiality is defined as the biological aspects of our subjectivity or as the economic factors determining our lives (one or the other and at times both).

Once it is put like this, the argument becomes a version of the debate within Marxism over the different instances of social determination and their hierarchy ('ideology' versus the 'economic') or else it becomes an accusation of idealism (Lacan) against materialism (Marx). I think this argument completely misses the importance of the emphasis on language in Lacan and of mental representation in Freud. The statement that 'the unconscious is structured like a language' was above all part of Lacan's attempt to establish a continuity between the seeming disorder of the symptom or dream and the normal language through which we recognise each other and speak. And the importance of the linguistic sign (Saussure's distinction between the signifier and the signified)[30] was that it provided a model internal to language itself of that form of indirect representation (the body speaking because there is something which cannot be said) which psychoanalysis uncovered in the symptomatology of its patients. Only if one thing can stand for another is the hysterical symptom something more than the logical and direct manifestation of physical or psychic (and social) degeneracy.

This is why the concept of the unconscious – as indicating an irreducible discontinuity of psychic life – is so important. Recognition of that discontinuity in us all is in a sense the price we have to pay for that earlier historical displacement.

FEMINISM AND THE UNCONSCIOUS

It is, however, this concept which seems to be lost whenever Freud has been challenged on those ideas which have been most problematic for feminism, in so far as the critique of Freudian phallocentrism so often relies on a return to empiricism, on an appeal to 'what actually happens' or what can be *seen* to be the case. Much of Ernest Jones's criticism of Freud, for example, stemmed from his conviction that girls and boys could not conceivably be ignorant of so elementary a fact as that of sexual difference and procreation.[31] And Karen Horney, in her similar but distinct critique, referred to 'the manifestations of so elementary a principle of nature as that of the mutual attraction of the sexes'.[32] We can compare this with Freud: 'from the point of view of psycho-analysis the exclusive sexual interest felt by men for women is also a problem that needs elucidating and is not a self-evident fact based upon an attraction that is ultimately of a chemical nature.'[33] The point is not that one side is appealing to 'biology' (or 'nature') and the other to 'ideas', but that Freud's opening premise is to challenge the self-evidence of both.

The feminist criticism of Freud has of course been very different since it has specifically involved a rejection of the evidence of this particular norm: the normal femininity which, in the earlier quarrel, Freud himself was considered to have questioned. But at this one crucial level – the idea of an unconscious which points to a fundamental division of psychic life and which therefore challenges any form of empiricism based on what is there to be observed (even when scientifically tested and tried) – the very different critiques are related. In *Psychoanalysis and Feminism*, Juliet Mitchell based at least half her argument on this point but it has been lost. Thus Shulamith Firestone, arguing in *The Dialectic of Sex* that the girl's alleged sense of inferiority in relation to the boy was the logical outcome of the observable facts of the child's experience, had to assume an unproblematic and one-to-one causality between psychic life and social reality with no possibility of dislocation or error.[34] The result is that the concept of the unconscious is lost (the little girl rationally recognises and decides her fate) and mothering is deprived of its active components (the mother is seen to be only subordinate and in no sense powerful for the child).[35] For all its more obvious political appeal, the idea that psychic life is the unmediated reflection of social relations locks the mother and child into a closed subordination which can then only be broken by the advances of empiricism itself:

> Full mastery of the reproductive process is in sight, and there has been significant advance in understanding the basic life and death process. The nature of ageing and growth, sleep and hibernation, the chemical functioning of the brain and the development of consciousness and memory are all beginning to be understood in their entirety. This acceleration promises to continue for another century, or however long it takes to achieve the goal of Empiricism: total understanding of the laws of nature.[36]

Shulamith Firestone's argument has been criticised by feminists who would not wish to question, any more than I would, the importance of her intervention for feminism.[37] But I think it is important that the part of her programme which is now criticised (the idea that women must rely on scientific progress to achieve any change) is so directly related to the empiricist concept of social reality (what can be *seen* to happen) which she offers. The empiricism of the goal is the outcome of the empiricism at the level of social reality and psychic life. I have gone back to this moment because, even though it is posed in different terms, something similar seems to be going on in the recent Marxist repudiation of Freud. Janet Sayers's critique of Juliet Mitchell, for example, is quite explicitly based on the concept of 'what actually and specifically happens' ('in the child's environment' and 'in the child's physical and biological development').[38]

UTOPIANISM OF THE PSYCHE

Something else happens in all of this which is probably the most central issue for me: the discarding of the concept of the unconscious seems to leave us with a type of utopianism of psychic life. In this context it is interesting to note just how close the appeal to biology and the appeal to culture as the determinants of psychic experience can be. Karen Horney switched from one to the other, moving from the idea that femininity was a natural quality, subject to checks, but tending on its course, to the idea that these same checks, and indeed most forms of psychic conflict, were the outcome of an oppressive social world. The second position is closer to that of feminism, but something is nonetheless missing from both sides of the divide. For what has happened to the unconscious, to that divided and disordered subjectivity which, I have argued, had to be recognised in us all if the category of hysteria as a peculiar property of one class of women was to be disbanded? Do not both of these movements make psychic conflict either an accident or an obstacle on the path to psychic and sexual continuity – a continuity which, as feminists, we recognise as a myth of our culture only to reinscribe it in a different form on the agenda for a future (post-revolutionary) date?

Every time Freud is challenged, this concept of psychic cohesion as the ultimate object of our political desires seems to return. Thus the French feminist and analyst, Luce Irigaray, challenges Lacan not just for the phallocentrism of his arguments, but because the Freudian account is seen to cut women off from an early and untroubled psychic unity (the primordial state of fusion with the mother) which feminists should seek to restore. Irigaray calls this the 'imaginary' of women (a reference to Lacan's idea of a primitive narcissism which was for him only ever a fantasy). In a world felt to be especially alienating for women, this idea of psychic oneness or primary narcissism has its own peculiar force. It appears in a different form in Michèle Barrett's and Mary McIntosh's excellent reply to Christopher Lasch's thesis that we are witnessing a regrettable decline in the patriarchal family.[39] Responding to his accusation that culture is losing its super-ego edge and descending into narcissism, they offer the particularly female qualities of mothering (Chodorow) and a defence of this very 'primary narcissism' in the name of women against Lasch's undoubtedly reactionary lament. The problem remains, however, that whenever the 'feminine' comes into the argument as a quality in this way we seem to lose the basic insight of psychoanalysis – the failure or difficulty of femininity for women, and that fundamental psychic division which in Freud's work was its accompanying and increasingly insistent discovery. If I question the idea that psychoanalysis is the 'new orthodoxy' for feminists, it is at least partly because of the strong political counterweight of this idea of femininity which appears to repudiate both these Freudian insights together.

To return to the relationship between Marxism and psychoanalysis with which I started, I think it is relevant that the most systematic attack we have had on the hierarchies and organisation of the male Left[40] gives to women the privilege of the personal in a way which divests it (*has* to divest it) of complexity at exactly this level of the conflicts and discontinuities of psychic life. Like many feminists, the slogan 'the personal is political' has been central to my own political development; just as I see the question of sexuality, as a political issue which *exceeds* the province of Marxism ('economic', 'ideological' or whatever), as one of the most important defining characteristics of feminism itself. But the dialogue between feminism and psychoanalysis, which is for me the arena in which the full complexity of that 'personal' and that 'sexuality' can be grasped, constantly seems to fail.

In this article, I have not answered all the criticisms of psychoanalysis. It is certainly the case that psychoanalysis does not give us a blueprint for political action, or allow us to deduce political conservatism or radicalism directly from the vicissitudes of psychic experience. Nor does the concept of the unconscious sit comfortably with the necessary attempt by feminism to claim a new sureness of identity for women, or with the idea of always conscious and deliberate political decision-making and control (psychoanalysis is *not* a voluntarism).[41] But its challenge to the concept of psychic identity is important for feminism in that it allows into the political arena problems of subjectivity (subjectivity *as* a problem) which tend to be suppressed from other forms of political debate. It may also help us to open up the space between different notions of political identity – between the idea of a political identity for feminism (what women require) and that of a feminine identity for women (what women are or should be), especially given the problems constantly encountered by the latter and by the sometimes too easy celebration of an identity amongst women which glosses over the differences between us.

Psychoanalysis finally remains one of the few places in our culture where our experience of femininity can be spoken as a problem that is something other than the problem which the protests of women are posing for an increasingly conservative political world. I would argue that this is one of the reasons why it has not been released into the public domain. The fact that psychoanalysis cannot be assimilated directly into a political programme as such does not mean, therefore, that it should be discarded, and thrown back into the outer reaches of a culture which has never yet been fully able to heed its voice.

11

Womanliness as a Masquerade

Joan Riviere

Every direction in which psychoanalytic research has pointed seems in its turn to have attracted the interest of Ernest Jones, and now that in recent years investigation has slowly spread to the development of the sexual life of women, we find as a matter of course one by him among the most important contributions to the subject. As always, he throws great light on his material, with his peculiar gift of both clarifying the knowledge we had already and also adding to it fresh observations of his own.

In his paper on 'The early development of female sexuality'[1] he sketches out a rough scheme of types of female development which he first divides into heterosexual and homosexual, subsequently subdividing the latter homosexual group into two types. He acknowledges the roughly schematic nature of his classification and postulates a number of intermediate types. It is with one of these intermediate types that I am today concerned. In daily life types of men and women are constantly met with who, while mainly heterosexual in their development, plainly display strong features of the other sex. This has been judged to be an expression of the bisexuality inherent in us all; and analysis has shown that what appears as homosexual or heterosexual character-traits, or sexual manifestations, is the end-result of the interplay of conflicts and not necessarily evidence of a radical or fundamental tendency. The difference between homosexual and heterosexual development results from differences in the degree of anxiety, with the corresponding effect this has on development. Ferenczi pointed out a similar reaction in behaviour,[2] namely, that homosexual men exaggerate their heterosexuality as a 'defence' against their homosexuality. I shall attempt to show that women who wish for masculinity may put on a mask of womanliness to avert anxiety and the retribution feared from men.

It is with a particular type of intellectual woman that I have to deal. Not long ago intellectual pursuits for women were associated almost exclusively with an overtly masculine type of woman, who in pronounced cases made no secret of her wish or claim to be a man. This has now changed. Of all the women engaged in professional work today, it would be hard to say whether the greater number are more feminine than masculine in their mode of life and character. In university life, in scientific professions and in business, one constantly meets women who seem to fulfil every criterion of complete feminine development. They are excellent wives and mothers, capable housewives; they maintain social life and assist culture; they have no lack of feminine interests, e.g. in their personal appearance, and when called upon they can still find time to play the part of devoted and disinterested mother-substitutes among a wide circle of relatives and friends. At the same time they fulfil the duties of their profession at least as well as the average man. It is really a puzzle to know how to classify this type psychologically.

Some time ago, in the course of an analysis of a woman of this kind, I came upon some interesting discoveries. She conformed in almost every particular to the description just given; her excellent relations with her husband included a very intimate affectionate attachment between them and full and frequent sexual enjoyment; she prided herself on her proficiency as a housewife. She had followed her profession with marked success all her life. She had a high degree of adaptation to reality and managed to sustain good and appropriate relations with almost everyone with whom she came in contact.

Certain reactions in her life showed, however, that her stability was not as flawless as it appeared; one of these will illustrate my theme. She was an American woman engaged in work of a propagandist nature, which consisted principally in speaking and writing. All her life a certain degree of anxiety, sometimes very severe, was experienced after every public performance, such as speaking to an audience. In spite of her unquestionable success and ability, both intellectual and practical, and her capacity for managing an audience and dealing with discussions, etc., she would be excited and apprehensive all night after, with misgivings whether she had done anything inappropriate, and obsessed by a need for reassurance. This need for reassurance led her compulsively on any such occasion to seek some attention or complimentary notice from a man or men at the close of the proceedings in which she had taken part or been the principal figure; and it soon became evident that the men chosen for the purpose were always unmistakable father-figures, although often not persons whose judgement on her performance would in reality carry much weight. There were clearly two types of reassurance sought from these father-figures: first, direct reassurance of the nature of compliments about her performance; secondly, and more important, indirect reassurance of the nature of sexual attentions from these men. To speak broadly, analysis of her behaviour after her performance showed that she was attempting to obtain sexual advances from the particular type of men by means of flirting and coquetting with them in a more or less veiled manner. The extraordinary incongruity of this attitude with her highly impersonal and objective attitude during her intellectual performance, which it succeeded so rapidly in time, was a problem.

Analysis showed that the Oedipus situation of rivalry with the mother was extremely acute and had never been satisfactorily solved. I shall come back to this later. But beside the conflict in regard to the mother, the rivalry with the father was also very great. Her intellectual work, which took the form of speaking and writing, was based on an evident identification with her father, who had first been a literary man and later had taken to political life; her adolescence had been characterised by conscious revolt against him, with rivalry and contempt of him. Dreams and phantasies of this nature, castrating the husband, were frequently uncovered by analysis. She had quite conscious feelings of rivalry and claims to superiority over many of the 'father-figures' whose favour she would then woo after her own performances! She bitterly resented any assumption that she was not equal to them, and (in private) would reject the idea of being subject to their judgment or criticism. In this she corresponded clearly to one type Ernest Jones has sketched: his first group of homosexual women who, while taking no interest in the other women, wish for 'recognition' of their masculinity from men and claim to be the equals of men, or in other words, to be men themselves. Her resentment, however, was not openly expressed; publicly she acknowledged her condition of womanhood.

Analysis then revealed that the explanation of her compulsive ogling and coquetting – which actually she was herself hardly aware of till analysis made it manifest – was as follows: it was an unconscious attempt to ward off the anxiety which would ensue on account of the reprisals she anticipated from the father-figures after her intellectual performance. The exhibition in public of her intellectual proficiency, which was in itself carried through successfully, signified an exhibition of herself in possession of the father's penis, having castrated him. The display once over, she was seized by horrible dread of the retribution the father would then exact. Obviously it was a step towards propitiating the avenger to endeavour to offer herself to him sexually. This phantasy, it then appeared, had been very common in her childhood and youth, which had been spent in the Southern States of America; if a negro came to attack her, she planned to defend herself by making him kiss her and make love to her (ultimately so that she could then deliver him over to justice). But there was a further determinant of the obsessive behaviour. In a dream which had a rather similar content to this childhood phantasy, she was in terror alone in the house; then a negro came in and found her washing clothes, with her sleeves rolled up and arms exposed. She resisted him, with the secret intention of attracting him sexually, and he began to admire her arms and caress them and her breasts. The meaning was that she had killed father and mother and obtained everything for herself (alone in the house), became terrified of their retribution (expected shots through the window), and defended herself by taking on a menial role (washing clothes) and by *washing off* dirt and sweat, guilt and blood, everything she had obtained by the deed, and 'disguising herself' as merely a castrated woman. In that guise the man found no stolen property on her which he need attack her to recover and, further, found her attractive as an object of love. Thus the aim of the compulsion was not merely to secure reassurance by evoking friendly feelings towards her in the man; it was chiefly to make sure of safety by masquerading as guiltless and innocent. It was a compulsive reversal of her intellectual performance; and the two together formed the 'double-action' of an obsessive act, just as her life as a whole consisted alternately of masculine and feminine activities.

Before this dream she had had dreams of people putting masks on their faces in order to avert disaster. One of these dreams was of a high tower on a hill being pushed over and falling down on the inhabitants of a village below, but the people put on masks and escaped injury!

Womanliness therefore could be assumed and worn as a mask, both to hide the possession of masculinity and to avert the reprisals expected if she was found to possess it – much as a thief will turn out his pockets and ask to be searched to prove that he has not the stolen goods. The reader may now ask how I define womanliness or where I draw the line between genuine womanliness and the 'masquerade'. My suggestion is not, however, that there is any such difference; whether radical or superficial, they are the same thing. The capacity for womanliness was there in this woman – and one might even say it exists in the most completely homosexual woman – but owing to her conflicts it did not represent her main development and was used far more as a device for avoiding anxiety than as a primary mode of sexual enjoyment.

I will give some brief particulars to illustrate this. She had married late, at 29; she had had great anxiety about defloration and had had the hymen stretched or slit before the wedding by a woman doctor. Her attitude to sexual intercourse before marriage was a set determination to obtain and experience the enjoyment and pleasure which she knew some women have in it, and the orgasm. She was afraid of impotence in exactly the same way as a man. This was partly a determination to surpass certain mother-figures who were frigid, but on deeper levels it was a determination not to be beaten by the man.[3] In effect, sexual enjoyment was full and frequent, with complete orgasm; but the fact emerged that the gratification it brought was of the nature of a reassurance and restitution of something lost, and not ultimately pure enjoyment. The man's love gave her back her self-esteem. During analysis, while the hostile castrating impulses towards the husband were in process of coming to light, the desire for intercourse very much abated, and she became for periods relatively frigid. The mask of womanliness was being peeled away, and she was revealed either as castrated (lifeless, incapable of pleasure), or as wishing to castrate (therefore afraid to receive the penis or welcome it by gratification). Once, while for a period her husband had had a love-affair with another woman, she had detected a very intense identification with him in regard to the rival woman. It is striking that she had had no homosexual experiences (since before puberty with a younger sister); but it appeared during analysis that this lack was compensated for by frequent homosexual dreams with intense orgasm.

In everyday life one may observe the mask of femininity taking curious forms. One capable housewife of my acquaintance is a woman of great ability, and can herself attend to typically masculine matters. But when, e.g. any builder or upholsterer is called in, she has a compulsion to hide all her technical knowledge from him and show deference to the workman, making her suggestions in an innocent and artless manner, as if they were 'lucky guesses'. She has confessed to me that even with the butcher and baker, whom she rules in reality with a rod of iron, she cannot openly take up a firm straightforward stand; she feels herself as it were 'acting a part', she puts on the semblance of a rather uneducated, foolish and bewildered woman, yet in the end always making her point. In all other relations in life this woman is a gracious, cultured lady, competent and well-informed, and can manage her affairs by sensible rational behaviour without any subterfuges. This woman is now aged 50, but she tells me that as a young woman she had great anxiety in dealings with men such as porters, waiters, cabmen, tradesmen, or any other potentially hostile father-figures, such as doctors, builders and lawyers; moreover, she often quarrelled with such men and had altercations with them, accusing them of defrauding her and so forth.

Another case from everyday observation is that of a clever woman, wife and mother, a university lecturer in an abstruse subject which seldom attracts women. When lecturing, not to students but to colleagues, she chooses particularly feminine clothes. Her behaviour on these occasions is also marked by an inappropriate feature: she becomes flippant and joking, so much so that it has caused comment and rebuke. She has to treat the situation of displaying her masculinity to men as a 'game', as something *not real*, as a 'joke'. She cannot treat herself and her subject seriously, cannot seriously contemplate herself as on equal terms with men; moreover, the flippant attitude enables some of her sadism to escape, hence the offence it causes.

Many other instances could be quoted, and I have met with a similar mechanism in the analysis of manifest homosexual men. In one such man with severe inhibition and anxiety, homosexual activities really took second place, the source of greatest sexual gratification being actually masturbation under special conditions, namely, while looking at himself in the mirror dressed in a particular way. The excitation was produced by the sight of himself with hair parted in the centre, wearing a bow tie. These extraordinary 'fetishes' turned out to represent a *disguise of himself* as his sister; the hair and bow were taken from her. His conscious attitude was a desire to *be* a woman, but his manifest relations with men had never been stable. Unconsciously the homosexual relation proved to be entirely sadistic and based on masculine rivalry. Phantasies of sadism and '*possession of a penis*' could be indulged only while reassurance against anxiety was being obtained from the mirror that he was safely 'disguised as a woman'.

To return to the case I first described. Underneath her apparently satisfactory heterosexuality it is clear that this woman displayed well-known manifestations of the castration complex. Horney was the first among others to point out the sources of that complex in the Oedipus situation; my belief is that the fact that womanliness may be assumed as a mask may contribute further in this direction to the analysis of female development. With that in view I will now sketch the early libido-development in this case.

But before this I must give some account of her relations with women. She was conscious of rivalry of almost any woman who had either good looks or intellectual pretensions. She was conscious of flashes of hatred against almost any woman with whom she had much to do, but where permanent or close relations with women were concerned she was none the less able to establish a very satisfactory footing. Unconsciously she did this almost entirely by means of feeling herself superior in some way to them (her relations with her inferiors were uniformly excellent). Her proficiency as a housewife largely had its root in this. By it she surpassed her mother, won her approval and proved her superiority among rival 'feminine' women. Her intellectual attainments undoubtedly had in part the same object. They too proved her superiority to her mother; it seemed probable that since she reached womanhood her rivalry with women had been more acute in regard to intellectual things than in regard to beauty, since she could usually take refuge in her superior brains where beauty was concerned.

The analysis showed that the origin of all these reactions, both to men and women, lay in the reaction to the parents during the oral-biting sadistic phase. These reactions took the form of the phantasies sketched by Melanie Klein[4] in her Congress paper, 1927. In consequence of disappointment or frustration during sucking or weaning, coupled with experiences during the primal scene which is interpreted in oral terms, extremely intense sadism develops towards both parents.[5] The desire to bite off the nipple shifts, and desires to destroy, penetrate and disembowel the mother and devour her and the contents of her body succeed it. These contents include the father's penis, her fæces and her children – all her possessions and love-objects, imagined as within her body.[6] The desire to bite off the nipple is also shifted, as we know, on to the desire to castrate the father by biting off his penis. Both parents are rivals in this stage, both possess desired objects; the sadism is directed against both and the revenge of both is feared. But, as always with girls, the mother is the more hated, and consequently the more feared. She will execute the punishment that fits the crime – destroy the girl's body, her beauty, her children, her capacity for having children, mutilate her, devour her, torture her and kill her. In this appalling predicament the girl's only safety lies in placating the mother and atoning for her crime. She must retire from rivalry with the mother and, if she can, endeavour to restore to her what she has stolen. As we know, she identifies herself with the father; and then she uses the masculinity she thus obtains by *putting it at the service of the mother*. She becomes the father and takes his place; so she can 'restore' him to the mother. This position was very clear in many typical situations in my patient's life. She delighted in using her great practical ability to aid or assist weaker and more helpless women, and could maintain this attitude successfully so long as rivalry did not emerge too strongly. But this restitution could be made on one condition only; it must procure her a lavish return in the form of gratitude and 'recognition'. The recognition desired was supposed by her to be owing for her self-sacrifices; more unconsciously what she claimed was recognition of her *supremacy* in *having* the penis to give back. If her supremacy were not acknowledged, the rivalry became at once acute; if gratitude and recognition were withheld, her sadism broke out in full force and she would be subject (in private) to paroxysms of oral-sadistic fury, exactly like a raging infant.

In regard to the father, resentment against him arose in two ways: (1) during the primal scene he took from the mother the milk, etc., which the child missed; (2) at the same time he gave to the mother the penis or children instead of to her. Therefore all that he had or took should be taken from him by her; he was castrated and reduced to nothingness, like the mother. Fear of him, though never so acute as of the mother, remained; partly, too, because his vengeance for the death and destruction of the mother was expected. So he too must be placated and appeased. This was done by masquerading in a feminine guise for him, thus showing him her 'love' and guiltlessness towards him. It is significant that this woman's mask, though transparent to other women, was successful with men, and served its purpose very well. Many men were attracted in this way, and gave her reassurance by showing her favour. Closer examination showed that these men were of the type who themselves fear the ultra-womanly woman. They prefer a woman who herself has male attributes, for to them her claims on them are less.

As the primal scene the talisman which both parents possess and which she lacks is the father's penis; hence her rage, also her dread and helplessness.[7] By depriving the father of it and possessing it herself she obtains the talisman – the invincible sword, the 'organ of sadism'; he becomes powerless and helpless (her gentle husband), but she still guards herself from attack by wearing towards him the mask of womanly subservience, and under that screen, performing many of his masculine functions herself – 'for him' – (her practical ability and management). Likewise with the mother: having robbed her of the penis, destroyed her and reduced her to pitiful inferiority, she triumphs over her, but again secretly; outwardly she acknowledges and admires the virtues of 'feminine' women. But the task of guarding herself against the woman's retribution is harder than with the man; her efforts to placate and make reparation by restoring and using the penis in the mother's service were never enough; this device was worked to death, and sometimes it almost worked her to death.

It appeared, therefore, that this woman had saved herself from the intolerable anxiety resulting from her sadistic fury against both parents by creating in phantasy a situation in which she became supreme and no harm could be done to her. The essence of the phantasy was her *supremacy* over the parent-objects; by it her sadism was gratified, she triumphed over them. By this same supremacy she also succeeded in averting their revenges; the means she adopted for this were reaction-formations and concealment of her hostility. Thus she could gratify her id-impulses, her narcissistic ego and her super-ego at one and the same time. The phantasy was the mainspring of her whole life and character, and she came within a narrow margin of carrying it through to complete perfection. But its weak point was the megalomanic character, under all the disguises, of the necessity for supremacy. When this supremacy was seriously disturbed during analysis, she fell into an abyss of anxiety, rage and abject depression; before the analysis, into illness.

I should like to say a word about Ernest Jones' type of homosexual woman whose aim is to obtain 'recognition' of her masculinity from men. The question arises whether the need for recognition in this type is connected with the mechanism of the same need, operating differently (recognition for services performed), in the case I have described. In my case direct recognition of the possession of the penis was not claimed openly; it was claimed for the reaction-formations, though only the possession of the penis made them possible. Indirectly, therefore, recognition was none the less claimed for the penis. This indirectness was due to apprehension lest her possession of a penis *should be* 'recognised', in other words 'found out'. One can see that with less anxiety my patient too would have openly claimed recognition from men for her possession of a penis, and in private she did in fact, like Ernest Jones' cases, bitterly resent any lack of this direct recognition. It is clear that in his cases the primary sadism obtains more gratification; the father has been castrated and shall even acknowledge his defeat. But how then is the anxiety averted by these women? In regard to the mother, this is done of course by denying her existence. To judge from indications in analyses I have carried out, I conclude that, first, as Jones implies, this claim is simply a displacement of the original sadistic claim that the desired object, nipple, milk, penis, should be instantly surrendered; secondarily, the need for recognition is largely a need for absolution. Now the mother has been relegated to limbo; no relations with her are possible. Her existence appears to be denied, though in truth it is only too much feared. So the guilt of having triumphed over both can be absolved only by the father; if he sanctions her possession of the penis by acknowledging it, she is safe. By *giving* her recognition, he *gives* her the penis and to her instead of to the mother; then she has it, and she may have it, and all is well. 'Recognition' is always in part reassurance, sanction, love; further, it renders her supreme again. Little as he may know it, to her the man has admitted his defeat. Thus in its content such a woman's phantasy-relation to the father is similar to the normal Oedipus one; the difference is that it rests on a basis of sadism. The mother she has indeed killed, but she is thereby excluded from enjoying much that the mother had, and what she does obtain from the father she has still in great measure to extort and extract.

These conclusions compel one once more to face the question: what is the essential nature of fully developed femininity? What is *das ewig Weibliche?* The conception of womanliness as a mask, behind which man suspects some hidden danger, throws a little light on the enigma. Fully developed hetero-sexual womanhood is founded, as Helene Deutsch and Ernest Jones have stated, on the oral-sucking stage. The sole gratification of a primary order in it is that of receiving the (nipple, milk) penis, semen, child from the father. For the rest it depends upon reaction-formations. The acceptance of 'castra-tion', the humility, the admiration of men, come partly from the over-estimation of the object on the oral-sucking plane; but chiefly from the renunciation (less intensity) of sadistic castration-wishes deriving from the later oral-biting level. 'I must not take, I must not even ask; it must be *given* me.' The capacity for self-sacrifice, devotion, self-abnegation expresses efforts to restore and make good, whether to mother- or to father-figures, what has been taken from them. It is also what Radó has called a 'narcissistic insurance' of the highest value.

It becomes clear how the attainment of full heterosexuality coincides with that of genitality. And once more we see, as Abraham first stated, that genitality implies attainment of a *post-ambivalent* state. Both the 'normal' woman and the homosexual desire the father's penis and rebel against frus-tration (or castration); but one of the differences between them lies in the difference in the degree of sadism and of the power of dealing both with it and with the anxiety it gives rise to in the two types of women.

12

Joan Riviere and the Masquerade

Stephen Heath

Joan Riviere was born Joan Verrall in 1883. Her education was later to be described by James Strachey, the general editor of the *Standard Edition* of Freud's works, as 'a little irregular'[1] but two things in it may be noted as of particular importance for her subsequent career: first, at the age of 17 she was sent off for a year to Gotha where she gained fluency in German; second, she was the niece of A.W. Verrall, the classical scholar, and spent a good deal of time mixing in Cambridge intellectual circles on her frequent visits to her uncle's home (where Strachey indeed would like to think he first met her). Through the Cambridge Verralls she was connected with the Society for Psychical Research and she may have arrived at Freud by the same path (Freud was made a corresponding member of the Society in 1911 and a year later provided a 'Note on the unconscious in psychoanalysis' for publication in its *Proceedings*). From 1916 to 1920 she was in analysis with Ernest Jones and by 1919 had patients of her own. The relationship with Jones was intense and fraught, a result certainly of strong transference and counter-transference and possibly too of an actual love-affair. She writes to Jones in 1918 of 'the long tragedy of my relationship with you'; he describes her as a patient as 'the worst failure I ever had'.[2]

That description is in a letter to Freud to whom Jones recommends Riviere for analysis in 1921 (she had already met Freud in 1920 at the first post-war International Congress of Psychoanalysis, held at The Hague):

It is a case of typical hysteria, almost the only symptoms being sexual anaesthesia and unorganised Angst, with a few inhibitions of a general nature.... She has a most colossal narcissism imaginable, to a great extent secondary to the refusal of her father to give her a baby and her subsequent masculine identification with him.[3]

The situation thus created is common enough in the early years of psychoanalysis, with Freud and a forceful male disciple exchanging a woman for analysis in a complex erotic imbroglio; and exchanging her for analysis too

139

in the sense that the woman is seen as a potential gain for the cause, 'a valuable translator and member of the society', as Jones puts it in Riviere's case[4] (the most striking example of such a triangle is no doubt that involving Freud, Jung and Sabina Spielrein[5]). In 1922 Jones is assuring Freud that his relationship with Riviere has never been a sexual one: 'She is not the type that attracts me erotically though I certainly have the admiration for her intelligence that I would have with a man.'[6] Which is just what Jones will then say in his *Sigmund Freud: Life and Work* of Freud's attraction to Riviere, will say in a brief paragraph sandwiched between mention of the famous question *Was will das Weib?* and comment on Freud's actual 'type of sexual object', 'a gentle feminine one':

> Freud was also interested in another type of woman, of a more intellectual and perhaps masculine cast. Such women several times played a part in his life, accessory to his men friends though of a finer calibre, but they had no erotic attraction for him. The most important of them were first of all his sister-in-law Minna Bernays, then in chronological order; Emma Eckstein, Loe Kann, Lou Andreas-Salomé, Joan Riviere, Marie Bonaparte.[7]

(It is worth noting in this list that Loe Kann, despite classification as being of this 'more intellectual and perhaps masculine cast', had a passionate affair with Jones who recommended her too for analysis with Freud.) Nothing else of the Jones–Freud–Riviere triangle gets into *Sigmund Freud: Life and Work*, only this quick reference to her and her type; as well as, in a different vein, quotation of 'an intimate impression' of Freud written by Riviere for *The Lancet* at the time of Freud's death.[8]

Subsequent to her analysis with Freud, Riviere was analysed by Melanie Klein with whom she worked closely in London, helping in the development of child analysis and practising generally as a lay analyst. Her major intellectual work was in translating Freud (most notably the four volumes of *Collected Papers*, 1924–5) and in overseeing translations for the *International Journal of Psychoanalysis*, many of which she did herself. To her we owe many of the English Freudian terms, many of our now familiar phrases – 'civilisation and its discontents', for example (where Freud himself had proposed 'man's discomforts in civilisation'). She died in 1962.

Her life remains to be written but reading the letter in which Jones presents her to Freud – 'typical hysteria', 'sexual anaesthesia', 'masculine identification' – is to find oneself at once in the world of her 'Masquerade' paper, just as Jones's discourse of types – the intellectual and the gentle feminine – gives us immediately the context of the masquerade as defence, defence in this system of male identities and consequent identifications. Relations between the paper and the life are doubtless strong, more than strong. What did it mean to be an intellectual and a woman, an intellectual woman? The question for Riviere's patient in the paper can hardly but have been a question for her too (as it was so widely in the writing of the period, the question of identity as a woman explored, for instance, in those novels contemporary with and contiguous to Riviere's life that make up Dorothy Richardson's *Pilgrimage*). Reminiscences by those who knew her bring up fragments, touches of her existence that seem to make a pattern here: a visual memory of her at an evening party, 'tall, strikingly handsome, distinguished-looking and somehow impressive'; the interruption of a work-session at lunchtime one Sunday when, her husband at home, 'Joan became the hostess . . . a delicious meal at a beautifully laid table'; her liking for cosmetics which she enjoyed 'in a quite weighty manner'; her taste in and knowledge of dresses (for a time she worked as a professional dressmaker).[9] If the pattern is that of the masquerade, however, we would then have to know what that means – defence against the implications of her intellectual and perhaps masculine cast? expression of genuine womanliness? subjection to the male régime of 'the woman'? derision of that régime? an ambiguous mixture of all or some of these things? Perhaps the one account to quote above all others is Katherine West's childhood memory, which gets the right feel, sets Riviere and the masquerade: the scene, the period, the assumptions, the identities, the recognition of the woman and the masculine equal and the problem of that, she 'of all things' a psychoanalyst:

> I still . . . cherish the vision of a friend of my mother's – a tall, Edwardian beauty with a picture hat and scarlet parasol – walking up and down the seashell path in lively conversation with a gentleman. Perhaps they were discussing theatres or the Post-Impressionists. Or perhaps they were talking about Freud – since this chic and decorative creature Joan Riviere was, of all things, Freud's first translator and a pioneer lay analyst.[10]

Published in the *International Journal of Psychoanalysis* in 1929, 'Womanliness as a masquerade' is now no doubt Riviere's best-known and most important piece of analytic writing. Its immediate context is that of the work done by analysts in the 1920s on sexual difference and, in particular, on female sexuality; including, of course, most crucially for Riviere, the work of Ernest Jones himself (Riviere refers at the outset to Jones's paper on 'The early development of female sexuality' and he in turn will use her paper in his 'The phallic phase'[11]). Freud's own writings respond to this whole debate but never specifically to 'Womanliness as a masquerade': Riviere has no entry in the index to the *Standard Edition* and the term 'masquerade' appears only twice in its twenty-four volumes, both times in the translation of texts written before Riviere's paper and with no connection whatsoever to the discussion of women and femininity.[12] It is not until more recent years that the idea of the masquerade has received significant attention and gained a certain currency, this with the renewal of the debate around female sexuality and its understanding at once through psychoanalysis and through feminist critique of psychoanalysis (the key moment is Lacan's commentary on Jones and the phallic phase in 1958, which then also retrieves Riviere and the masquerade[13]). The idea has subsequently known a wider cultural extension and found a place in thinking about questions of representation and sexual difference, notably in connection with film and cinema.

The paper itself is straightforward, up to a point. Its concern is with 'women who wish for masculinity' and who may then put on 'a mask of womanliness' as a defence, 'to avert anxiety and the retribution feared from men' (p.130); given which, it can be seen immediately as a contribution to discussion of the evolution of the Oedipus complex in women (the title, in fact, of a paper by Jeanne Lampl-de Groot published in the *International Journal* in the previous year[14]). The case from which Riviere develops her argument involves a successful intellectual woman who seeks reassurance from men after her public engagements, reassurance above all in the form of sexual attentions: 'To speak broadly, analysis of her behaviour after her performances showed that she was attempting to obtain sexual advances from the particular type of men by means of flirting and coquetting with them in a more or less veiled manner. The extraordinary incongruity of this attitude with her highly impersonal and objective attitude during her intellectual performance, which it succeeded so rapidly in time, was a problem' (pp.131–2). The problem can be solved by reference to Oedipal rivalry: in her successful professional career, the woman rivals and takes the place of the father; in her acknowledgement nevertheless of womanliness, the flirting and coquetting, she placates him: 'it was an unconscious attempt to ward off the anxiety which would ensue on account of the reprisals she anticipated from the father-figures after her intellectual performance' (p.132). Having exhibited herself in possession of the father's penis, having thus castrated him, she then seeks protection from his expected anger, offering herself now as the castrated woman to the particular type of men, 'unmistakable father-figures' (p.131). Hence her life as a whole, which 'consisted alternately of masculine and feminine activities' (p.133).

Riviere then extends her discussion and proposes a fuller explanation in terms of the castration complex and its sources in the Oedipal situation. Both her parents, father and mother, are the patient's rivals, objects of her sadistic fury: 'In consequence of disappointment or frustration during sucking or weaning, coupled with experience during the primal scene which is interpreted in oral terms, extremely intense sadism develops towards both parents' (p.135). The primal scene confronts her with her lack of the father's penis – 'the talisman which both parents possess' (p.136) – and produces rage and dread. The masquerading woman becomes the father through her masculine success, dominating him (her gentle husband), but conciliating him all the same (her mask of womanliness); equally, she robs the mother of the penis, taken from the father, but guards against retaliation of her victory by the self-sacrifice she makes for weaker women: 'The essence of the phantasy was her *supremacy* over parent-objects; by it her sadism was gratified, she triumphed over them. By this same supremacy she also succeeded in averting their revenges; the means she adopted for this were reaction-formations and concealment of her hostility. Thus she could gratify her id-impulses, her narcissistic ego and her super-ego at one and the same time' (p.137).

So we have Riviere's masquerade – the 'mask of womanliness' (p.133), '"disguising herself" as merely a castrated woman' (p.133), 'masquerading as guiltless and innocent' (p.133), 'masquerading in a feminine guise' (p.136). A woman identifies as a man – takes on masculine identity – and then identifies herself after all as a woman – takes up a feminine identity. What could be more simple? Except that at the centre of Riviere's paper is the *question* of the feminine identity:

The reader may now ask how I define womanliness or where I draw the line between genuine womanliness and the 'masquerade'. My suggestion is not, however, that there is any such difference; whether radical or superficial, they are the same thing. The capacity for womanliness was there in this woman – and one might even say it exists in the most completely homosexual woman – but owing to her conflicts it did not represent her main development and was used far more as a device for avoiding anxiety than as a primary mode of sexual enjoyment. (p.133)

In the masquerade the woman mimics an authentic – genuine – womanliness but then authentic womanliness is such a mimicry, *is* the masquerade ('they are the same thing'); to be a woman is to dissimulate a fundamental masculinity, femininity is that dissimulation. At times Riviere seems critical of the masquerade, both as travesty of womanliness ('compulsive ogling and coquetting', p.132) and as inappropriate betrayal of true ability (as with the university lecturer who 'cannot treat herself and her subject seriously', p.134); at others she seems to see it as answering to 'the essential nature of fully developed femininity' (p.138). But then again, that femininity – 'I must not take, I must not even ask; it must be *given* me' (p.138) – is a masquerade, a way of dealing with 'sadistic castration wishes' (p.138).

The attainment of full heterosexuality, which coincides with genitality, is at that price, the price of the masquerade that is the woman. Or that is 'the woman', the male fiction, construction, condition. Jones and Freud (according to Jones) will deny erotic attraction to Riviere in these terms, she is masculine not feminine, at the same time as the erotic attraction is there; she is after all of the same type as Loe Kann. Riviere is admirable and disturbing and so disturbed: the letter in which Jones presents her to Freud is premonitory of the 'Masquerade' paper, right down to the characterisation of her as despising 'all the rest of us, especially the women.'[15] The problem is not the mask but its assumption or not, its fit or misfit, with the latter pointing to it as mask, womanliness as a mask, 'behind which man suspects some hidden danger' (p.138). As indeed he would: if there is a mask, then there is a behind-the-mask and we need to know what is behind, to be *sure*. Man's suspicion is the old question, *Was will das Weib?, das ewig Weibliche*, all the others always the same. Riviere's position in her paper is difficult: the masquerade is the woman's thing, hers, but is also exactly *for* the man, a male presentation, as he would have her (and, Riviere will say, as the mother would have her, making up the woman over again, not the stealer but the receiver of the penis). Which leaves Riviere where? 'What is *das ewig Weibliche?* The conception of womanliness as a mask, behind which man suspects some hidden danger, throws a little light on the enigma' (p.138). Whose enigma? What light? Collapsing genuine womanliness and the masquerade together, Riviere undermines the integrity of the former with the artifice of the latter. That she then concludes, provides the psychoanalytic explanation, changes nothing, on the contrary: the identity of the woman – the assumption of 'the woman' – slips; which is then enigma, danger, darkness needing light, and that identity here becomes struggle, rebellion 'against frustration (or castration)' (p.138), the contradiction of her identification in the world, of being 'the woman'. Riviere's paper knows that contradiction, in its writing as in its thesis.

The strongest commentator on and respondent to the masquerade is no doubt Nietzsche, troubled with woman and truth and masks and veils and feminism. He writes, in *Beyond Good and Evil*: 'Comparing man and woman in general one may say: woman would not have the genius for finery [*das Genie des Putzes*] if she did not have the instinct for the *secondary* role.'[16] The finery goes with the secondary – 'the acceptance of "castration", the humility, the admiration of men', as Riviere will have it (p.138). Woman is secondary and so supplementary and so an act: 'her great art is the lie, her supreme concern is appearance and beauty'; which is after all, 'let us confess it', what we men 'love and honour'.[17] But then, meanwhile, 'female voices are raised which ... make one tremble': 'there are threatening and medically explicit statements of what woman *wants* of man.'[18] Nietzsche is already caught on the *Was will das Weib?* and the problem is, of course, that woman wants, that she makes a difference to man and that men, Nietzsche first and foremost, feel something wanted of them, which is fear, threat, the medically explicit, as Nietzsche says, conflating along with his time feminism, hysteria and sexuality. Better if she did not want; Nietzsche, hopefully, doubts she can, doubts whether woman 'really *wants* or *can* want', and specifically not 'enlightenment about herself', her pretence to which is just another '*adornment* for herself [*einen neuen Putz für sich*]' – 'self-adornment [*das Sich-Putzen*] pertains to the eternal-womanly, does it not?'[19] The intellectual woman, the feminist (the two are synonymous for Nietzsche), is a lie, a self-adorner, but then woman is a lie, adornment is her truth.

Is her sexual truth; hence the enigma (who is she, how can we know her, what does she want?): woman in the sexual act is just that, in an *act*. In *The Gay Science* Nietzsche spells it out:

> Finally, *women*. Reflect on the whole history of women: do they not *have* to be first of all and above all else actresses? Listen to physicians who have hypnotised women; finally, love them – let yourself be 'hypnotised by them'! What is always the end result? That they 'put on something' even when they take off everything [*dass sie 'sich geben', selbst noch wenn sie – sich geben*]. Woman is so artistic.[20]

The German is clear: even when they give themselves, women only ' "give themselves" '. Truth goes into quotation marks, with women everything is mask, masquerade; which is essence and trouble, what we love and honour and what we hate and fear. The philosopher is fascinated and threatened, seduced and mocked: woman is the vanishing point for which he lacks any true perspective, since the perspective *he* has guarantees he cannot know *her*, while the impossibility of knowing her is itself *his* perspective, women produced as 'the woman', *das ewig Weibliche*, the function of this discourse of mask and behind, that mask behind which man suspects some hidden danger.

Listen to physicians who have hypnotised women. Listen to analysts the history of whose psychoanalysis starts with hypnosis, women, hysteria. And hysteria is what? *Failed* masquerade. The hysteric will not play the game, misses her identity as woman: 'Speaking as a whole', writes Freud, 'hysterical attacks, like hysteria in general, revive a piece of sexual activity in women which existed during their childhood and at that time revealed an essentially masculine character.'[21] Playing the game is how a Lacanian analyst, Moustapha Safouan, puts it with reference to the patient described in Riviere's paper: 'When Joan Riviere's patient falls into the masquerade, it is out of rivalry. What I call playing the game, is abandoning the masquerade inasmuch as it covers such a rivalry.'[22] The game to be played is that of being the phallus. With the mother as initial object, the child seeks to be the phallus she wants, lacks-desires (the phallic phase); with the father as law, the child is forbidden that fantasy and pushed into division, sexual difference (the castration complex). No one has the phallus, it is a signifier, the initial signifier of 'the lack-in-being that determines the subject's relation to the signifier'.[23] The phallus inscribes the subject in a relation of desire as division, the subject's lack-in-being, and assigns the subject to sexual difference, boy or girl as having or not having the phallus. No one has the phallus but the order of the phallus as initial signifier identifies as having or not having: the subject is constituted in lack *and* the woman represents lack. In the Oedipal moment of the articulation of sexual difference as identity, male and female, the woman concedes to phallic *jouissance* (Riviere's attainment of full heterosexuality coincident with genitality): 'she invests the man as having the phallus. But she cannot thus invest him without the wish to be, herself, for him, the phallus... in the end she finds her being not as woman but as phallus (this is the sense of the fundamental alienation of her being).'[24] In other words, she becomes the woman men want, the term of phallic identity, phallic exchange.

So Lacan credits Riviere with pin-pointing in the masquerade 'the feminine sexual attitude': the woman's 'on-the-off-chance of preparing herself so that the fantasy of The man in her finds its moment of truth.'[25] The masquerade serves to show what she does not have, a penis, by showing – the adornment, the putting-on – something else, the phallus she becomes, as woman to man, sustaining his identity and an order of exchange of which she is the object – 'the fantasy of The man in her finds its moment of truth': 'Such is the woman behind her veil: it is the absence of the penis that makes her phallus, object of desire.'[26] Adornment *is* the woman, she exists veiled; only thus can she represent lack, be what is wanted: lack 'is never presented other than as a reflection on a veil'.[27] Disguising herself as a castrated woman, the woman represents man's desire and finds her identity as, precisely, woman – genuine womanliness and the masquerade are the same thing, as Riviere insists, or, in the words of the Lacanian analyst Eugènie Lemoine-Luccioni, 'the veil is constitutive of the feminine libidinal structure'.[28]

It is the question of the *constitutive* – and with it the status of the feminine, the identity of the woman – that is crucial here. Its psychoanalytic context (Lacanian-Freudian) includes the following emphases: (1) The subject is given divided in the symbolic; the drama of the subject in language is the experience of its lack in being and that experience is a movement of desire: 'desire is a relation of being to lack... not lack of this or that but lack in being by which the being exists'.[29] Thus nothing can make up division, no object can satisfy desire – what is *wanting* is always wanting, division is the condition of subjectivity. (2) Sexual division is the crucial articulation of symbolic division, it enacts the fundamental splitting of subjectivity itself. The phallus is the term – the signifier – of this articulation-enactment; it comes to figure lack and so to order desire. In Juliet Mitchell's words: 'The phallus – with its status as potentially absent – comes to stand in for the necessarily *missing* object of desire at the level of sexual division.'[30] (3) That no one has the phallus is an expression of its reality as signifier of lack: if division cannot be made up, desire satisfied, then the phallus is not an end, not some final truth, but, paradoxically, the supreme signifier of an impossible identity. (4) Insisting on sexual identity as constructed from division, from the castration complex which gives the phallic mark of sexual distinction, and not ordained in nature, psychoanalysis stresses that identity as precarious, uncertain. (5) Nevertheless, precisely, psychoanalysis describes that construction in terms of an assignment of identity, male and female, the attainment – or not – of heterosexuality round the phallus and castration. (6) For Freud both sexes repudiate femininity; this is the bedrock that analysis strikes: 'the repudiation of femininity can be nothing else than a biological fact, a part of the great riddle of sex.'[31] Pre-Oedipally, both sexes have a masculine relation to the mother, seeking to be the phallus she wants; the prohibition of the mother under the law of the father – the recognition of castration – inaugurates the Oedipus complex for the girl, she now shifting her object love to the father who seems to have the phallus and identifying with the mother who, to her fury, does not: henceforth the girl will desire to have the phallus, which is the bedrock repudiation for her, the point in analytic work more than any other at which the analyst's efforts are felt to have been in vain, 'trying to persuade a woman to abandon her wish for a penis on the ground of its being unrealisable'.[32]

With these emphases in mind as the psychoanalytic context, we can return to the masquerade. The masquerade is a representation of femininity but then femininity is representation, the representation of the woman: 'images and symbols of the woman's cannot be isolated from images and symbols of the woman.'[33] Representation gives not essential but constructed identity, which is uncertain and, as the perspectives slide, precisely masquerade, mask, disguise, threat, danger. Michèle Montrelay notes that 'man has always called the feminine defences and masquerade *evil*'[34] and we can remember Riviere's comment on man's suspicion of some 'hidden danger' behind the mask, as well as Nietzsche's demonstration of that very suspicion, the woman's always ' "giving herself" '. The woman is situated as subject *vis-à-vis* the symbolic, lack in being, the phallus as mark of sexual division, but she lacks nothing in the real, has a problematic relation (to say the least) to castration and the Oedipus complex. Somewhere women do not *fit*, and for Freud and Lacan returning late in their careers to the *Was will das Weib?* Just as the scandal of women that torments Nietzsche is what can the phallus signify to them, what can it say of them? They 'give themselves' even when they give themselves, they are never who they, phallically, are, never *really* the woman.

The masquerade says that the woman exists at the same time that, as masquerade, it says she does not. This tourniquet of reassurance and disturbance can be considered both from the side of the man and from that of the woman. He has the woman, who is, however, fantasy (whence her confirmation in show, spectacle, cinema). She becomes the woman that she is not, assumes a femininity in a movement that Safouan calls 'playing the game' but also 'the fundamental alienation of her being'.

'Alienation' is a social and political term which is here used in the psychoanalytic abstract:

> Let us limit ourselves to the psychoanalytic side of the question. If symbolic castration results in a benefit for the man as regards having, since it conditions 'the attribution of the penis to his person', all is not loss for the woman. But it is as regards being that the benefit is situated for her, since it is her very lack that confers on her her 'price' – a price without equal as there is nothing to pay for it![35]

Alienation quickly becomes a *structural* condition of being a woman (overlying the alienation which for Lacan is a structural condition of subjectivity in general, the subject's division in the symbolic) and can be transposed into playing the game (and in which the woman is said to benefit, said to profit). Alienation is playing the game which is the act of womanliness and the act is her identity (remember Nietzsche on the genius of women), she *sticks* to it. The problem for Rivere's patient is her *distance* from womanliness, the gap between her and femininity – *she*, the case-history says, is disturbed.

At a meeting of the Lacan School a woman analyst comments: 'The nature of femininity is to be cause of man's desire and, as corollary, not to be able to be recognised other than by a man is the nature of femininity. I know that the MLF [Women's Liberation Movement] will be super-angry but I'll carry on...'[36] It is not clear why the MLF should be 'super-angry' (my rendering of the here trivialising *furax*, a kid's slang version of *furieux*, furious) at what can be taken at once as a statement of the male economy of femininity within which women are held, forced to masquerade – *at the cost* of their desire (Luce Irigaray: 'the masquerade...is what women do...in order to participate in man's desire, but at the cost of giving up theirs'[37]). Women as subjects are subjected, men too, but the masquerade-femininity is the representation of this subjection to men, a male order, and so must be broken: 'Women always experience at certain moments of their lives that "femininity" is a masquerade', writes Monique Plaza in the first issue of the journal *Questions féministes*,[38] and we can reread Rivere's patient as experiencing just that, just that alienation.

For the psychoanalyst, however, the social-political analysis of the masquerade towards which the idea of an alienation can pull must be problematic. The analyst who thinks the MLF will be super-angry does so because she is announcing exactly a nature of femininity, what being a woman is in the human articulation of identity round the phallus. Riviere herself runs the masquerade back into 'genuine womanliness' and in Oedipal terms makes the latter an attainment, not an alienation but a fulfilment (there is a moment too when she seems almost to posit a given 'capacity for womanliness', the property of every woman, p.133). In other words, the masquerade comes out as a basic fact of female identity, which can then only doubt and question any social-political analysis of it. If the masquerade goes, taking femininity with it, what is left? Thus another woman analyst: 'When women give up the masquerade, what do they find in bed? Women analysts, how do they cause erections? This difficulty is the price they pay when they leave the masquerade.'[39]

This is crude enough (though its particular concern with phallic identity and exchange can be turned round and read back into the world of Riviere's patient, as into the world of the writing of her paper, the reality of the Freud–Jones–Riviere triangle, their problem with her, the woman analyst, as erotic type) but the question is insistent and important: what is left behind the mask of womanliness? The Oedipal story replies with masculinity; in Freud's words, 'the development of femininity remains exposed to disturbance by the residual phenomena of the early masculine period'.[40] The display of femininity, the masquerade, hides an unconscious masculinity; which is Riviere's account of womanliness as the defence against masculinity that the normal woman achieves, just as it is Nietzsche's worry precisely at that womanliness as defence, the fear of it as mask and so of what may lie behind (the intellectual woman, the feminist, the hysteric, a different sexuality). On the other side, over and against the Oedipal story, resisting the masculine answer, are replies that look to something lost, really the woman's. Both answers come together, have a certain oneness, the one truth they envisage, phallus or anti-phallus, the man/the woman (Irigaray again: 'she does not constitute herself as *one*, does not oppose the masculine truth with a feminine truth; which would be tantamount once more to playing the game of castration'[41]).

No one has the phallus but the phallus is the male sign, the man's assignment; so Safouan talks about his benefit in having 'the attribution of the penis to his person'. The man's masculinity, his male world, is the assertion of the phallus to support his having it. To the woman's masquerade there thus corresponds male display (*parade* is Lacan's term), that display so powerfully described by Virginia Woolf in *Three Guineas*: 'Your clothes in the first place make us gape with astonishment . . . every button, rosette and stripe seems to have some symbolical meaning.'[42] All the trappings of authority, hierarchy, order, position make the man, his phallic identity: 'if the penis was the phallus, men would have no need of feathers or ties or medals . . . Display [*parade*], just like the masquerade, thus betrays a flaw: no one has the phallus.'[43] Which can be read ironically in the reactions of the university lecturer to whom Riviere briefly refers:

When lecturing, not to students but to colleagues, she chooses particularly feminine clothes. Her behaviour on these occasions is also marked by an inappropriate feature: she becomes flippant and joking, so much so that it has caused comment and rebuke. She has to treat the situation of displaying her masculinity to men as a 'game', as something *not real*, as a 'joke'. (p.134)

Riviere reads clothes and behaviour as inappropriate, though at the same time appropriate to women as women, but we can turn things round to this woman displaying *their* masculinity to men as a game, as a joke, much as Woolf does in *Three Guineas* (a strong social-political, feminist joke): she cannot, indeed, contemplate herself on equal terms with men – she isn't, and why should she? For her colleagues, for that *rank* of men (*not* for her students, there she simply does her job), she puts on a show of the femininity they demand, but inappropriately, keeping her distance, and returns masculinity to them as equally unreal, another act, a charade of power. But then masculinity is real in its effects, femininity too, the charade is *in* power (Woolf's theme again in *Three Guineas*); this woman's life is marked by power and effects, is caught up in the definitions of masculinity/ femininity, the identifications of the man and the woman. Her behaviour and dress are about that; Oedipally reading one way only, Riviere misreads, and protest becomes merely sadism – sexual politics gives way to a psycho- logy of sex.

   In the end we come back to a now familiar problem. Psychoanalysis gives us sexual identity as construction and an understanding of that construction that makes good sense; reading 'Womanliness as a masquerade' is surely evidence enough of this. At the same time, the terms of that understanding give us a pattern of development – for instance, the little girl's passage 'from her masculine phase to the feminine one to which she is biologically destined'[44] – which seems to fix things for ever in the given, and oppressive, identities, with no connections through to the *social-historical* realities that it also seems accurately to be describing; 'Womanliness as a masquerade' surely provides evidence of this too. The argument crystallises again today round femininity and woman's identity, for obvious reasons. Psychoanalysis tells us that iden- tity is precarious and that women will bear the traces of its difficult achieve- ment; but it *is* an identity and it is, normally, achieved, and individual women can be understood – analysed – in relation to it. Riviere does just this with the patient in her paper and the paper gives us the psychical and the social together and simultaneously keeps them apart, returning to the former over the latter. No doubt it is an articulation of the psychical and the social in the construction of sexuality and sexual identity that we need to break the dead- lock, the articulation that psychoanalysis lays a basis for and continually suggests but never makes. Easier said than done.

And cinema? The masquerade is obviously at once a whole cinema, the given image of femininity. So it is no surprise that cinema itself can be seen as a prime statement of the masquerade, nor then that the masquerade as a concept should have a presence today in film analysis, thinking about film. The collective analysis by the *Cahiers du cinéma* editorial group of Sternberg's *Morocco* in 1970 is one moment of its introduction; Claire Johnston's account of Tourneur's *Anne of the Indies* in 1975 is another.[45]

A whole cinema ... Cinema has played to the maximum the masquerade, the signs of the exchange femininity, has ceaselessly reproduced its – their – social currency: from genre to genre, film to film, the same spectacle of the woman, her body highlighted into the unity of its image, this cinema image, set out with all the signs of its femininity (all the 'dress and behaviour'). Which is not to say that women in those films are only those signs, that image, but simply that cinema works with the masquerade, the inscription of the fantasy of femininity, the identity of the woman. 'Works with' in the sense of runs on, and in the sense that the masquerade is a work of film and cinema, something to be made up again, *re*inscribed.

The films of the classic Hollywood cinema – more or less contemporary with Riviere's paper and her main analytic contributions – know the difficulties of the masquerade and genuine womanliness, the problematic of who *she* is. The *Cahiers du cinéma* analysis takes *Morocco*, Marlene Dietrich directed by Sternberg who had made her image in *The Blue Angel* only months before and who is fascinated by the very cinema of cinema, the extremes of elaboration. Dietrich wears all the accoutrements of femininity *as* accoutrements, does the poses as poses, gives the act as an act (as in so many films, she is a cabaret performer); writing of a much later performance by her, Sylvia Bovenschen talks of watching 'a woman demonstrate the representation of a woman's body'.[46] We are at an extreme: Dietrich gives the masquerade in excess and so *proffers* the masquerade, take it or leave it, holding and flaunting the male gaze; not a defence against but a derision of masculinity (remember the bric-à-brac of male attire that Dietrich affects in her most famous poses – top hat, dress jacket, cane).

Max Ophuls again develops the masquerade as pure cinema, the hyperspectacle of fantasy. *Madame de* ... sets out the woman, no name, just Madame de ..., the object–possession–identity, the luxurious feminine of jewellery, furs, mirrors, and the man, the men, all their display of uniforms, military rituals, codes of honour. Everything turns on a pair of earrings: 'I've a right to do what I like with them', she says at the beginning of the film, but no, she hasn't; she doesn't *have*, she *is*. The circulation of the earrings produces the spectacle of the film, all the show of femininity, and the catastrophe to which its narrative leads, closing on her death; the masquerade again in excess – but then it *always* is: *was will das Weib?*, the trouble of her identity.

Hitchcock does it differently. In *Suspicion* and again in *Rebecca* Joan Fontaine is offered us as genuine, which means a certain submissive insignificance, the absence of the masquerade that the film will nevertheless quote in order to fill its spectacle contract (in *Suspicion*, for example, the close-ups of Joan Fontaine as she calms her horse) at the same time that it will explicitly reject it (in *Rebecca*, for example, the ball-dress scene where she fails to be the spectacle of the woman, is different from the dangerous Rebecca). Spectacle and narrative, image and movement, cinema in its films exasperates the masquerade and also tries to get women right, know her identity as reassurance – which rightness itself, however, can only be masquerade, fetishisation, a whole cinema: the genuineness of the Joan Fontaine character is just another image, womanliness *is* masquerade.

The fetishisation of the masquerade that cinema captures is the male distance: having, possession, the woman as phallus as the term of the fantasy of the man, her identity for him. Mary Ann Doane has recently been emphasising women's lack of distance here or, to put it another way, the claustrophobia of this cinema:

> Above and beyond a simple adoption of the masculine position in relation to the cinematic sign, the female spectator is given two options: the masochism of overidentification or the narcissism entailed in becoming one's own object of desire, in assuming the image in the most radical way. The effectivity of masquerade lies precisely in its potential to manufacture a distance for the image, to generate a problematic within which the image is manipulable, producible, and readable by the woman.[47]

The problem is thus the refusal of the masquerade, making films outside of cinema, its images (so Anne Friedberg will see Lizzie Borden's *Born in Flames* in this way: 'you never fetishise the body through masquerade ... the film seems consciously deaestheticised'[48]), or perhaps its use, breaking the closeness of femininity for women (Doane's suggestion, taking the masquerade as artifice, destabilising the image – remember Riviere's lecturer again). The former is a question of representation – what is an alternative image and an alternative to the image? – while the latter is a question in representation – what are the breaks, the contradictions, the possible skewings in the system? The former is the utopian actuality of a new spectatorship, the latter the current disturbance of the old positions (in fact, Doane stresses the difficulties here, of seeing through the masquerade in a different way – Riviere's lecturer disturbs but is also caught up in the given identities in the very form of her disturbance).

I know nothing of Riviere's experience of the cinema. Her life remains to be written and, unlike Woolf or Richardson or H. D. or Bryher (all of them contemporaries of her paper, literary figures with an awareness of psycho-analysis), she seems to have written nothing herself directly concerning film. Of course, we can wonder: the year of the 'Masquerade' paper saw the release in Berlin of Pabst's *Pandora's Box*, a study in feminine identity and the masquerade in the male system of the woman; the previous year had seen the publication in *Close Up* (the London film journal with which Bryher, H. D. and Richardson were involved) of its first article by Freud's close colla-borator Hanns Sachs, 'Film psychology'. Perhaps, probably, Riviere knew of these things, and many others, but that is all we can say. So we are left with her paper and the possibilities of the idea of the masquerade, the various ways it can go, in thinking about cinema as in thinking generally about the construction and representation of sexual identity. We are left with that and with her other writings and her translations; and then with the world of the paper, her world – the seashell path, the scarlet parasol, the conversation that should have been on theatres but might have been on Freud, this woman 'of all things'...[49]

13

Critically Queer

Judith Butler

Discourse is not life; its time is not yours.
(Michel Foucault, 'Politics and the Study of Discourse')

How is it that a term that signalled degradation has been turned – 'refunc-
tioned' in the Brechtian sense – to signify a new and affirmative set of
meanings? Is this a simple reversal of valuations such that 'queer' means
either a past degradation or a present or future affirmation? Is this a reversal
that retains and reiterates the abjected history of the term? When the term
has been used as a paralysing slur, as the mundane interpellation of pathologised sexuality, it has produced the user of the term as the emblem and
vehicle of normalisation; the occasion of its utterance, as the discursive
regulation of the boundaries of sexual legitimacy. Much of the straight
world has always needed the queers it has sought to repudiate through the
performative force of the term. If the term is now subject to a reappropria-
tion, what are the conditions and limits of that significant reversal? Does the
reversal reiterate the logic of repudiation by which it was spawned? Can the
term overcome its constitutive history of injury? Does it present the discursive occasion for a powerful and compelling fantasy of historical reparation?
When and how does a term like 'queer' become subject to an affirmative
resignification for some when a term like 'nigger', despite some recent efforts
at reclamation, appears capable of only reinscribing its pain? How and
where does discourse reiterate injury such that the various efforts to recon-
textualise and resignify a given term meet their limit in this other, more
brutal, and relentless form of repetition?[1]

In *On the Genealogy of Morals*, Nietzsche introduces the notion of the
'sign-chain' in which one might read a utopian investment in discourse, one
that re-emerges within Foucault's conception of discursive power. Nietzsche
writes, 'the entire history of a "thing", an organ, a custom can be a continuous sign-chain of ever new interpretations and adaptations whose causes
do not even have to be related to one another but, on the contrary, in some
cases succeed and alternate with one another in a purely chance fashion' (p.
77). The 'ever new' possibilities of resignification are derived from the
postulated historical discontinuity of the term. But is this postulation itself

suspect? Can resignifiability be derived from a pure historicity of 'signs'? Or must there be a way to think about the constraints on and in resignification that takes account of its propensity to return to the 'ever old' in relations of social power? And can Foucault help us here or does he, rather, reiterate Nietzschean hopefulness within the discourse of power? Investing power with a kind of vitalism, Foucault echoes Nietzsche as he refers to power as 'ceaseless struggles and confrontations ... produced from one moment to the next, at every point, or rather in every relation from one point to another.'[2]

Neither power nor discourse are rendered anew at every moment; they are not as weightless as the utopics of radical resignification might imply. And yet how are we to understand their convergent force as an accumulated effect of usage that both constrains and enables their reworking? How is it that the apparently injurious effects of discourse become the painful resources by which a resignifying practice is wrought? Here it is not only a question of how discourse injures bodies, but how certain injuries establish certain bodies at the limits of available ontologies, available schemes of intelligibility. And further, how is it that those who are abjected come to make their claim through and against the discourses that have sought their repudiation?

PERFORMATIVE POWER

Eve Sedgwick's recent reflections on queer performativity ask us not only to consider how a certain theory of speech acts applies to queer practices, but how it is that 'queering' persists as a defining moment of performativity.[3] The centrality of the marriage ceremony in J. L. Austin's examples of performativity suggests that the heterosexualisation of the social bond is the paradigmatic form for those speech acts which bring about what they name. 'I pronounce you...' puts into effect the relation that it names. But from where and when does such a performative draw its force, and what happens to the performative when its purpose is precisely to undo the presumptive force of the heterosexual ceremonial?

Performative acts are forms of authoritative speech: most performatives, for instance, are statements that, in the uttering, also perform a certain action and exercise a binding power.[4] Implicated in a network of authorisation and punishment, performatives tend to include legal sentences, baptisms, inaugurations, declarations of ownership, statements which not only perform an action, but confer a binding power on the action performed. If the power of discourse to produce that which it names is linked with the question of performativity, then the performative is one domain in which power acts *as* discourse.

Importantly, however, there is no power, construed as a subject, that acts, but only, to repeat an earlier phrase, a reiterated acting that *is* power in its persistence and instability. This is less an 'act', singular and deliberate, than a nexus of power and discourse that repeats or mimes the discursive gestures of power. Hence, the judge who authorises and instals the situation he names invariably *cites* the law that he applies, and it is the power of this citation that gives the performative its binding or conferring power. And though it may appear that the binding power of his words is derived from the force of his will or from a prior authority, the opposite is more true: it is *through* the citation of the law that the figure of the judge's 'will' is produced and that the 'priority' of textual authority is established.[5] Indeed, it is through the invocation of convention that the speech act of the judge derives its binding power; that binding power is to be found neither in the subject of the judge nor in his will, but in the citational legacy by which a contemporary 'act' emerges in the context of a chain of binding conventions.

Where there is an 'I' who utters or speaks and thereby produces an effect in discourse, there is first a discourse which precedes and enables that 'I' and forms in language the constraining trajectory of its will. Thus there is no 'I' who stands *behind* discourse and executes its volition or will *through* discourse. On the contrary, the 'I' only comes into being through being called, named, interpellated, to use the Althusserian term, and this discursive constitution takes place prior to the 'I'; it is the transitive invocation of the 'I'. Indeed, I can only say 'I' to the extent that I have first been addressed, and that address has mobilised my place in speech; paradoxically, the discursive condition of social recognition *precedes and conditions* the formation of the subject: recognition is not conferred on a subject, but forms that subject. Further, the impossibility of a full recognition, that is, of ever fully inhabiting the name by which one's social identity is inaugurated and mobilised, implies the instability and incompleteness of subject-formation. The 'I' is thus a citation of the place of the 'I' in speech, where that place has a certain priority and anonymity with respect to the life it animates: it is the historically revisable possibility of a name that precedes and exceeds me, but without which I cannot speak.

QUEER TROUBLE

The term 'queer' emerges as an interpellation that raises the question of the status of force and opposition, of stability and variability, *within* performativity. The term 'queer' has operated as one linguistic practice whose purpose has been the shaming of the subject it names or, rather, the producing of a subject *through* that shaming interpellation. 'Queer' derives its force precisely through the repeated invocation by which it has become linked to accusation, pathologisation, insult. This is an invocation by which a social bond among homophobic communities is formed through time. The interpellation echoes past interpellations, and binds the speakers, as if they spoke in unison across time. In this sense, it is always an imaginary chorus that taunts 'queer!' To what extent, then, has the performative 'queer' operated alongside, as a deformation of, the 'I pronounce you...' of the marriage ceremony? If the performative operates as the sanction that performs the heterosexualisation of the social bond, perhaps it also comes into play precisely as the shaming taboo which 'queers' those who resist or oppose that social form as well as those who occupy it without hegemonic social sanction.

On that note, let us remember that reiterations are never simply replicas of the same. And the 'act' by which a name authorises or deauthorises a set of social or sexual relations is, of necessity, *a repetition*. 'Could a performative succeed,' asks Derrida, 'if its formulation did not repeat a "coded" or iterable utterance ... if it were not identifiable in some way as a "citation"?'[6] If a performative provisionally succeeds (and I will suggest that 'success' is always and only provisional), then it is not because an intention successfully governs the action of speech, but only because that action echoes prior actions, and *accumulates the force of authority through the repetition or citation of a prior, authoritative set of practices*. What this means, then, is that a performative 'works' to the extent that *it draws on and covers over* the constitutive conventions by which it is mobilised. In this sense, no term or statement can function performatively without the accumulating and dissimulating historicity of force.

This view of performativity implies that discourse has a history[7] that not only precedes but conditions its contemporary usages, and that this history effectively decentres the presentist view of the subject as the exclusive origin or owner of what is said.[8] What it also means is that the terms to which we do, nevertheless, lay claim, the terms through which we insist on politicising identity and desire, often demand a turn *against* this constitutive historicity. Those of us who have questioned the presentist assumptions in contemporary identity categories are, therefore, sometimes charged with depoliticising theory. And yet, if the genealogical critique of the subject is the interrogation of those constitutive and exclusionary relations of power through which contemporary discursive resources are formed, then it follows that the critique of the queer subject is crucial to the continuing *democratisation* of queer politics. As much as identity terms must be used, as much as 'outness' is to be affirmed, these same notions must become subject to a critique of the exclusionary operations of their own production: For whom is outness a historically available and affordable option? Is there an unmarked class character to the demand for universal 'outness'? Who is represented by *which* use of the term, and who is excluded? For whom does the term present an impossible conflict between racial, ethnic, or religious affiliation and sexual politics? What kinds of policies are enabled by what kinds of usages, and which are backgrounded or erased from view? In this sense, the genealogical critique of the queer subject will be central to queer politics to the extent that it constitutes a self-critical dimension within activism, a persistent reminder to take the time to consider the exclusionary force of one of activism's most treasured contemporary premises.

As much as it is necessary to assert political demands through recourse to identity categories, and to lay claim to the power to name oneself and determine the conditions under which that name is used, it is also impossible to sustain that kind of mastery over the trajectory of those categories within discourse. This is not an argument *against* using identity categories, but it is a reminder of the risk that attends every such use. The expectation of self-determination that self-naming arouses is paradoxically contested by the historicity of the name itself: by the history of the usages that one never controlled, but that constrain the very usage that now emblematises autonomy; by the future efforts to deploy the term against the grain of the current ones, and that will exceed the control of those who seek to set the course of the terms in the present.

If the term 'queer' is to be a site of collective contestation, the point of departure for a set of historical reflections and futural imaginings, it will have to remain that which is, in the present, never fully owned, but always and only redeployed, twisted, queered from a prior usage and in the direction of urgent and expanding political purposes. This also means that it will doubtless have to be yielded in favour of terms that do that political work more effectively. Such a yielding may well become necessary in order to accommodate – without domesticating – democratising contestations that have and will redraw the contours of the movement in ways that can never be fully anticipated in advance.

It may be that the conceit of autonomy implied by self-naming is the paradigmatically presentist conceit, that is, the belief that there is a one who arrives in the world, in discourse, without a history, that this one makes oneself in and through the magic of the name, that language expresses a 'will' or a 'choice' rather than a complex and constitutive history of discourse and power which compose the invariably ambivalent resources through which a queer and queering agency is forged and reworked. To recast queer agency in this chain of historicity is thus to avow a set of constraints on the past and the future that mark at once the *limits* of agency and its most *enabling conditions*. As expansive as the term 'queer' is meant to be, it is used in ways that enforce a set of overlapping divisions: in some contexts, the term appeals to a younger generation who want to resist the more institutionalised and reformist politics sometimes signified by 'lesbian and gay'; in some contexts, sometimes the same, it has marked a predominantly white movement that has not fully addressed the way in which 'queer' plays – or fails to play – within non-white communities; and whereas in some instances it has mobilised a lesbian activism,[9] in others the term represents a false unity of women and men. Indeed, it may be that the critique of the term will initiate a resurgence of both feminist and anti-racist mobilisation within lesbian and gay politics or open up new possibilities for coalitional alliances that do not presume that these constituencies are radically distinct from one another. The term will be revised, dispelled, rendered obsolete to the extent that it yields to the demands which resist the term precisely because of the exclusions by which it is mobilised.

We no more create from nothing the political terms that come to represent our 'freedom' than we are responsible for the terms that carry the pain of social injury. And yet, neither of those terms are as a result any less necessary to work and rework within political discourse.

In this sense, it remains politically necessary to lay claim to 'women', 'queer', 'gay', and 'lesbian', precisely because of the way these terms, as it were, lay their claim on us prior to our full knowing. Laying claim to such terms in reverse will be necessary to refute homophobic deployments of the terms in law, public policy, on the street, in 'private' life. But the necessity to mobilise the necessary error of identity (Spivak's term) will always be in tension with the democratic contestation of the term which works against its deployments in racist and misogynist discursive regimes. If 'queer' politics postures independently of these other modalities of power, it will lose its democratising force. The political deconstruction of 'queer' ought not to paralyse the use of such terms, but, ideally, to extend its range, to make us consider at what expense and for what purposes the terms are used, and through what relations of power such categories have been wrought. Some recent race theory has underscored the use of 'race' in the service of 'racism', and proposed a politically informed inquiry into the process of *racialisation*, the formation of race.[10] Such an inquiry does not suspend or ban the term, although it does insist that an inquiry into formation is linked to the contemporary question of what is at stake in the term. The point may be taken for queer studies as well, such that 'queering' might signal an injury into (a) the *formation* of homosexualities (a historical inquiry which cannot take the stability of the term for granted, despite the political pressure to do so) and (b) the *deformative* and *misappropriative* power that the term currently enjoys. At stake in such a history will be the differential formation of homosexuality across racial boundaries, including the question of how racial and reproductive relations become articulated through one another.

One might be tempted to say that identity categories are insufficient because every subject position is the site of converging relations of power that are not univocal. But such a formulation underestimates the radical challenge to the subject that such converging relations imply. For there is no self-identical who houses or bears these relations, no site at which such relations converge. This converging and interarticulation *is* the contemporary fate of the subject. In other words, the subject as a self-identical entity is no more.

It is in this sense that the temporary totalisation performed by identity categories is a necessary error. And if identity is a necessary error, then the assertion of 'queer' will be necessary as a term of affiliation, but it will not fully describe those it purports to represent. As a result, it will be necessary to affirm the contigency of the term: to let it be vanquished by those who are excluded by the term but who justifiably expect representation by it, to let it take on meanings that cannot now be anticipated by a younger generation whose political vocabulary may well carry a very different set of investments. Indeed, the term 'queer' itself has been precisely the discursive rallying point for younger lesbians and gay men and, in yet other contexts, for lesbian interventions and, in yet other contexts, for bisexuals and straights for whom the term expresses an affiliation with anti-homophobic politics. That it can become such a discursive site whose uses are not fully constrained in advance ought to be safeguarded not only for the purposes of continuing to democratise queer politics, but also to expose, affirm, and rework the specific historicity of the term.

GENDER PERFORMATIVITY AND DRAG

How, if at all, is the notion of discursive resignification linked to the notion of gender parody or impersonation? First, what is meant by understanding gender as an impersonation? Does this mean that one puts on a mask or persona, that there is a 'one' who precedes that 'putting on', who is something other than its gender from the start? Or does this miming, this impersonating precede and form the 'one', operating as its formative precondition rather than its dispensable artifice?

The construal of gender-as-drag according to the first model appears to be the effect of a number of circumstances. One of them I brought on myself by citing drag as an example of performativity, a move that was taken then, by some, to be *exemplary* of performativity. If drag is performative, that does not mean that all performativity is to be understood as drag. The publication of *Gender Trouble* coincided with a number of publications that did assert that 'clothes make the woman', but I never did think that gender was like clothes, or that clothes make the woman. Added to these, however, are the political needs of an emergent queer movement in which the publicisation of theatrical agency has become quite central.[11]

The practice by which gendering occurs, the embodying of norms, is a compulsory practice, a forcible production, but not for that reason fully determining. To the extent that gender is an assignment, it is an assignment which is never quite carried out according to expectation, whose addressee never quite inhabits the ideal s/he is compelled to approximate. Moreover, this embodying is a repeated process. And one might construe repetition as precisely that which *undermines* the conceit of voluntarist mastery designated by the subject in language.

As *Paris Is Burning* made clear, drag is not unproblematically subversive. It serves a subversive function to the extent that it reflects the mundane impersonations by which heterosexually ideal genders are performed and naturalised and undermines their power by virtue of effecting that exposure. But there is no guarantee that exposing the naturalised status of heterosexuality will lead to its subversion. Heterosexuality can augment its hegemony *through* its denaturalisation, as when we see denaturalising parodies that reidealise heterosexual norms *without* calling them into question.

On other occasions, though, the transferability of a gender ideal or gender norm calls into question the abjecting power that it sustains. For an occupation or reterritorialisation of a term that has been used to abject a population can become the site of resistance, the possibility of an enabling social and political resignification. And this has happened to a certain extent with the notion of 'queer'. The contemporary redeployment enacts a prohibition and a degradation against itself, spawning a different order of values, a political affirmation from and through the very term which in a prior usage had as its final aim the eradication of precisely such an affirmation.

It may seem, however, that there is a difference between the embodying or performing of gender norms and the performative use of discourse. Are these two different senses of 'performativity', or do they converge as modes of citationality in which the compulsory character of certain social imperatives becomes subject to a more promising deregulation? Gender norms operate by requiring the embodiment of certain ideals of femininity and masculinity, ones that are almost always related to the idealisation of the heterosexual bond. In this sense, the initiatory performative, 'It's a girl!' anticipates the eventual arrival of the sanction, 'I pronounce you man and wife'. Hence, also, the peculiar pleasure of the cartoon strip in which the infant is first interpellated into discourse with 'It's a lesbian!' Far from an essentialist joke, the queer appropriation of the performative mimes and exposes both the binding power of the heterosexualising law *and its expropriability*.

To the extent that the naming of the 'girl' is transitive, that is, initiates the process by which a certain 'girling' is compelled, the term or, rather, its symbolic power, governs the formation of a corporeally enacted femininity that never fully approximates the norm. This is a 'girl', however, who is compelled to 'cite' the norm in order to qualify and remain a viable subject. Femininity is thus not the product of a choice, but the forcible citation of a norm, one whose complex historicity is indissociable from relations of discipline, regulation, punishment. Indeed, there is no 'one' who takes on a gender norm. On the contrary, this citation of the gender norm is necessary in order to qualify as a 'one', to become viable as a 'one', where subject-formation is dependent on the prior operation of legitimating gender norms.

It is in terms of a norm that compels a certain 'citation' in order for a viable subject to be produced that the notion of gender performativity calls to be rethought. And precisely in relation to such a compulsory citationality that the theatricality of gender is also to be explained. Theatricality need not be conflated with self-display or self-creation. Within queer politics, indeed, within the very signification that is 'queer', we read a resignifying practice in which the desanctioning power of the name 'queer' is reversed to sanction a contestation of the terms of sexual legitimacy. Paradoxically, but also with great promise, the subject who is 'queered' into public discourse through homophobic interpellations of various kinds *takes up* or *cites* that very term as the discursive basis for an opposition. This kind of citation will emerge as *theatrical* to the extent that it *mimes and renders hyperbolic* the discursive convention that it also *reverses*. The hyperbolic gesture is crucial to the exposure of the homophobic 'law' that can no longer control the terms of its own abjecting strategies.

To oppose the theatrical to the political within contemporary queer politics is, I would argue, an impossibility: the hyperbolic 'performance' of death in the practice of 'die-ins' and the theatrical 'outness' by which queer activism has disrupted the closeting distinction between public and private space have proliferated sites of politicisation and AIDS awareness through-out the public realm. Indeed, an important set of histories might be told in which the increasing politicisation *of* theatricality for queers is at stake (more productive, I think, than an insistence on the two as polar opposites within queerness). Such a history might include traditions of cross-dressing, drag balls, street walking, butch-femme spectacles, the sliding between the 'march' (New York City) and the parade (San Francisco); die-ins by ACT UP, kiss-ins by Queer Nation; drag performance benefits for AIDS (by which I would include both Lypsinka's and Liza Minnelli's in which she, finally, does Judy[12]); the convergence of theatrical work with theatrical activism;[13] performing excessive lesbian sexuality and iconography that effectively counters the desexualisation of the lesbian; tactical interruptions of public forums by lesbian and gay activists in favour of drawing public attention and outrage to the failure of government funding of AIDS research and outreach.

The increasing theatricalisation of political rage in response to the killing inattention of public policy-makers on the issue of AIDS is allegorised in the recontextualisation of 'queer' from its place within a homophobic strategy of abjection and annihilation to an insistent and public severing of that inter-pellation from the effect of shame. To the extent that shame is produced as

the stigma not only of AIDS, but also of queerness, where the latter is understood through homophobic causalities as the 'cause' and 'manifestation' of
the illness, theatrical rage is part of the public resistance to that interpellation
of shame. Mobilised by the injuries of homophobia, theatrical rage reiterates
those injuries precisely through an 'acting out', one that does not merely
repeat or recite those injuries, but that also deploys a hyperbolic display of
death and injury to overwhelm the epistemic resistance to AIDS and to the
graphics of suffering, or a hyperbolic display of kissing to shatter the
epistemic blindness to an increasingly graphic and public homosexuality.
[. . .]

GENDERED AND SEXUAL PERFORMATIVITY

How then does one link the trope by which discourse is described as
'performing' and that theatrical sense of performance in which the hyperbolic status of gender norms seems central? What is 'performed' in drag is, of
course, *the sign* of gender, a sign that is not the same as the body that it
figures, but that cannot be read without it. The sign, understood as a gender
imperative – 'girl!'– reads less as an assignment than as a command and, as
such, produces its own insubordinations. The hyperbolic conformity to the
command can reveal the hyperbolic status of the norm itself, indeed, can
become the cultural sign by which that cultural imperative might become
legible. Insofar as heterosexual gender norms produce inapproximable
ideals, heterosexuality can be said to operate through the regulated production of hyperbolic versions of 'man' and 'woman'. These are for the most
part compulsory performances, ones which none of us choose, but which
each of us is forced to negotiate. I write 'forced to negotiate' because the
compulsory character of these norms does not always make them effica-
cious. Such norms are continually haunted by their own inefficacy; hence,
the anxiously repeated effort to instal and augment their jurisdiction.

The resignification of norms is thus a function of their *inefficacy*, and so
the question of subversion, of *working the weakness in the norm*, becomes a
matter of inhabiting the practices of its rearticulation. The critical promise of
drag does not have to do with the proliferation of genders, as if a sheer
increase in numbers would do the job, but rather with the exposure or the
failure of heterosexual regimes ever fully to legislate or contain their own
ideals. Hence, it is not that drag *opposes* heterosexuality; or that the proliferation of drag will bring down heterosexuality, on the contrary, drag
tends to be the allegorisation of heterosexuality and its constitutive melanch-
olia. As an allegory that works through the hyperbolic, drag brings into
relief what is, after all, determined only in relation to the hyperbolic: the
understated, taken-for-granted quality of heterosexual performativity. At its

best, then, drag can be read for the way in which hyperbolic norms are dissimulated as the heterosexual mundane. At the same time these same norms, taken not as commands to be obeyed, but as imperatives to be 'cited', twisted, queered, brought into relief as heterosexual imperatives, are not, for that reason, necessarily subverted in the process.

It is important to emphasise that although heterosexuality operates in part through the stabilisation of gender norms, gender designates a dense site of significations that contain and exceed the heterosexual matrix. Although forms of sexuality do not unilaterally determine gender, a non-causal and non-reductive connection between sexuality and gender is nevertheless crucial to maintain. Precisely because homophobia often operates through the attribution of a damaged, failed, or otherwise abject gender to homosexuals, that is, calling gay men 'feminine' or calling lesbians 'masculine', and because the homophobic terror over performing homosexual acts, where it exists, is often also a terror over losing proper gender ('no longer being a real or proper man' or 'no longer being a real and proper woman'), it seems crucial to retain a theoretical apparatus that will account for how sexuality is regulated through the policing and the shaming of gender.

We might want to claim that certain kinds of sexual practices link people more strongly than gender affiliation,[14] but such claims can only be nego- tiated, if they can, in relation to specific occasions for affiliation; there is nothing in either sexual practice or in gender to privilege one over the other. Sexual practices, however, will invariably be experienced differentially depending on the relations of gender in which they occur. And there may be forms of 'gender' within homosexuality which call for a theorisation that moves beyond the categories of 'masculine' and 'feminine'. If we seek to privilege sexual practice as a way of transcending gender, we might ask at what cost the *analytic* separability of the two domains is taken to be a distinction in fact. Is there perhaps a specific gender pain that provokes such fantasies of a sexual practice that would transcend gender difference altogether, in which the marks of masculinity and femininity would no longer be legible? Would this not be a sexual practice paradigmatically fetishistic, trying not to know what it knows, but knowing it all the same? This question is not meant to demean the fetish (where would we be without it?), but it does mean to ask whether it is only according to a logic of the fetish that the radical separability of sexuality and gender can be thought.

In theories such as Catharine MacKinnon's, sexual relations of subordination are understood to establish differential gender categories, such that 'men' are those defined in a sexually dominating social position and 'women' are those defined in subordination. Her highly deterministic account leaves no room for relations of sexuality to be theorised apart from the rigid framework of gender difference or for kinds of sexual regulation that do not take gender as their primary objects (i.e., the prohibition of sodomy, public sex, consensual homosexuality). Hence, Gayle Rubin's influential distinction between the domains of sexuality and gender in 'Thinking Sex' and Sedgwick's reformulation of that position have constituted important theoretical opposition to MacKinnon's deterministic form of structuralism.[16]

My sense is that now this very opposition needs to be rethought in order to muddle the lines between queer theory and feminism.[17] For surely it is as unacceptable to insist that relations of sexual subordination determine gender position as it is to separate radically forms of sexuality from the workings of gender norms. The relation between sexual practice and gender is surely not a structurally determined one, but the destabilising of the heterosexual presumption of that very structuralism still requires a way to think the two in a dynamic relation to one another.

In psychoanalytic terms, the relation between gender and sexuality is in part negotiated through the question of the relationship between identification and desire. And here it becomes clear why refusing to draw lines of causal implication between these two domains is as important as keeping open an investigation of their complex interimplication. For, if to identify as a woman is not necessarily to desire a man, and if to desire a woman does not necessarily signal the constituting presence of a masculine identification, whatever that is, then the heterosexual matrix proves to be an *imaginary* logic that insistently issues forth its own unmanageability. The heterosexual logic that requires that identification and desire be mutually exclusive is one of the most reductive of heterosexism's psychological instruments: if one identifies *as* a given gender, one must desire a different gender. On the one hand, there is no one femininity with which to identify, which is to say that femininity might itself offer an array of identificatory sites, as the proliferation of lesbian femme possibilities attests. On the other hand, it is hardly descriptive of the complex dynamic exchanges of lesbian and gay relationships to presume that homosexual identifications 'mirror' or replicate one another. The vocabulary for describing the difficult play, crossing, and destabilisation of masculine and feminine identifications within homosexuality has only begun to emerge within theoretical language: the non-academic language historically embedded in gay communities is here much more instructive. The thought of sexual difference *within* homosexuality has yet to be theorised in its complexity.

For one deciding issue will be whether social strategies of regulation, abjection, and normalisation will not continue to relink gender and sexuality such that the oppositional analysis will continue to be under pressure to theorise their interrelations. This will not be the same as reducing gender to prevailing forms of sexual relations such that one 'is' the effect of the sexual position one is said to occupy. Resisting such a reduction, it ought to be possible to assert a set of non-causal and non-reductive relations between gender and sexuality, not only to link feminism and queer theory, as one might link two separate enterprises, but to establish their constitutive inter-relationship. Similarly, the inquiry into both homosexuality and gender will need to cede the priority of *both* terms in the service of a more complex mapping of power that interrogates the formation of each in specified racial regimes and geopolitical spatialisations. And the task, of course, does not stop here, for no one term can serve as foundational, and the success of any given analysis that centres on any one term may well be the marking of its own limitations as an exclusive point of departure.

The goal of this analysis, then, cannot be pure subversion, as if an under-mining were enough to establish and direct political struggle. Rather than denaturalisation or proliferation, it seems that the question for thinking discourse and power in terms of the future has several paths to follow: how to think power as resignification together with power as the conver-gence or interarticulation of relations of regulation, domination, constitu-tion? How to know what might qualify as an affirmative resignification – with all the weight and difficulty of that labour – and how to run the risk of reinstalling the abject at the site of its opposition? But how, also, to rethink the terms that establish and sustain bodies that matter?

The film *Paris Is Burning* has been interesting to read less for the ways in which it deploys denaturalising strategies to reidealise whiteness and hetero-sexual gender norms than for the less stabilising rearticulations of kinship it occasioned. The drag balls themselves at times produce high femininity as a function of whiteness and deflect homosexuality through a transgendering that *reidealises* certain bourgeois forms of heterosexual exchange. And yet, if those performances are not immediately or obviously subversive, it may be that it is rather in the *reformulation of kinship*, in particular, the redefining of the 'house' and its forms of collectivity, mothering, mopping, reading, and becoming legendary, that the appropriation and redeployment of the categ-ories of dominant culture enable the formation of kinship relations that function quite supportively as oppositional discourse. In this sense, it would be interesting to read *Paris Is Burning* against, say, Nancy Chodor-ow's *The Reproduction of Mothering* and ask what happens to psychoana-lysis and kinship as a result. In the former, the categories like 'house' and 'mother' are derived from that family scene, but also deployed to form alternative households and community. This *resignification* marks the work-ings of an agency that is (a) not the same as voluntarism, and that (b) though *implicated* in the very relations of power it seeks to rival, is not, as a consequence, reducible to those dominant forms.

Performativity describes this relation of being implicated in that which one opposes, this turning of power against itself to produce alternative modalities of power, to establish a kind of political contestation that is not a 'pure' opposition, a 'transcendence' of contemporary relations of power, but a difficult labour of forging a future from resources inevitably impure.

How will we know the difference between the power we promote and the power we oppose? Is it, one might rejoin, a matter of 'knowing?' For one is, as it were, in power even as one opposes it, formed by it as one reworks it, and it is this simultaneity that is at once the condition of our partiality, the measure of our political unknowingness, and also the condition of action itself. The incalculable effects of action are as much a part of their subversive promise as those that we plan in advance.

The effects of performatives, understood as discursive productions, do not conclude at the terminus of a given statement or utterance, the passing of legislation, the announcement of a birth. The reach of their signifiability cannot be controlled by the one who utters or writes, since such productions are not owned by the one who utters them. They continue to signify in spite of their authors, and sometimes against their authors' most precious intentions.

It is one of the ambivalent implications of the decentring of the subject to have one's writing be the site of a necessary and inevitable expropriation. But this yielding of ownership over what one writes has an important set of political corollaries, for the taking up, reforming, deforming of one's words does open up a difficult future terrain of community, one in which the hope of ever fully recognising oneself in the terms by which one signifies is sure to be disappointed. This not owning of one's words is there from the start, however, since speaking is always in some ways the speaking of a stranger through and as oneself, the melancholic reiteration of a language that one never chose, that one does not find as an instrument to be used, but that one is, as it were, used by, expropriated in, as the unstable and continuing condition of the 'one' and the 'we', the ambivalent condition of the power that binds.

14

Gender or Sex?

Diane Elam

GENDER OR SEX?

This history of women should be written in a kind of suspension, written in a present that is not at ease with either its past or its future. The category of women imposes an uncertainty which is also an openness, and feminism should not be afraid to forbid itself epistemological authority. Between clear and distinct knowledge and ignorance lies politics. Yet before turning to the ungrounded politics of women's solidarity, it is important to interrogate what kind of category 'women' constitutes. A significant debate has taken place within feminism as to whether women is a category of gender or of sex, and as to the precise nature of the distinction between gender and sex.

It will be no surprise that I say right away that this distinction is not necessarily a helpful one. However, it is important to take account of the fundamental issue that feminists have sought to get hold of by means of it: is 'women' primarily a natural or a cultural category? The rough distinction between sex and gender can be made as follows: either sex is privileged as a biological attribute upon which a gender ideology is imposed, or sex is denied as merely the ideological mystification that obscures cultural facts about gender. Thus, if women are a sex, they are oppressed by gender; if women are understood as a gender, they are oppressed by sex. I fear that the desire to decide this issue is a significant problem for feminism. Whichever way feminists argue – whether women are understood as naturally sexed or as culturally gendered – the result is a kind of vicious circle.
[...]

The strict opposition between sex and gender, nature and culture, is the product of the desire that women have an identity above all – be it natural or cultural. I would like to suggest that the way out of the impasse between these stark extremes is not to resolve the argument between the two straw-women – earth mother and stereotype victim. Rather, a closer examination of the stakes in the gender/sex distinction may lead us to understand women as a category without recourse to a notion of identity as such.
[...]

The distinction between gender and sex attempts to deal with the categorical problem of 'women'. The role of psychoanalysis has been crucial in suggesting that apparently 'natural' attributes of sex are in fact the effect of psychic representations of gender. This is somewhat paradoxical, since Freud himself was, of course, primarily concerned to return patients' aberrant psychic representations to what he considered to be the natural sexual roles of male activity and female passivity.[1]

Rather than follow in Freud's patriarchal footsteps, a number of feminists have found Lacan's rereading of Freud a valuable contribution towards an understanding of gender-roles as masks rather than norms. And it is important in the context of my discussion of feminism and deconstruction to look more precisely at what Lacan's work has involved. Lacan makes his position on the relationship between gender and sex clearest in his by now famous parable of the two children on the train:

> A train arrives at a station. A little boy and a little girl, brother and sister, are seated in a compartment face to face next to the window through which the buildings along the station platform can be seen passing as the train pulls to a stop. 'Look,' says the brother, 'we're at Ladies!'; 'Idiot!' replies his sister, 'Can't you see we're at Gentlemen.'[2]

What the two children see, of course, are the signs over the station toilets, and what strikes the reader immediately is that the children have each made a mistake and don't know it. But while the children probably could be convinced that they had misunderstood where they were, it is unlikely that they would also understand the significance of their original error. Such is the stuff of parables, and the psychoanalyst steps in to identify six important points:

First, like the children we are ignorant of the structure that holds the gender/sex relationship in place. As a result, we are likely to be susceptible to the power the structure holds over us without even realising it. That is to say, we will not be able to recognise the extent to which sex/gender systems control and limit our actions.

Second, each child understands where they are in terms of the other: the sister sees 'Gentlemen', the brother 'Ladies'. This aspect of the parable not only calls attention to the force of binary logic in the gender/sex relationship but also underlines the way in which it is based on difference more than identity : we satisfy our prescribed gender role more through a knowledge of what we are *not* than what we are. And yet this knowledge is not the result of direct experience, since we are forbidden direct access to the place of the Other: the girl is not allowed to go behind the door marked Gentlemen; the boy is forbidden entry to Ladies. Something of the other sex/gender always remains a secret.

Third, sex/gender differentiation occurs as the result of language, not of natural or biological fact. In making this point, Lacan is not attempting to develop yet another instrumentalist account of language to explain sex/ gender differentiation. Saussure's insistence on the unmotivated character and differential functioning of the sign is important to Lacan here. Gender is not established on the basis of any intrinsic sexual properties of the subject, but rather in opposition to the sign of the other gender. The signified meaning of woman or man arises from the interplay of the opposed signifiers of gender, from the presence or absence of the phallus. But this is not to argue that there is a one to one correspondence between signifier and signified, which Saussure's work might lead us to believe. As Lacan demonstrates, at the most basic level, the signifier (or sound image) 'Ladies' refers both to the signified (concept) of a set of toilets *and* to the group of women in general. A similar multiple correspondence occurs with the signifier 'Gentlemen'. In each case, this crucial multiplication of signifieds suggests that woman might refer to more than a biological female, man to more than a biological male. Ultimately, as Jane Gallop notices, the 'whole normalising moralism of biologistic psychology' is upset because a natural correspondence between biological sex and proper gender roles does not exist.[3] That is to say, in Lacan's parable the 'normal' has no biologistic grounds to which a psychological moralism could appeal.

Fourth, the entire system of assigning signifiers to signifieds is, as Saussure understood, ultimately arbitrary. There is no natural or justifiable reason why one toilet or group of people should be called 'Ladies' and the other 'Gentlemen'. Nor is there any *a priori* justification for enforcing this division. Rather, enforcement is justified through a number of social conventions. Significantly, Lacan's parable makes no mention of the classic psychoanalytic notion of the Oedipal complex and resulting castration anxiety as a primary avenue for gender differentiation. The very absence of this central paradigm – where the girl is supposed to spend her life trying either to represent the phallus or to get the phallus (for instance, penis envy leads to the desire for children, which stands for the phallus) and the boy acquires a life-long preoccupation with the need to have the phallus that, at any moment, could be taken away from him – suggests that gender differentiation is not necessarily tied to parenting or reducible to developmental Oedipal interactions.

Fifth, no matter how much we might point out the arbitrariness of the division of individual subjects on the basis of sex/gender correspondence, this system is nonetheless rigidly enforced. The little girl must still sit in the seat which makes her think she is at 'Gentlemen', the little boy must believe himself to be stopped at 'Ladies'. Lacan's parable would indicate, then, that it is no accident that public restrooms in the West continue to enforce a code of urinary segregation based on sex and gender distinctions. It is perhaps a further irony that the pictures which accompany or replace the written designations on Western toilet facilities do not necessarily bear a strict resemblance to those individuals who are hailed by them. Women will not necessarily wear the familiar skirt which inevitably adorns the women's room, and men in kilts and djellebas will not particularly resemble their trousered counterparts. But the fact remains that there must, underneath it all, be a moment of visual accountability. Women who fail to resemble sufficiently stereotypic women will be likely to find themselves accosted by law enforcement officals and asked to prove why they should be using the women's not the men's room – presence of the wrong set of genitals indicates the presence of a pervert.[4] Obviously, the stakes here go beyond who is simply allowed to use which toilet. The enforcement of sex and gender divisions aids and abets heterosexist societies and also leads to unjust divisions of labour that correspond to economic disparity.[5]

Sixth, Lacan's parable does not so much suggest that anatomy is destiny (in the fashion of much Freudian analysis), as it implies that culture has handed out tickets for gender seats on the basis of anatomy. Females are suppose to stand in the line that makes them into women, males line up to become men. Or as Jacqueline Rose points out, it is 'not that anatomical difference *is* sexual difference (the one as strictly deducible from the other), but that anatomical difference comes to *figure* sexual difference, that is, becomes the sole representative of what that difference is allowed to be.'[6]

The Lacanian six-point analysis goes a long way in explaining how the two-party system of male and female sex is made to correspond with the appropriate gender. I would even argue that the catchy parable is helpful for understanding that the entire gender/sex system rests upon arbitrary, socially constructed criteria. However, Lacan's train does not carry feminism as far as it needs to go. The ride on the gender/sex railroad may prove informative, but it hardly exhausts the possible terrain that can be covered nor takes into account whether or not the entire train needs to be derailed.

Deconstruction intersects with feminism precisely here: as an extension of the psychoanalytic account of the structure of gender/sex, an extension which involves a switching of tracks. To begin with, for Joan Scott, psychoanalysis is not sufficiently historical and lays too much emphasis on the individual. Nonetheless, her analysis in *Gender and the Politics of History* begins in much the same place as does Lacan's. She sets up the now familiar opposition where gender is a socially constructed category imposed on the pre-determined sexed body. But Scott is not altogether comfortable with the residue of biological determinism that this relationship implies, nor is she pleased with the way in which gender has been isolated from other categories of difference. As a result, she urges that 'a genuine historicisation and deconstruction of the terms of sexual difference' need to take place. This, she contends, would shift the emphasis away from sex and onto gender so that gender could be 'redefined and restructured in conjunction with a vision of political and social equality that includes not only sex but class and race'.[7]

In *Technologies of Gender* Teresa de Lauretis, like Scott, places sexual difference on the side of biological determinism and gender on the side of cultural construction. Also like Scott, de Lauretis privileges gender, which she understands as not only a classificatory term in grammar but also a representation of a relation that is an ongoing social construction.[8] For her, sexual difference 'constrains feminist critical thought within the conceptual frame of a universal sex opposition', which makes it difficult, if not impossible, to articulate differences among and within women (p. 2).

However, de Lauretis is even less satisfied than Scott or Lacan with the simple distinction between sex and gender. As a result, she proposes that 'we need a notion of gender that is not so bound up with sexual difference as to be virtually coterminous' with it (p. 2). According to de Lauretis, we must unravel and deconstruct the sex/gender relationship so that gender is no longer seen either as unproblematically proceeding from biologically determined sex, or as an imaginary construct that is completely beside the point.[9] Alternately, she proposes that 'gender is not a property of bodies or something originally existent in human beings'; rather it is a 'product and process of a number of social technologies' which create a matrix of differences and cross any number of languages as well as cultures (p. 3). In short, de Lauretis's feminist theory of gender 'points to a conception of the subject as multiple, rather than divided or unified' (p. x).

But de Lauretis's deconstructive engagement with the sex/gender distinction only goes so far. She wants to retain a notion of the subject, arguing that deconstructions of the subject effectively 'recontain women in femininity (Woman)' and 'reposition female subjectivity *in* the male subject' (p. 24). For de Lauretis, 'gender marks the limit of deconstruction, the rocky bed (so to speak) of the "abyss of meaning"' (p. 48). I am less inclined than de Lauretis, however, to believe that we have indeed hit rock bottom, that at the bottom of the deconstructive abyss lie the jagged edges of gender.

Rather than abandon feminism's alliance with deconstruction where de Lauretis does, Judith Butler goes on to question even our basic presuppositions about the sex/gender relationship. Butler sees no reason to believe that sex, as natural fact, precedes cultural inscriptions of gender: 'Gender is not to culture as sex is to nature.'[10] As far as Butler is concerned, then, Lacan's two children on the train do not first each receive a (biological) sex and then a gender (a cultural meaning for that sex). Instead, gender as a discursive element actually gives rise to a belief in pre-discursive or inner sex. That is to say, sex is retrospectively a product of gender so that, in sense, gender comes *before* sex:

It's not that there is some kind of *sex* that exists in hazy biological form that is somehow *expressed* in the gait, the posture, the gesture; and that some sexuality then expresses both that apparent gender or that more or less magical sex. If gender is drag, and if it is an imitation that regularly produces the ideal it attempts to approximate, then gender is a perform-ance that *produces* the illusion of an inner sex or essence or psychic gender core.... In effect, one way that gender gets naturalised is through being constructed as an inner psychic or physical *necessity*.[11]

If sex is the retrospective projection of gender, its fictional origin, Butler does not however argue that gender is the 'real thing'. Rather, she calls it 'drag' or 'performance', a particular kind of imitation. Not the imitation of a real sex but an imitation of an ideal that is its own projection, that does not exist anywhere else. This gender ideal can never be stabilised, but must ceaselessly be repeated with each performance of gender. To put this another way, we might say that gendered bodies are like actors in an unscripted play desperately trying to imitate a life that no one has ever led. They try so desperately because they believe that if they get it right, they will be allowed to leave the stage and lead that life. The significance of this argument (in the somewhat Beckettian formulation I have given it) lies in a refusal of the simple alternatives of sex and gender, nature and culture. Nature is the retro-projected illusion of a real origin to culture, yet that illusion is *necessary* to culture, the very ground of its capacity to represent itself.

Butler's aim is not, therefore, to deconstruct gender in order to reveal the natural sex which gender had obscured. Nor is she suggesting that gender is a cultural rock on which deconstruction founders. Rather, what the work of deconstruction will reveal is that there is no bedrock (to use de Lauretis' metaphor) of gender or sex at the bottom of the abyss. The relationship between sex and gender is a continuously self-deconstructing one which produces structures that are called natural only because we have forgotten that they are structures.

Paul de Man makes this point clearer when he explains that:

The deconstruction of a system of relationships always reveals a more fragmented stage that can be called natural with regard to the system that is being undone. Because it also functions as the negative truth of the deconstructive process, the 'natural' pattern authoritatively substitutes its relational system for the one it helped to dissolve. In so doing, it conceals the fact that it is itself one system of relations among others, and it presents itself as the sole and true order of things, as nature and not as structure. But since a deconstruction always has for its target to reveal the existence of hidden articulations and fragmentations within assumedly monadic totalities, nature turns out to be a self-deconstructing term. It engenders endless other 'natures' in an eternally repeated pattern of regression. Nature deconstructs nature. ....[12]

What de Man wants us to recognise is that the work of deconstruction may reveal that nature is a structure (the 'natural' is a cultural construct). However, this new found 'culture' in its turn implies a new nature, behind it as it were. Once this new nature is posited, it in turn gives rise to another deconstruction, another culture, another implied nature, and so on. The point here is not that culture deconstructs a pre-existing nature but that culture actually produces nature as its fictional origin.

To understand how this works specifically with regard to the sex/gender relationship, it is worth taking a closer look at some commonly held assumptions about sex. It would not take much of an argument to point out that sex has traditionally been understood in the West as a biological feature which requires no cultural assembly. Human beings come in two sexes, male and female, and each individual is supposed to be decidably one or the other.

But what happens when some assembly is required in order to make sure that there are still only two discernible sexes (and genders)? It is the answer to this question that best illustrates how gender actually gives rise to two 'natural' sexes. The best presentation of this information to date is Suzanne Kessler's excellent essay, 'The Medical Construction of Gender'.[13] Kessler looks at what happens when physicians are faced with infants with genitals which are not unambiguously female or male. In these instances, Kessler notes that 'case management involves perpetuating the notion that good medical decisions are based on interpretations of the infant's real "sex" rather than on cultural understandings of gender' (p. 10). Physicians assume, and parents are led to believe, that each infant has a natural sex and that the medical task is simply to reveal it. As Kessler puts it, 'the emphasis is not on the doctors creating gender but in their completing the genitals' (p. 16).

In discovering this 'natural' sex, Kessler observes that doctors tend to refer to an 'underdeveloped phallus' rather than an 'overdeveloped clitoris', which suggests that an infant is first of all male until proven otherwise. And more often than not, he is proven otherwise. 'What is ambiguous', she notices, 'is not whether this is a penis but whether it is "good enough" to remain one' (p. 13). Thus, as Kessler explains, 'as long as the decision rests largely on the criterion of genital appearance, and male is defined as having a "good-sized" penis, more infants will be assigned to the female gender than to the male' (p. 13). Again and again, the principal criterion for femaleness is the absence of *sufficient* maleness:

> The formulation 'good penis equals male; absence of good penis equals female', is treated in the literature and by the physicians interviewed as an objective criterion, operative in all cases. There is a striking lack of

attention to the size and shape requirements of the female genitals, other than that the vagina be able to receive a penis. (p. 20)[14]

The point of Kessler's article is to illustrate how physicians create a 'natural' sex on the basis of shared cultural values about gender roles (p. 18). Kessler concludes that 'the belief that gender [and sex] consists of two exclusive types is maintained and perpetuated by the medical community in the face of incontrovertible physical evidence that this is not mandated by biology' (p. 25). The upshot of this, to return to Lacan's example of the two children on the train, is that as far as medical science is concerned, individuals are not allowed to stand in the aisles when the train pulls into the station; everyone must sit in a single seat, use a single toilet, be hailed by one and only one of two sexes/genders.

What Kessler so thoroughly demonstrates is that physicians begin with cultural gender stereotypes and work backward to discover a supposedly natural sex which comes in only two types: female and male. The exclusivity of the two types is then assured in that the male type is given priority, and the female defined as 'all those not having a good sized penis'. While Kessler deals with extremes, it is nonetheless easy to see that the more common relationship between sex and gender works in precisely the same way. First, sex is established in relation to visual criteria (breasts or beards, clitoris or penis), and gender roles (clothing, mannerisms, voice tone, jobs) are established on the basis of sex-identification. However, it is the awareness of gender-roles that leads us to go looking for supposedly natural sexes.

But it is not only medicine's attention to genitalia or the general public's visual acumen that indicate how gender works to construct sex. In *Gender Blending* Holly Devor takes a revealing look at hormone studies:

Human behaviour patterns commonly used in hormone studies as indicators of biologically based femininity include: interest in weddings and marriage, preference for marriage over career, interest in infants and children, and an enjoyment of childhood play with dolls. Evidence of biologically based masculinity is defined in terms of childhood enjoyment of toys and games requiring high levels of activity, in self-assurance, and in holding career aspirations as more important than parenting.[15]

Devor goes on to explain that by the age of two, children understand that they are members of a gender grouping which consists of stereotypes like those used for hormonal studies.[16] 'Popular conceptions of femininity and masculinity', she observes, 'revolve around hierarchical appraisals of the "natural" roles of males and females.' What this leads to in mainstream North American society is a patriarchal gender schema that 'reserves highly valued attributes for males and actively supports the high evaluation of any characteristics which might inadvertently become associated with male-ness.'[17]

Taking Devor's and Kessler's work into consideration may lead us to wonder whether the West could ever understand the un-naturalness of its own assumptions about nature and break away from gender stereotypes. On this score, feminists attempting to critique received assumptions about the naturalness of sex and gender roles have found Lacanian psychoanalysis helpful, even though it can be complicitous with the very positions that feminism opposes. Because Lacanian psychoanalysis has displayed a less than loyal relationship to feminist projects, it is worth taking some time to trace how Lacan managed to support both the feminist and patriarchal causes. And in so doing, I hope to perform a deconstructive reading which shows, as Elizabeth Grosz urges, 'how psychoanalysis both participates in and departs from phallo(logo)centrism in ways that are not clearly distinguished'.[18]

As I tried to make clear earlier, Lacan's work has been useful for feminism insofar as it outlines the traditional understanding of the sex/gender relationship in the West. But beyond this point, in his now well-known *Encore* seminar, Lacan also began a controversial discussion about the psychoanalytic nature of feminine sexuality. Here Lacan is quick to stress that 'there is no such thing as *The* woman, where the definite article stands for the universal'.[19] On first glance, this statement sets Lacan's work apart from beliefs in static gender-roles or strict correlations between sex and gender. Going even further, Lacan argues that this division of woman upsets the phallic sexual relation which, as Rose and Mitchell point out, 'the woman has classically come to support' (p. 137). As an alternative, Lacan proposes a feminine sexuality that would be supplementary and not complementary to phallic sexuality, 'a *jouissance* beyond the phallus', as he puts it (p. 145).

But all is not well for feminism in *jouissance* land, where women are not having as much fun as Lacan claims. Feminist critics of Lacan's theory of feminine sexuality have been numerous – too numerous, in fact, to do justice to them all here. But I would like, nonetheless, to chart the trajectory of some frequent and well-founded objections. To begin with, despite all his protestations to the contrary, Lacan actually threatens to return women and women's sexuality to the same rigid, psychoanalytic models from which he claims to be departing. On this score, it seems particularly apt that a statue (Bernini's *Santa Teresa*) serves as his central example of feminine sexuality. Lacan brashly contends that:

> You only have to go and look at Bernini's statue [of Saint Theresa] in Rome to understand immediately that she's coming, there is no doubt about it. And what is her *jouissance*, her *coming* from? It is clear that the

essential testimony of the mystics is that they are experiencing it but know nothing about it. (p. 147)

In one look Lacan thinks he knows all about women's pleasure – a *jouissance* that the mystics themselves could not know. And since the statue is not going to talk back to him – such is the benefit of taking your examples from marble slabs – the woman herself is hardly going to contradict him. Lacan, it would seem, returns women's pleasure to a state of passivity which would even make Freud happy.[20]

This is not a particularly feminist conclusion on Lacan's part, to say the least, and Luce Irigaray quickly exposes his phallocentric hands:

> The question whether, in [Lacan's] logic, [women] can articulate anything at all, whether they can be heard, is not even raised. For raising it would mean granting that there may be some other logic, and one that upsets his own. That is, a logic that challenges mastery.
>
> And to make sure this does not come up, the right to experience pleasure is awarded to a statue. ...
>
> In Rome? So far away? To look? At a statue? Of a saint? Sculpted by a man? What pleasure are we talking about? Whose pleasure? For where the pleasure of the Theresa in question is concerned, her own writings are perhaps more telling.[21]

Examples of feminine pleasure, like Lacan's, are nothing more than a solace for men, guaranteeing to them that there is something foreign, fantasmatic, other to what is intolerable in their world.[22] Understanding woman as always and only a fixed model (even a model such as Saint Theresa, fixed in an attitude of mobility and self-abandon) necessarily reduces woman to the condition of the patriarchy: to be for herself a representation, lost in the act of modelling herself.

Statue of a mystic. Woman as statue. Woman as mystic. Such are the leaps of logic in Lacan's argument and the source of another serious problem with his work. It is easy for Lacan's theory of feminine sexuality to amount to little more than another instance of the mystification of woman as fixed model of the truth. This is the problem with Lacan's work that Derrida outlines in great detail in 'Le facteur de la vérité'. What Derrida demonstrates is that as far as Lacan is concerned woman is always where she is looked for. Woman has no universal, but she does lack universally. She has no truth, but femininity marks the truth of castration. As Derrida puts it:

> The link of Femininity and Truth is the ultimate signified of [Lacan's] deciphering. ... He gives to Woman or to Femininity a capital letter that elsewhere he often reserves for Truth. ... Femininity is the Truth (of)

castration, is the best figure of castration, because in the logic of the signifier it has always already been castrated.[23]

Although Lacan refuses directly to make woman a universal – there is no such thing as the woman – before he's done with her, 'Woman', 'women', and 'femininity' (Lacan readily collapses the terms) actually become the psychoanalytic pure particular, an ultimate pre-discursive signifier which comes before the discursive phallus. Hers is the true identity of pre-discursive lack.

So Lacanian psychoanalysis proves at times to be just another form of phallogocentrism, while medical science all too often puts its confidence in conventional, heterosexist paradigms of sex and gender. In these circumstances, all is not well for feminism, despite deconstruction's attempts to intervene. Women seem ontologically determined from the start, even if this 'start' is retrospectively projected. It is worth asking, then, whether it is possible to break the established links between sex (as biological factor), gender, and sexuality. What can feminism and deconstruction do to move beyond conditions that inevitably prove oppressive for women?

Monique Wittig finds that the only answer is an all-out destruction of gender and sex. To understand why this must be so, Wittig argues that gender is 'the linguistic index of the political opposition between the sexes and the domination of women', while sex is a political and philosophical category 'that founds society as heterosexual'.[24] That is to say, Wittig's point is that within society women are marked by sex, while within language they are marked by gender. Given this distinction, though, any power granted to sex and gender categories is grounded on ontological falsehoods. Gender, she maintains, 'is an ontological impossibility because it tries to accomplish the division of Being'.[25] According to Wittig, lesbianising language performs a linguistic overhaul which reveals, by contrast, that Being is not divided, that the categories of gender and sex only get in the way of understanding ourselves as total subjects. With sex and gender out of the way, with distinctions between women and men no longer operative, society will be made up of ontologically total subjects, thanks to the linguistic revolution of lesbianisation.

It may be tempting to believe that total subjects lie on the other side of the gender/sex divide, that all the king's persons and all the king's horses could put the subject back together again. But deconstruction has taught us to be suspicious of such totalising schemes which, as Butler recognises, unwittingly set up a 'normative model of humanism as the framework for feminism'. Butler is quick to point out the serious problems with Wittig's argument:

> Where it seems that Wittig has subscribed to a radical project of lesbian emancipation and enforced a distinction between 'lesbian' and 'woman',

she does this through the defence of the pregendered 'person', characterised as freedom. This move not only confirms the presocial status of human freedom, but subscribes to that metaphysics of substance that is responsible for the production and naturalisation of the category of sex itself.[26]

Feminism's answer to the problem of established links between sex, gender, and sexuality should not be a philosophical embrace of presocial human freedom and neutralised Being. The dialectical neutralisation of Being always ensures phallocentric mastery; presocial human freedom appeals to phallocentric universals.[27] Put simply, there is no liberated, total subject which unfortunately became divided [...] I have just as little interest in pursuing the possibility of a gender and sex free, total subject as I do in trying to establish the true nature of sex or gender. Feminism should not be about establishing the true nature of sexual or gender difference, nor about abolishing it. Rather, the focus should be on keeping sexual difference – understood as the complex interplay of sex and gender roles – open as the space of a radical uncertainty.

But with that said, I have still not suggested *how* feminism and deconstruction would assure this space of radical uncertainty. For as Cornell reminds us, 'we can't just drop out of gender or sex-roles and pick them up again when we feel like it'.[28] Sex and gender-roles seem all too often unradically certain. Given a general resistance to change and a social interest in maintaining set gender and sex-roles, I would agree with Cornell that 'we must take off from within sexual difference and not simply pretend to be beyond it'.[29] The question more precisely becomes how to operate within the established terms of sexual difference, examining where those lines of difference have been drawn, while at the same time upsetting the terms and redrawing the lines.

One such avenue for change has been a combination of hormonal therapy and genital reconstruction which has helped individuals change their first biologically identified sex. One might say, then, that women have yet to be determined biologically. While some view medical sex-change procedures to be the reconstruction of the true sex which nature got wrong, such an argument has all of the problems that go along with other considerations of sex as a natural attribute. I would argue instead that sex change procedures generate a second sex which is neither more natural nor more cultural than the first. The very possibility of change itself calls attention to the unnaturalness of sex and gender-roles. This becomes even more evident when apparently radical medical practices designed to change an individual's sex rely on very conventional understandings of what it means to be either sex: the size of primary and secondary sex traits, voice timbre, quantity of body hair, overall body shape. After all is said and done, the result is still the same old two: female and male, woman and man.[30]

There is nothing necessarily feminist or deconstructive about these procedures, which tend to establish the same divisions of sexual difference, even if through unconventional means. Moving away from medical approaches, Devor appeals to what she calls 'gender blending', the mixing of sex and gender such that strangers sometimes 'mistakenly attribute them with membership in a gender with which the gender blenders themselves do not identify, i.e. females who think of themselves as women are mistaken for men'.[31] Devor argues that an increased attention to gender blending 'could serve as a transitional step between the present patriarchal sexist gender schema and a future state wherein the concept of gender would become obsolete and meaningless'.[32]

On the surface, Devor's argument resembles Wittig's. But Devor's interest in abolishing traditional gender and sex roles is not to pursue a presocial total subject; her goal is the creation of a diverse range of sex/gender combinations such that the terms themselves could no longer create the grounds for discrimination and prescriptive sex/gender combinations. This interest in multiplication and diversity has been a feature of much of Derrida's deconstructive engagement with issues of sexual difference. Derrida stresses the importance of not understanding sexual difference in terms of sexual *opposition*. That is, we must move beyond understanding sexual difference as a binary opposition, which has long been the problem for both philosophical and psychoanalytic interpretations.[33]

In order to do this, Derrida encourages an examination of the 'ready-to-wear', 'off-the-rack universals' with which we symbolically determine sexual opposition.[34] His rather unlikely example is a Van Gogh painting of two shoes. What interests Derrida so much are the casual assumptions that Heidegger and Meyer Schapiro have made about the painting. In their consideration of the painting, both Heidegger and Schapiro draw conclusions about the class and gender of the owner of the shoes:

> It is true that neither Heidegger nor Schapiro seems to give thematic attention to the sex of reattachment. The one reattaches, prior to any examination of the question, to peasantry, but passes without warning from peasantry to the peasant woman. The other, having examined the question, reattaches to some city-dwelling painter, but never asks himself why they should be man's shoes nor why the other, not content with saying 'peasantry', sometimes adds 'the peasant woman'. Sometimes, and even most often.[35]

Derrida is fascinated by the way in which both Heidegger and Schapiro jump to such conclusions about two shoes which do not explicitly denote the class or gender of their owner. He argues that a whole set of ready-to-wear assumptions about sex and class have been unthinkingly applied in order to reach these conclusions and even to assume, as both Heidegger and Schapiro do, that the two shoes form a pair. What is genuinely remarkable is the stunning obviousness of Derrida's observation that these shoes are *not* a pair, and that no one seems to have been able to see this before. While Van Gogh's shoes, or Heidegger's and Schapiro's interpretations of them, may not seem of much significance for feminism, Derrida's point is that the conclusions the viewers draw about the shoes rest, in each case, on opposition – left/right, male/female, city/country, peasant/painter – and the ability to *see* these oppositions. In order to talk about, perhaps even to see, these objects, the critics have to insist that there is a pair there, even Schapiro who claims to oppose his own scholarly empiricism to Heidegger's mystic ramblings. While it would be valuable to discuss the implications of each of these pairs, for the purposes of my argument here, I want to underline one point that Derrida makes in his essay: sex becomes visible and thinkable in Western philosophy only when it is thought as a complementary pairing, male and female, penis and vagina, inside and outside.[36]

Derrida proposes an alternative to this way of thinking sexual difference which is not unlike Devor's in its implications. Derrida wants to believe in the possibility of a non-binary, non-oppositional, 'sexual otherwise'. This would consist of 'the multiplicity of sexually marked voices', 'of non-identified sexual marks whose choreography can carry, divide, multiply the body of each "individual"'.[37] Thus, sexualities, like sexual differences, would proliferate, confirming Irigaray's statement that for women there is 'no possible law for their pleasure, no more than there is any possible discourse'.[38] The cognitive abyss of sexual difference is where we are, before we know where it is we are.

Not all feminists have been comfortable with this news from nowhere, and Derrida's remarks have been often criticised for being merely utopian, for phantasmatically moving away from what women really experience.[39] However, I would have to agree with Cornell that Derrida's attempt to move beyond binary or oppositional definitions of sexual difference is one of the more valuable aspects of his work for feminism. Cornell correctly points out that Derrida's 'writing is explicitly utopian in that it evokes an elsewhere to our current system, in which sex is lived within the established "heterosexual" matrix as a rigid gender identity'.[40] And it is such utopian thinking that becomes important for feminism, because it 'demands the continual exploration and re-exploration of the possible and yet also the unrepresentable'.[41]

Summaries and Notes

1 ANNA TRIPP, INTRODUCTION

1. *In Our Time*, BBC Radio 4, broadcast on 7 January 1999, chaired by Melvyn Bragg and featuring Helena Cronin and Germaine Greer.
2. Cronin, quoted by Bragg, *In Our Time* (my italics).
3. Genesis, The Old Testament.
4. Greer, *In Our Time*.
5. Essay 5, p. 59. (My italics.)
6. Liz York, *Impertinent Voices: Subversive Strategies in Contemporary Women's Poetry* (London, 1991), p. 5.
7. Joan Wallach Scott contends that the 'concern with gender as an analytical category has emerged only in the late twentieth century' (Scott, *Gender and the Politics of History* [New York, 1988], p. 41). However Catherine Belsey points out that 'At least since the seventeenth century, women who have written in protest about the injustices of a male-dominated society have recognised the social construction of gender difference' (essay 3, p. 31).
8. Of course, in languages other than English – French, for example – this distinction may be somewhat different or less readily available.
9. *The Oxford Dictionary of Etymology* (Oxford, 1966).
10. Robert Stoller, *Sex and Gender: On the Development of Masculinity and Femininity* (London, 1968).
11. Ibid. p. ix.
12. Ibid. p. xiii.
13. See, for example, Germaine Greer, *The Female Eunuch* (London, 1971), and Kate Millet, *Sexual Politics* (London, 1977 [first published 1969]) and Ann Oakley, *Sex, Gender and Society* (London, 1972).
14. It is important to note, however, that many forms of feminism contain, to a greater or lesser extent, some sort of essentialist element. Ironically perhaps, there are even some feminists who would agree wholeheartedly with Cronin that men are 'essentially' or 'naturally' territorial, aggressive and promiscuous (warmongers and potential rapists) and that women are 'essentially' and 'naturally' nurturing and intuitive (warm and caring earth mothers).
15. Belsey, essay 3, p. 35.
16. Virginia Woolf, *A Room of One's Own* (London, 1977), p. 41.
17. The reader, of course, may suspect this statement of intent of being somewhat tongue-in-cheek, given that modernist writing is often characterised by anxiety about the fractured and fugitive nature of truth.
18. Woolf, 'Women and Fiction', p. 26.
19. Elizabeth V. Spelman, *Inessential Woman* (London, 1990), pp. 8–9.
20. Jean-François Lyotard, *The Postmodern Condition: A Report on Knowledge*, trans. Geoff Bennington and Brian Massumi (Manchester, 1984), p. 8.

21. See, for example, Belsey's essay, 'A Future for Materialist Feminist Criticism?', for a more detailed discussion of what feminism may have to gain from an alliance with postmodernism.
22. Essay 14, p. 169.
23. Hélène Cixous, 'Sorties: Out and Out: Attacks/Ways Out/Forays', in Catherine Belsey and Jane Moore (eds), *The Feminist Reader: Essays in Gender and the Politics of Literary Criticism*, 2nd edn (Basingstoke, 1997), pp. 91–103.
24. Judith Butler, *Bodies That Matter: On the Discursive Limits of 'Sex'* (New York, 1993), p. 7.
25. Belsey's reading of *Macbeth*, in 'A Future for Materialist Feminist Criticism?', confirms this by emphasising the debates around the meanings of 'woman' and the 'difference within the term "man"' in this play.
26. Essay 11.
27. Belsey, 'A Future for Materialist Feminist Criticism?', p. 259.
28. Essay 4, p. 48.
29. Gillian Beer, 'Representing Women: Re-presenting the Past', in Belsey and Moore (eds), *The Feminist Reader*, pp. 77–90, 81.
30. Millett, *Sexual Politics*.
31. Juliet Mitchell, *Psychoanalysis and Feminism* (London, 1974).
32. Essay 10, p. 124.
33. Beer, 'Representing Women', in Belsey and Moore (eds), *The Feminist Reader*, p. 83.
34. Jonathan Culler, *Literary Theory: A Very Short Introduction* (Oxford, 1997), p. 59.
35. Holly Devor, *Gender Blending: Confronting the Limits of Duality* (Bloomington, IN, 1989), p. 52.
36. Essay 8, p. 102.
37. Angela Carter, *The Passion of New Eve* (London, 1982), p. 63 (Carter's italics).
38. Judith Butler, *Gender Trouble: Feminism and the Subversion of Identity* (New York, 1990), pp. 6–7.
39. Thomas Laqueur, *Making Sex: Body and Gender from the Greeks to Freud* (Cambridge, MA, 1990). Suzanne J. Kessler,'The Medical Construction of Gender: Case Management of Intersexed Infants', in *Signs: Journal of Women in Culture and Society*, 16: 1 (1990), 3–26. Anne Fausto-Sterling, *Myths of Gender: Biological Theories about Women and Men* (New York, 1979).
40. Kessler, 'The Medical Construction of Gender', p. 18.
41. Essay 11, p. 134.
42. Ibid., p. 133.
43. Essay 12, p. 150.
44. Butler, *Bodies That Matter*, p. xi.
45. Essay 14, p. 173.
46. Butler, *Gender Trouble*, p. ix (Butler's italics).
47. Ibid., p. viii.
48. Ibid.
49. See *Gender Trouble*, p. 151 for Butler's definition and discussion of this term.
50. Sonya Andermahr, Terry Lovell and Carol Wolkowitz, in *A Concise Glossary of Feminist Theory* (London, 1997), p. 180, claim that the term 'queer theory' was coined by Teresa de Lauretis in 1991.
51. Eve Kosofsky Sedgwick, *The Epistemology of the Closet* (Hemel Hempstead, 1991).

52. Michel Foucault, *The History of Sexuality, Volume 1: An Introduction*, trans. Robert Hurley (New York, 1980).
53. Identity politics takes as its starting point the affirmation of a pre-existing common identity (for example as 'women' or as 'lesbians') by a group of people.
54. Raman Selden, Peter Widdowson and Peter Brooker, *A Reader's Guide to Contemporary Literary Theory*, 4th edn (London, 1997), p. 255.
55. Joseph Bristow, *Sexuality* (London, 1997), p. 4.
56. Judith Butler, 'Melancholy Gender/Refused Identification' in Berger, Wallis and Watson (eds), *Constructing Masculinity*, pp. 21–36, 25.
57. Marjorie Garber, *Vested Interests: Cross-Dressing and Cultural Anxiety* (Harmondsworth, 1993), p. 16. See also Garber's *Vice Versa: Bisexuality and the Eroticism of Everyday Life* (London, 1996).
58. Essay 14, p. 181.
59. Devor, *Gender Blending*, pp. 153–4.

2. VIRGINIA WOOLF, 'WOMEN AND FICTION'

(From Virginia Woolf, *A Room of One's Own* (London, 1977), pp. 26–40.)

Summary

'Women and Fiction' addresses the causes and effects of material inequalities between the sexes and articulates a keen awareness of the role of history, culture and language in the production of differential understandings of what it means to be a woman or a man. The narrative gives a characteristically modernist sense of the fractured and fugitive nature of truth; this includes 'the truth about women', which is found to be inherently contradictory, historically variable and ultimately plural and evasive.

The narrator explicitly identifies the society of the time as a patriarchy, in which it is overwhelmingly men who occupy positions of power and influence, and considers evidence of – and possible reasons for – misogyny and anxiety in certain male-authored texts about women. However, it is also implied that conventionally masculine attributes, such as territorial aggression, are taught rather than natural. This piece ends on a prophetic note, considering the inevitability of historical change and speculating on possibilities for the future of women.

Notes

1. ' "Men know that women are an overmatch for them, and therefore they choose the weakest or the most ignorant. If they did not think so, they never could be afraid of women knowing as much as themselves." ... In justice to the sex, I think it but candid to acknowledge that, in a subsequent conversation, he told me that he was serious in what he said.' – Boswell, *The Journal of a Tour to the Hebrides*.
2. 'The ancient Germans believed that there was something holy in women, and accordingly consulted them as oracles.' – Frazer, *Golden Bough*.

3. CATHERINE BELSEY, 'A FUTURE FOR MATERIALIST FEMINIST CRITICISM?'

(From Valerie Wayne (ed.), *The Matter of Difference: Materialist Feminist Criticism of Shakespeare* (Hemel Hempstead, 1991), pp. 257–70.)

Summary

In this essay, Catherine Belsey moves debates about materialist feminism into a postmodern context. Materialist feminism is generally understood as a feminism which takes into account wider social and economic structures, the role of class, specific institutions, and the operations of historical difference in constructions of sex and gender – rather than treating these things as purely physiological and psychological or as universal and essential. Belsey points out, however, that materialist feminism should also encompass an understanding of the role played by language and culture: gender, she argues, is an ongoing effect of meanings and definitions culturally and linguistically produced and circulated, albeit definitions that have very real material consequences.

The possibility of resistance to existing definitions of gender, this essay suggests, arises from the fact that patriarchal power is not monolithic, consistent or static. Belsey considers the strategies feminist writing and feminist criticism have employed in the past and speculates about what forms they may take in the future. Given the role that language plays in perpetuating patriarchal definitions of gender, language is considered to be an important battleground for gender politics: Belsey thus suggests that an awareness of style is indispensable to feminists.

Notes

1. Judith Newton and Deborah Rosenfelt, 'Introduction: toward a materialist-feminist criticism', in their *Feminist Criticism and Social Change: Sex, class and race in literature and culture* (New York and London, 1985), pp. xv–xxxix, xvi–xviii and *passim*.
2. Shakespeare references are to the one-volume edition of *The Complete Works*, ed. Peter Alexander (London, 1951).
3. It could be argued that the crisis of epistemology is to be found sporadically at many historical moments since the Renaissance. Lyotard, for example, scandalously finds postmodernism in the sixteenth century: 'It seems to me that the essay (Montaigne) is postmodern' (Jean-Francois Lyotard, 'What is postmodernism?', in *The Postmodern Condition: A Report on Knowledge*, trans. Geoff Bennington and Brian Massumi [Manchester, 1984], p. 81).
4. Lyotard, *The Postmodern Condition*, p. xxiv.
5. Alice A. Jardine, *Gynesis: Configurations of Woman and Modernity* (Ithaca, NY, and London, 1985). See especially pp. 19–24, 38–49, 52–64, 82 and 92–7.
6. For an earlier discussion of this aspect of the issue see Shelia Rowbotham, 'The Trouble with "Patriarchy"', and Sally Alexander and Barbara Taylor, 'In Defence of "Patriarchy"', in Mary Evans (ed), *The Woman Question: Readings on the Subordination of Women* (London, 1982), pp. 73–83 (rpt. from R. Samuel [ed.], *People's History and Socialist Theory* [London, 1981], pp. 364–73).

 7. I have discussed the debate between new historicism and cultural materialism in
    more detail in 'Towards cultural history — in theory and practice', *Textual
    Practice*, 3 (1989), 159–72.
 8. Lyotard, 'What is Postmodernism?', esp. pp. 78–82.
 9. Catherine Belsey, *The Subject of Tragedy: Identity and Difference in Renaissance
    Drama* (London and New York, 1985), pp. 83–6.
10. Mary Jacobus, 'The Difference of View', in her *Women Writing and Writing
    About Women* (London; New York, 1979), pp. 10–21. Reprinted in Catherine
    Belsey and Jane Moore (eds), *The Feminist Reader: Essays in gender and the
    politics of literary criticism* (London and New York, 1989), pp. 49–62.
11. Barbara Johnson, *A World of Difference* (Baltimore and London, 1987), pp. 3–4.
12. Rachel Bowlby, 'Flight reservations', *The Oxford Literary Review*, 10 (1988),
    61–72, 68.
13. Ibid., p. 70.

4. ADRIENNE RICH, 'TOWARD A MORE FEMINIST CRITICISM'

(From Adrienne Rich, *Blood, Bread and Poetry: Selected Prose 1979–1985* (London,
1987), pp. 85–99.)

Summary

This essay opens up important debates about the relationship between literary-
critical analyses of gender in the academy and 'grassroots' feminist struggles taking
place in societies at large. Rich calls to account a certain group of feminists who,
she feels, have become overly institutionalised and comfortable within academia.
Such feminists, she argues, are overwhelmingly and solipsistically white, middle-
class and heterosexual; they are unselfconscious about their own position of
privilege, and treat whiteness and heterosexuality as uninterrogated and universal
norms. Rich calls for an acknowledgement that women are not – and never will be – a
homogeneous and unified group: for feminists this means that communication
and solidarity can never be taken for granted. In order for feminism to succeed,
Rich suggests, women in various situations and walks of life must of course commun-
icate with each other, but this communication must be based not only on a
search for common ground but also on a constant attention to – and respect for –
difference.

Notes

This was the opening address, Feminist Studies in Literature Symposium,
University of Minnesota, Minneapolis, 1981.

1. Kate Millett, *Sexual Politics* (Garden City, NY, 1970), p. xii.
2. Barbara Smith, 'Toward a Black Feminist Criticism', in *All the Women Are White,
   All the Blacks Are Men, but Some of Us Are Brave: Black Women's Studies*, ed.
   Gloria T. Hull, Patricia Bell Scott and Barbara Smith (Old Westbury, NY, 1982),
   p. 154.
3. Jan Clausen, *A Movement of Poets*, pamphlet (Brooklyn, NY, 1981).
4. Gloria T. Hull, 'Researching Alice Dunbar-Nelson', in *All the Women Are White*,
   pp. 193–4.

5. Ibid, p. 193.
6. Myra Jehlen, 'Archimedes and the Paradox of Feminist Criticism', *Signs: Journal of Women in Culture and Society*, 6, no. 4 (Summer 1981), 571–600.
7. Judith Gardiner, Elly Bulkin, Rena Grasso Patterson, and Annette Kolodny, 'An Interchange on Feminist Criticism: On "Dancing through the Minefield"', *Feminist Studies*, 8, no. 3 (Fall 1982), 636.
8. Hull, 'Researching Dunbar-Nelson', pp. 193-4.
9. [A.R., 1986: Mab Segrest, 'Southern Women Writing: Toward a Literature of Wholeness', in *My Mama's Dead Squirrel: Lesbian Essays on Southern Culture* (Ithaca, NY, 1985).]
10. Elly Bulkin (ed.), *Lesbian Fiction: An Anthology* (Watertown, MA, Persephone, 1981); and Elly Bulkin and Joan Larkin (eds), *Lesbian Poetry* (Watertown, MA, 1981; distributed by Gay Press, Boston, Massachusetts).
11. Gloria Anzaldúa, 'Speaking in Tongues: A Letter to Third World Women Writers', in *This Bridge Called My Back*, ed. Cherríe Moraga and Gloria Anzaldúa (Watertown, MA, 1981).
12. Irena Klepfisz, 'The Journal of Rachel Robotnik', *Conditions*, 6 (1980), 1. [A.R., 1986: Reprinted in Irena Klepfisz, *Different Enclosures* (London, 1985).]

5. CHANDRA TALPADE MOHANTY, 'UNDER WESTERN EYES: FEMINIST SCHOLARSHIP AND COLONIAL DISCOURSES'

(From Chandra Talpade Mohanty, Ann Russo and Lourdes Torres (eds), *Third World Women and The Politics of Feminism* (Bloomington, IN, 1991), pp. 51–80.)

Summary

This essay is concerned with the hegemony of Western feminisms. Certain Western feminists, Mohanty argues, produce in their writing a notion of 'the Third World Woman', thus implying that all women in the so-called 'Third World' are the same, and that they simply represent more primitive and oppressed versions of Western women. These women are often discussed as if they are entirely powerless victims with little if any self-determination or freedom to make choices. Mohanty's essay offers a vital and timely reminder to Western feminists that Western categories and analyses of gender cannot be applied universally or cross-culturally, and that individual subjects should always be treated as products of specific and ongoing histories and complex sets of cultural, socio-political and economic relations. To attempt simply to 'export' Western feminism, Mohanty implies, would be a colonising gesture. Gender politics must be context-specific: only through an understanding of the contradictions and resistances that occur locally within power structures and ideologies can effective feminist analysis and action can take place.

Notes

This is an updated and modified version of an essay published in *Boundary* 2,12, no. 3/13, no.1 (Spring/Fall 1984), and reprinted in *Feminist Review*, no. 30 (Autumn 1988).

This essay would not have been possible without S. P. Mohanty's challenging and careful reading. I would also like to thank Biddy Martin for our numerous discussions about feminist theory and politics. They both helped me think through some of the arguments herein.

1. Cf. particularly contemporary theorists such as Paul A. Baran, *The Political Economy of Growth* (New York, 1962), Samir Amin, *Imperialism and Unequal Development* (New York, 1977), and Audre Gunder-Frank, *Capitalism and Underdevelopment in Latin America* (New York, 1967).

2. Cf. especially Cherríe Moraga and Gloria Anzaldúa (eds), *This Bridge Called My Back: Writings By Radical Women of Color* (New York, 1983), Barbara Smith, *Home Girls: A Black Feminist Anthology* (New York, 1983), Gloria Joseph and Jill Lewis, *Common Differences: Conflicts in Black and White Feminist Perspectives* (Boston, 1981), and Cherríe Moraga, *Loving in the War Years* (Boston, 1984).

3. Terms such as *third* and *first world* are very problematical, both in suggesting oversimplified similarities between and among countries labelled thus, and in implicitly reinforcing existing economic, cultural and ideological hierarchies which are conjured up in using such terminology. I use the term *'third world'* with full awareness of its problems, only because this is the terminology available to us at the moment. The use of quotation marks is meant to suggest a continuous questioning of the designation. Even when I do not use quotation marks, I mean to use the term critically.

4. I am indebted to Teresa de Lauretis for this particular formulation of the project of feminist theorising. See especially her introduction in de Lauretis, *Alice Doesn't: Feminism, Semiotics, Cinema* (Bloomington, IN, 1984); see also Sylvia Winter, 'The Politics of Domination', unpublished manuscript.

5. This argument is similar to Homi Bhabha's definition of colonial discourse as strategically creating a space for a subject people through the production of knowledges and the exercise of power. The full quote reads: '[colonial discourse is] an apparatus of power... an apparatus that turns on the recognition and disavowal of racial/cultural/historical differences. Its predominant strategic function is the creation of a space for a subject people through the production of knowledges in terms of which surveillance is exercised and a complex form of pleasure/unpleasure is incited. It (i.e. colonial discourse) seeks authorisation for its strategies by the production of knowledges by coloniser and colonised which are stereotypical but antithetically evaluated' (Bhabha, 'The Other Question – The Stereotype and Colonial Discourse', *Screen*, 24, no.6 [1983], 23).

6. Anouar Abdel-Malek, *Social Dialectics: Nation and Revolution* (Albany, NY, 1981).

7. Ibid. pp. 145–6.

8. A number of documents and reports on the UN International Conferences on Women, Mexico City, 1975, and Copenhagen, 1980, as well as the 1976 Wellesley Conference on Women and Development, attest to this. Nawal el Saadawi, Fatima Mernissi and Mallica Vajarathon characterise this conference as 'American-planned and organised', situating third world participants as passive audiences. They focus especially on the lack of self-consciousness of Western women's implication in the effects of imperialism and racism in their assumption of an 'international sisterhood' (el Saadawi, Mernissi and Vajarathon, 'A Critical Look at the Wellesley Conference', *Quest* 4, no.2 [Winter 1978], 101–7). A recent essay by Valerie Amos and Pratibha Parmar characterises as 'imperial' Euro-American feminism which seeks to establish itself as the only legitimate feminism

(Amos and Parmar, 'Challenging Imperial Feminism,' *Feminist Review*, 17 [1984], 3–19).

9. The Zed Press Women in the Third World series is unique in its conception. I choose to focus on it because it is the only contemporary series I have found which assumes that 'women in the third world' are a legitimate and separate subject of study and research. Since 1985, when this essay was first written, numerous new titles have appeared in the Women in the Third World series. Thus, I suspect that Zed has come to occupy a rather privileged position in the dissemination and construction of discourses by and about third world women. A number of the books in this series are excellent, especially those which deal directly with women's resistance struggles. In addition, Zed Press consistently publishes progressive feminist, anti-racist, and anti-imperialist texts. However, a number of texts written by feminist sociologists, anthropologists, and journalists are symptomatic of the kind of Western feminist work on women in the third world that concerns me. Thus, an analysis of a few of these particular works in this series can serve as a representative point of entry into the discourse I am attempting to locate and define. My focus on these texts is therefore an attempt at an internal critique: I simply expect and demand more from this series. Needless to say, progressive publishing houses also carry their own authorising signatures.

10. Michelle Rosaldo's term, in 'The Use and Abuse of Anthropology: Reflections on Feminism and Cross-Cultural Understanding', *Signs*, 53 (1980), 389–417.

11. Elsewhere I have discussed this particular point in detail in a critique of Robin Morgan's construction of 'women's herstory' in her introduction to *Sisterhood is Global: The International Women's Movement Anthology* (New York, 1984). See my 'Feminist Encounters: Locating the Politics of Experience', *Copyright*, 1, 'Fin de Siècle 2000', 30–44, esp. 35, 37.

12. Amos and Parmar, 'Challenging Imperial Feminism', p. 7.

13. Fran Hosken, 'Female Genital Mutilation and Human Rights', *Feminist Issues*, 1, no.3 (1981), 11.

14. Ibid., p. 14.

15. Ibid.

16. Another example of this kind of analysis is Mary Daly's *Gyn/Ecology: The Metaethics of Radical Feminism* (Boston, 1978). Daly's assumption in this text, that women as a group are sexually victimised, leads to her very problematic comparison between the attitudes toward women witches and healers in the West, Chinese footbinding, and the genital mutilation of women in Africa. According to Daly, women in Europe, China, and Africa constitute a homogeneous group as victims of male power. Not only does this label (sexual victims) eradicate the specific historical and material realities and contradictions which lead to and perpetuate practices such as witch hunting and genital mutilation, but it also obliterates the differences, complexities, and heterogeneities of the lives of, for example, women of different classes, religions and nations in Africa. As Audre Lorde pointed out, women in Africa share a long tradition of healers and goddesses that perhaps binds them together more appropriately than their victim status (Lorde, 'An Open Letter to Mary Daly', in Moraga and Anzaldúa, *This Bridge Called My Back*, pp. 94–7). However, both Daly and Lorde fall prey to universalistic assumptions about 'African Women' (both negative and positive). What matters is the complex, historical range of power differences, commonalities, and resistances that exist among women in Africa which construct African women as 'subjects' of their own politics.

17. See Felicity Eldhom, Olivia Harris and Kate Young, 'Conceptualising Women', *Critique of Anthropology 'Women's Issue'*, no.3 (1977) for a good discussion of the necessity to theorise male violence within specific societal frameworks, rather than assume it as a universal fact.
18. Lindsay, *Comparative Perspectives of Third World Women: The Impact of Race, Sex and Class* (New York, 1983), pp. 298, 306.
19. Maria Rosa Cutrufelli, *Women of Africa: Roots of Oppression* (London, 1983), p. 13.
20. Ibid., p. 33.
21. Rosaldo, 'The Use and Abuse of Anthropology', p. 400.
22. Elizabeth Cowie, 'Woman as Sign', *m/f*, 1 (1978), 49–63.
23. Juliette Minces, *The House of Obedience: Women in Arab Society* (London 1980), esp. p. 23.
24. Mina Modares, 'Women and Shi'ism in Iran', *m/f*, 5 and 6 (1981), 61–82.
25. Patricia Jeffery, *Frogs in a Well: Indian Women in Purdah* (London, 1979).
26. Modares, 'Women and Shi'ism in Iran', p. 63.
27. Marina Lazreg, 'Feminism and Difference: The Perils of Writing as a Woman on Women in Algeria', *Feminist Issues*, 14, no. 1 (Spring 1988), 81–107, 87.
28. Irene Tinker and Michelle Bo Bramsen (eds), *Women and World Development* (Washington, DC, 1972), Ester Boserup, *Women's Role in Economic Development* (New York, 1970), and Perdita Huston, *Third World Women Speak Out* (New York, 1979). These views can also be found in differing degrees in collections such as Wellesley Editorial Committee (ed.), *Women and National Development: The Complexities of Change* (Chicago, 1977), and *Signs*, Special Issue, 'Development and the Sexual Division of Labour', 7, no.2 (Winter 1981). For an excellent introduction of WID issues, see ISIS, *Women in Development: A Resource Guide for Organisation and Action* (Philadephia, 1984). For a politically focused discussion of feminism and development and the stakes for poor third world women, see Gita Sen and Caren Grown, *Development Crises and Alternative Visions: Third World Women's Perspectives* (New York, 1987).
29. Huston, *Third World Women Speak Out.*
30. Ibid., p. 115.
31. Maria Mies, *The Lace Makers of Narsapur: Indian Housewives Produce for the World Market* (London, 1982).
32. Ibid. p. 157.
33. See essays by Vanessa Maher, Diane Elson and Ruth Pearson, and Maila Stevens in Kate Young, Carol Walkowitz, and Roslyn McCullagh (eds), *Of Marriage and the Market: Women's Subordination in International Perspective* (London, 1981); and essays by Vivian Mota and Michelle Mattelart in June Nash and Helen I. Safa (eds), *Sex and Class in Latin America: Women's Perspectives on Politics, Economics and the Family in the Third World* (South Hadley, MA, 1980). For examples of excellent, self-conscious work by feminists writing about women in their own historical and geographical locations, see Marnia Lazreg on Algerian Women, Gayatri Chakravorty Spivak's 'A Literary Representation of the Subaltern: A Women's Text from the Third World', in her *In Other Worlds: Essays in Cultural Politics* (New York, 1987), pp. 241–68, and Lata Mani's essay 'Contentious Traditions: The Debate on SATI in Colonial India', *Cultural Critique*, 7 (Fall 1987), 119–56.
34. Ann Deardon (ed.), *Arab Women* (London, 1975), pp. 4–5.
35. Ibid. pp. 7, 10.
36. Hosken, 'Female Genital Mutilation', p. 15.

37. For detailed discussion, see Azar Tabari, 'The Enigma of the Veiled Iranian Women', *Feminist Review*, 5 (1980), 19–32.
38. Olivia Harris, 'Latin American Women – An Overview', in Harris (ed.), *Latin American Women* (London, 1983), pp. 4–7. Other MRG Reports include Deardon (ed.), *Arab Women*, and Rounaq Jahan (ed.), *Women in Asia* (London, 1980).
39. Eldhom, Harris and Young,'Conceptualising Women'.
40. Beverly Brown, 'Displacing the Difference' – Review, *Nature, Culture and Gender', m/f*, 8 (1983), 79–89. Marilyn Strathern and Carol McCormack (eds), *Nature, Culture and Gender* (Cambridge, 1980).
41. Madhu Kishwar and Ruth Vanita, *In Search of Answers: Indian Women's Voices from Manushi* (London, 1984).
42. Michel Foucault, *History of Sexuality: Volume One* (New York, 1980), pp. 135–45.
43. For succinct discussions of Western radical and liberal feminisms, see Hester Eisenstein, *Contemporary Feminist Thought* (Boston, 1983) and Zilah Eisenstein, *The Radical Future of Liberal Feminism* (New York, 1981).
44. Amos and Parmar describe the cultural stereotypes present in Euro-American feminist thought: 'The image is of the passive Asian woman subject to oppressive practices within the Asian family with an emphasis on wanting to "help" Asian women liberate themselves from their role. Or there is the strong, dominant Afro-Caribbean woman, who despite her "strength" is exploited by the "sexism" which is seen as being a strong feature in relationships between Afro-Caribbean men and women' ('Challenging Imperial Feminism', p. 9). These images illustrate the extent to which *paternalism* is an essential element of feminist thinking which incorporates the above stereotypes, a paternalism which can lead to the definition of priorities for women of colour by Euro-American feminists.
45. I discuss the question of theorising experience in my 'Feminist Encounters', and in an essay co-authored with Biddy Martin, 'Feminist Politics: What's Home Got to Do with It?', in Teresa de Lauretis (ed.), *Feminist Studies/Critical Studies* (Bloomington, IN, 1986), pp. 191–212.
46. This is one of Foucault's central points in his reconceptualisation of the strategies and workings of power networks.
47. Foucault, *History of Sexuality and Power/Knowledge* (New York, 1980).
48. Jacques Derrida, *Of Grammatology* (Baltimore, MD, 1974).
49. Julia Kristeva, *Desire in Language* (New York, 1980).
50. Gilles Deleuze and Felix Guattari, *Anti-Oedipus: Capitalism and Schizophrenia* (New York, 1977).
51. Edward Said, *Orientalism* (New York, 1978).
52. Luce Irigaray, 'This Sex Which Is Not One' and 'When the Goods Get Together', in Elaine Marks and Isabel de Courtivron (eds), *New French Feminisms* (New York, 1981).
53. Elizabeth Berg, 'The Third Woman', *Diacritics* (Summer 1982), 11–20.
54. Hélène Cixous, 'The Laugh of the Medusa', in Marks and Courtivron (eds), *New French Feminisms*.
55. William V. Spanos, 'Boundary 2 and the Polity of Interest: Humanism, the "Centre Elsewhere" and Power', *Boundary* 2, 12, no. 3/13, no 1 (Spring/Fall 1984).
56. For an argument which demands a *new* conception of humanism in work on third world women, see Marnia Lazreg, 'Feminism and Difference'. While Lazreg's position might appear to be diametrically opposed to mine, I see it as a

provocative and potentially positive extension of some of the implications that follow from my arguments. In criticising the feminist rejection of humanism in the name of 'essential Man', Lazreg points to what she calls an 'essentialism of difference' within these very feminist projects. She asks: 'To what extent can Western feminism dispense with an ethics of responsibility when writing about different women? The point is neither to subsume other women under one's own experience nor to uphold a separate truth for them. Rather, it is to allow them to *be* while recognising that what they are is just as meaningful, valid, and comprehensible as what we are ... Indeed, when feminists essentially deny other women the humanity they claim for themselves, they dispense with any ethical constraint. They engage in the act of splitting the social universe into us and them, subject and objects' (pp. 99–100).

This essay by Lazreg and an essay by S. P. Mohanty ('Us and Them: On the Philsophical Bases of Political Criticism', *Yale Journal of Criticism*, 2 [March 1989], 1–31) suggest positive directions for self-conscious cross-cultural analyses, analyses which move beyond the deconstructive to a fundamentally productive mode in designating overlapping areas for cross-cultural comparison. The latter essay calls not for a 'humanism' but for a reconsideration of the question of the 'human' in a posthumanist context. It argues that (1) there is no necessary 'incompatibility between the deconstruction of Western humanism' and such 'a positive elaboration' of the human, and moreover that (2) such an elaboration is essential if contemporary political-critical discourse is to avoid the incoherences and weaknesses of a relativist position.

6. LYNNE SEGAL, 'LOOK BACK IN ANGER: MEN IN THE FIFTIES'

(From Lynne Segal, *Slow Motion: Changing Masculinities, Changing Men* (London, 1990), pp. 1–25.)

Summary

'Women', Virginia Woolf pointed out in 1929, 'do not write books about men'. She goes on to urge her contemporary female audience of the importance of studying 'the other sex'. Some 60 years later, Lynne Segal takes up this challenge. Writing from a feminist perspective, she analyses the roles and representations of British men in the 1950s, a time when gender relations were being renegotiated after the chaos of the Second World War. This period, Segal suggests, was characterised by profound male anxiety, and contemporary understandings of what it meant to be a man were deeply divided. On the one hand, there was a widespread belief that men were becoming domesticated (although studies reveal that in actuality men rarely participated in housework or childcare); on the other hand there was a backlash against this supposedly emasculating trend, witnessed in the individualistic 'angry young men' of contemporary literature, the misogyny of contemporary humour, an intensification of homophobia and a fear of effeminacy. The extract ends by asking to what extent things have now changed: in this way Segal's arguments serve the useful purpose of lending historical depth to the two essays that follow.

Notes

1. Fay Weldon (1971), *Down Among the Women* (Harmondsworth), p. 106.
2. Walter Allen (1960), Review of *Lucky Jim* (first published 1954), reprinted in G. Feldman and M. Gartenberg (eds), *Protest* (London), p. 286.
3. Kenneth Allsop (1964), *The Angry Decade* (London), p. 203.
4. Storm Jameson in ibid., p. 201.
5. Jean McCrindle (1987), 'The Left as Social Movement' talk given at *Out of Apathy Conference*, on 30 years of the British New Left, organised by Oxford University Socialist Discussion Group, 14th November.
6. Quoted in Denise Riley (1983), *War in the Nursery* (London), p. 193.
7. Michael Young and Peter Willmott (1962), *Family and Kinship in East London* (Harmondsworth), p. 30.
8. John and Elizabeth Newson (1963), *Patterns of Infant Care in an Urban Community* (London). p. 143.
9. Anthony Sampson (1962), *Anatomy of Britain* (London), p. 73.
10. Peter Biskind (1983), *Seeing is Believing* (New York), p. 252.
11. Elizabeth Wilson (1980), *Only Halfway to Paradise: Women in Postwar Britain 1945–68* (London), p. 69.
12. Colin Willock (1958), *The Man's Book* (London).
13. Geoffrey Gorer (1955), *Exploring English Character* (London), p. 153.
14. Ibid., p. 66.
15. Betty Thorne (1987), 'Life in Our Street (1960)' in Mary Stott (ed.), *Women Talking – An Anthology from The Guardian's Women's Page* (London), p. 85.
16. 'J. B. H.' 'Bored Mum and "Talkback"'' (1959) in Stott ibid., pp. 240–1.
17. Ibid.
18. J. D. Salinger (1951), *The Catcher in the Rye* (Harmondsworth).
19. Alan Sillitoe (1961), 'What Comes on Monday' in *New Left Review*, 4 (July/August), 59.
20. Alan Sillitoe (1960), *Saturday Night and Sunday Morning* (London), p. 36.
21. Ibid., p. 65.
22. Ibid., p. 126.
23. Nigel Grey (1974), *The Silent Majority – A Study of the Working Class in Post-War British Fiction* (London), p. 129.
24. Alan Sinfield (ed.) (1983), *Society and Literature 1945–1970*, p. 2.
25. Quoted in ibid., p. 4.
26. David Lodge (1982), Afterword to *Ginger You're Barmy* (Harmondsworth), pp. 215–16.
27. John Osborne, 'Sex and Failure', in Feldman and Gartenberg (eds), *Protest*.
28. Quoted in Sinfield, *Society*, p. 27.
29. Ibid.
30. Colin MacInnes (1959), *Absolute Beginners* (London).
31. Quoted in Sinfield, *Society*, p. 177.
32. Richard Hoggart (1957), *The Uses of Literacy* (Harmondsworth), p. 246.
33. Geoffrey Gorer, 'The Perils of Hypergamy', in Feldman and Gartenberg, *Protest*, p. 315.
34. In Sinfield, *Society*, p. 26.
35. Eve Kosofsky Sedgwick (1985), *Between Men: English Literature and Male Homosexual Desire* (New York).
36. Craig Owens (1987), 'Outlaws: Gay Men in Feminism' in A. Jardine and P. Smith (eds), *Men in Feminism* (London), p. 221.

37. B. Seebohm Rowntree and G. R. Lavers (1951), *English Life and Leisure* (London), p. 212.
38. Ibid., p. 215.
39. See Jonathan Dollimore, 'The Challenge of Sexuality', in Sinfield, *Society*, p. 52.
40. See Tony Gould (1983), *Inside Outsider – The Life and Times of Colin MacInnes* (London), p. 64.
41. Ibid., p. 99.
42. Quentin Crisp (1968), *The Naked Civil Servant* (London).
43. Quoted in Dollimore, 'Challenge of Sexuality', p. 74.
44. James Baldwin (1963), *Another Country* (London); (1957) *Giovanni's Room* (London).
45. In Gould, *Inside Outsider*, p. 89.
46. Trevor Royle (1986), *The Best Years of Their Lives* (London), p.xiii.
47. B. S. Johnson (1973), *All Bull* (London); see also Lodge, Afterword and Sillitoe, *Saturday Night and Sunday Morning*.
48. Colin MacInnes (1966), 'Pacific Warriors', in *New Society*, 30 June.
49. Royle, *Best Years of Their Lives*, p. 116.
50. Ray Gosling (1960), 'Dream Boy', *New Left Review* (May/June), 3, 31.
51. David Morgan (1987), 'It Will Make a Man of You: Notes on National Service, Masculinity and Autobiography', *Studies in Sexual Politics*, no. 17, University of Manchester, p. 48.
52. Ibid., p. 82.
53. Ken Walpole (1983), *Dockers and Detectives* (London).
54. Ibid., p. 62.
55. Helen Hacker (1957). 'The New Burdens of Masculinity' in *Marriage and Family Living*, 19, p. 229.
56. Willock, *The Man's Book*, p. viii.
57. Ibid. pp. 352–4.
58. In Peter Lewis (1978), *The Fifties* (London), p. 63.
59. Quoted in Jean McCrindle (1982), 'Reading *The Golden Notebook* in 1962' in J. Taylor (ed.), *Notebooks/Memoirs/Archives: Reading and Rereading Doris Lessing* (London), p. 49.
60. Doris Lessing (1972), *The Golden Notebook* (St Albans), p. 395.
61. Quoted in Jean McCrindle, 'Reading', p. 53.
62. Ibid., p. 50.
63. Ibid., p. 51.
64. Margaret Drabble (1963), *A Summer Bird-Cage* (Harmondsworth), p. 29.
65. David Cooper (1964), 'Sartre on Genet', *New Left Review* (25 May/June), 71.
66. Stuart Hall (1987), Introductory talk at *Out of Apathy Conference*, cited in note 5.
67. Raphael Samuel (1987), 'Class and Classlessness' talk given at *Out of Apathy Conference*.
68. Jean McCrindle 'Reading', p. 55.
69. Ibid.
70. Ibid.
71. Ibid., p. 53.

7. JONATHAN RUTHERFORD, 'MR NICE (AND MR NASTY)'

(From Jonathan Rutherford, *Forever England: Reflections on Masculinity and Empire* (London, 1997), pp. 139–63.)

Summary

This essay examines masculinities in the 1990s, and draws on an eclectic range of material in the development of its argument. Rutherford is interested in the ways in which masculinities are formed in relation to other categories, such as Englishness, class and sexuality. For example, his analysis of *Four Weddings and a Funeral* focuses on what this film reveals about inconsistencies and blindspots in the construction of English male heterosexuality and ethnicity; his analysis of the 'backlash' against feminism shows how this is caught up in a wider conservative mythology. However, Rutherford's ultimate focus is on the ways in which masculinities are intersected and inflected by understandings and experiences of racial difference. 'Mr Nasty' and 'Mr Nice' are used to represent what Rutherford feels are two typical stances taken up by white men in response to racial difference: while the former is openly antagonistic, the latter plays the role of considerate (and patronising) host – but neither acknowledges the constructed and relational nature of 'whiteness' and English ethnicity. Calling on the work of Frantz Fanon, Rutherford sets out to explore – and ultimately to deconstruct – the ways in which white, heterosexual masculinities are formulated in opposition to a notion of a subordinate other.

Notes

1. Paul Mungo (1995), 'Hugh me?' in *GQ* magazine.
2. From Will Hutton (1995), 'Why the poor remain silent' in the *Guardian*, 30 October.
3. Social Trends 1996, p. 59.
4. Report in the *Guardian*, 31 August 1993.
5. Report in the *Guardian*, 21 December 1993.
6. Ibid.
7. Neil Lyndon, 'Feminism's fundamental flaws' in the *Independent on Sunday*, 29 March 1992.
8. Ibid.
9. Neil Lyndon, 'Feminism's fundamental flaws'.
10. Enoch Powell (1970), 'The Enemy Within' in *Powell and the 1970 General Election*, ed. John Wood, Elliot Right Way Books.
11. Ibid., p 107.
12. Digby Anderson and Graham Dawson, 'Popular but Unrepresented: the Curious Case of the Normal Family', in *Family Portraits*, ed. Anderson and Digby, Social Affairs Unit 1986, p. 11.
13. Sandra Scarr, Barbera K. Caporulo, Barnardo M. Ferdman, Roni B. Tower and Janet Caplan, 'Development Status and School Achievements of Minority and Non-Minority Children from Birth to 18 years in a British Midlands Town', *British Journal of Developmental Psychology*, No. 1, 983.
14. Patricia Morgan (1995), *Farewell to the Family?*, Institute of Economic Affairs, p. 153.

15. Paul Gilroy (1993), *The Black Atlantic: Modernity and Double Consciousness* (London), p. 85.
16. See Les Back (1994), 'The 'White Negro' revisited: race and masculinities in South London', in *Dislocating Masculinities Comparative Ethnographies*, ed. Andrea Cornwall and Nancy Lindisfarne (London).
17. Quote taken from Sharon Krum (1995), 'Now hear this' in the *Guardian*, 12 September. See also Michael Eric Dyson (1996), *Between God and Gangsta Rap* (Oxford), and Helen Kolawole (1996), 'sisters take the rap... but talk back' in *Girls! Girls! Girls! Essays on Women and Music*, ed. Sarah Cooper.
18. Fanon's failure to address gender makes his work of more limited value in debates around sexual differences and black and white femininities.
19. Jean-Paul Sartre (1986), *Being and Nothingness* (London).
20. Sartre's central tenet that human culture and society is founded upon the antinomies of Self and Other derives from Hegel's account of the 'independence and dependence of self-consciousness' (see *The Phenomenology of Spirit*). For a discussion on the similarities between Hegel's dialectic of recognition and the discourse of 'race' see Robert Young (1990), *White Mythologies Writing History and the West* (London). For example: 'Hegel articulates a philosophical structure of the appropriation of the other as a form of knowledge which uncannily simulates the project of nineteenth-century imperialism; the construction of knowledges which all operate through forms of expropriation and incorporation of the other mimics at a conceptual level the geographical and economic absorption of the non-European world by the West' (p. 3). Perhaps the single aim of postcolonial theories has been to find an alternative to the Hegelian dialectic of recognition which can avoid the exclusionary practice of identity. But given that the nineteenth-century epistemologies of psychoanalysis and Marxism are themselves rooted in Hegelian philosophy, the problem of finding another way to speak of racial and sexual differences remains unresolved.
21. There are two intellectual origins of this scene. The first can be found in Sartre's section on 'The Look' (p. 252) where he describes the experience of looking through a keyhole and being caught in the act (pp. 259–60). The scenario introduces a third figure into his equation of Self and Other; the voyeur, the subject behind the door and the person who catches the voyeur. In this moment of discovery and humiliation, Sartre reproduces Freud's scenario of masochism in 'A Child is Being Beaten' (1919) (see *PFL*, Vol.10). The second is Jacques Lacan's essay, 'The mirror stage as formative of the function of the "I" as revealed in psychoanalytic experience'. Lacan argues that the infant establishes its ego identity (its 'I') through a misrecognition of its wholeness in a mirror image of itself. This mirror stage inaugurates identifications with other people and forms the psychoanalytic foundations of relations between Self and Other.
22. S. Freud (1918b[1914]), 'From the History of an Infantile Neurosis (The 'Wolf Man')', *PFL*, Vol.9, p. 87.
23. Ibid, p. 280.
24. In his essay 'The Ego and the Id', Freud describes the 'more complete Oedipus Complex' with its 'positive and negative' trajectories. He writes: 'one gets the impression that the simple Oedipus Complex is by no means its commonest form, but rather represents a simplification or schematisation', see *PFL*, Vol. 11, p. 372.
25. Jean-Paul Sartre (1972), *Being and Nothingness* (London).

8. HOMI K. BHABHA, 'ARE YOU A MAN OR A MOUSE?'

(From Maurice Berger, Brian Wallis and Simon Watson (eds), *Constructing Masculinity* (New York, 1995), pp. 57–65.)

Summary

Punning and playful, and drawing on psychoanalytic and poststructuralist theory, this essay is written in a style which draws deliberate attention to the slippery, polysemic nature of the signifier. Bhabha opens by considering the ways in which masculinity masquerades as the human norm – the standard or generic case – in our language and in our culture. Bhabha does not wish to disavow masculinity, but he stresses the need to cease speaking of it in universalising terms and to expose its constructed and differential nature. Masculinity is never as monolithic and stable as it might first appear to be, and, from the title of this essay onwards, Bhabha draws attention to the anxieties and conflicts inherent in understandings and experiences of what it means to be a man.

The argument is illustrated by, amongst other things, a reading of Kazuo Ishiguro's Booker Prize-winning novel, *The Remains of the Day*. Here, Bhabha is particularly interested in relationships between patriarchal versions of masculinity and forms of nationalism or 'amor patriae', and the role played by 'phallic respect' for charismatic patriarchs in the psychology of fascism.

Notes

Portions of this essay have been published in a different form in my essay 'Anxious Nations, Nervous States', in Joan Copjec (ed.), *Supposing the Subject* (London and New York, 1994).

1. Maurice Berger, comp., 'Man Trouble: A Special Project', *Artforum*, 32, no.8 (April 1994), 74–83, 119–22.
2. Wayne Koestenbaum, ' "My" Masculinity', in ibid., p. 79.
3. Todd Haynes, 'Lines of Flight', in ibid., p. 79.
4. Herbert Sussman, 'His Infinite Variety', in ibid., p. 119.
5. Peter Middleton, *The Inward Gaze: Masculinity and Subjectivity in Modern Culture* (New York and London, 1992), p. 3.
6. Freud, 'Notes Upon a Case of Obsessional Neurosis' (1909), *The Standard Edition of the Complete Psychological Works of Sigmund Freud*, trans. James Strachey (London, 1954), vol.7. p. 128.
7. Ibid., p. 118.
8. Johann G. Fichte, *Addresses to the German Nation* (1807-1808) (Chicago, 1968).
9. Ibid., p. 83.
10. Ibid., p. 173.
11. Samuel Weber, *Return to Freud: Jacques Lacan's Dislocation of Psychoanalysis* (Cambridge, 1991), p. 154.
12. Ibid., p. 155.
13. Ibid.
14. Lacan, quoted in ibid., p. 158.
15. Lacan, quoted in ibid., p. 160 (my emphasis).
16. Michael Kinsley, 'Is Democracy Losing its Romance?' *Time*, 143 (Jan. 17 1994), 68.

17. Kazuo Ishiguro, *The Remains of the Day* (New York, 1990), p. 199.
18. H. C. Irwin, 'The Character of a Fine Gentleman', *The English Review*, 37 (1923), 643.
19. Peter Osborne, 'Small-Scale Victories, Large-Scale Defeats: Walter Benjamin's Politics of Time', in Andrew Benjamin and Peter Osborne (eds), *Walter Benjamin's Philosophy: Destruction and Experience* (London and New York, 1994), p. 93.
20. E. W. D. Tennant, 'Herr Hitler and his Policy', *The English Review*, 56 (1933), 373 (my emphasis).
21. Arlene Raven, 'Adrian Piper: You and Me', *Pretend*, exhibition catalogue (London, Ikon Gallery, 1991), p. 18.

9. ANNE FAUSTO-STERLING, 'HOW TO BUILD A MAN'

(From Maurice Berger, Brian Wallis and Simon Watson (eds), *Constructing Masculinity* (New York, 1995), pp. 127–34.)

Summary

How does one become a man? In setting out to answer this question, Fausto-Sterling starts at the very beginning, with the development of the foetus. She acknowledges that, in current thinking, gender is now widely acknowledged as a social construct; understandings of sex, however, remain more ambivalent, often based on the belief that sex is a biological fact underlying and preceding social discourse. This essay begins to explore how such 'facts' are *established for us* in biological and medical theory and practice. Sex, Fausto-Sterling argues – far from being a clear blueprint – is more complex and multifaceted, more open to interpretation and modification, than is generally supposed. There is more than one criterion for establishing 'sex' and, in some cases, the indicators seem to contradict one another. However, scientists and doctors are as much products of their culture as anybody else, and, as this essay shows, their culturally specific preconceptions inform the ways in which they interpret and act on evidence. If a baby is born 'intersexed', Fausto-Sterling reveals, doctors will operate in order to protect our cultural misconception that, in matters of sex (and gender), we are always simply and exclusively one thing or the other.

Notes

1. For a popular account of this picture, see John Money and Patricia Tucker, *Sexual Signatures: On Being a Man or a Woman* (Boston, 1975).
2. The data do not actually match the presence/absence model, but this does not seem to bother most people. For a discussion of this point, see Anne Fausto-Sterling, 'Life in the XY Corral', *Women's Studies International Forum*, 12 (1989), 319–31; Anne Fausto-Sterling, 'Society Writes Biology/Biology Constructs Gender', *Daedalus*, 116 (1987), 61–76; and Anne Fausto-Sterling, *Myths of Gender: Biological Theories about Women and Men* (New York, 1992).
3. I use the phrase 'male hormone' and 'female hormone' as shorthand. There are, in fact, no such categories. Males and females have the same hormones, albeit in different quantities and sometimes with different tissue distributions.

4. Patricia Donahue, David M. Powell, and Mary M. Lee, 'Clinical Management of Intersex Abnormalities', *Current Problems in Surgery*, 8 (1991), 527.
5. Robert H. Danish, Peter A. Lee, Thomas Mazur, James A. Amrhein, and Claude J. Migeon, 'Micropenis II: Hypogonadotropic Hypogonadism', *Johns Hopkins Medical Journal*, 146 (1980), 177–84.
6. Suzanne J. Kessler, 'The Medical Construction of Gender: Case Management of Intersexed Infants', *Signs*, 16 (1990).

10. JACQUELINE ROSE, 'FEMININITY AND ITS DISCONTENTS'

(From Jacqueline Rose, *Sexuality in the Field of Vision* (London, 1986), pp. 83–103.)

Summary

In this essay, Rose makes a case for the radical potential of the work of Sigmund Freud, and argues that feminism has much to gain by employing psychoanalytic concepts and insights. What psychoanalysis and feminism have in common, she argues, is a desire to denaturalise social 'givens' and to underline the complacency of common sense, both of which operate as ideological brakes on the possibility of change. Particular attention is paid here to Freud's notion of the unconscious, as that which continually destabilises or resists the possibility of a comfortable or coherent gender identity. An alliance with psychoanalysis, Rose implies, offers feminism a way out of the deadlock between biological determinism on the one hand and cultural determinism on the other: in Rose's reading of Freud, femininity is neither a set of natural attributes nor cultural *fait accompli*, but a laborious and sometimes bungled acquisition. Freudian psychoanalysis is, according to Rose, one of the only discourses in our culture which recognises that learning to occupy the roles designated for women by our culture is not a natural, easy or inevitable process.

Notes

1. First published in *Feminist Review*, 14 (Summer 1983), 5–21, this essay was originally requested by the editors of *Feminist Review* to counter the largely negative representation of psychoanalysis which had appeared in the journal, and as a specific response to Elizabeth Wilson's 'Psychoanalysis: Psychic Law and Order', *Feminist Review*, 8 (Summer 1981). (See also Janet Sayers, 'Psychoanalysis and Personal Politics: A Response to Elizabeth Wilson', *Feminist Review*, 10 [1982].) As I was writing the piece, however, it soon became clear that Elizabeth Wilson's article and the question of *Feminist Review's* own relationship to psychoanalysis could not be understood independently of what has been – outside the work of Juliet Mitchell for feminism – a fairly consistent repudiation of Freud within the British Left. In this context, the feminist debate over Freud becomes part of a larger question about the importance of subjectivity to our understanding of political and social life. That this was in fact the issue became even clearer when Elizabeth Wilson and Angie Weir published an article, 'The British Women's Movement' in *New Left Review*, 148 (November–December 1984), which dismissed the whole area of subjectivity and psychoanalysis from feminist politics together with any work by feminists (historians

200 *Gender*

and writers on contemporary politics) who, while defining themselves as socialist feminists, nonetheless query the traditional terms of an exclusively class-based analysis of power.

2. Wilson, 'Psychoanalysis', p. 63.
3. *Psychoanalysis and Feminism*.
4. Perry Anderson, 'Components of the National Culture', *New Left Review*, 50 (July–August 1968).
5. David Cooper, 'Freud Revisited' and 'Two Types of Rationality', *New Left Review*, 20 (May–June 1963) and 29 (January–February 1965); R. D. Laing 'Series and Nexus in the Family' and 'What is Schizophrenia?', *New Life Review*, 15 (May–June 1962) and 28 (November–December 1964).
6. Anderson, 'Origins of the Present Crisis', *New Left Review*, 23 (January–February 1964); see also E. P. Thompson, 'The Peculiarities of the English', *Socialist Register* 1965.
7. Louis Althusser, 'Freud and Lacan', trans. Ben Brewster, *New Left Review*, 55 (March–April 1969); Jacques Lacan, 'The Mirror Phase', trans. Jan Meil, *New Left Review*, 51 (September–October 1968).
8. Juliet Mitchell, 'Why Freud?', *Shrew* (November–December 1970), and *Psychoanalysis and Feminism*.
9. Michael Rustin, 'A Socialist Consideration of Kleinian Psychoanalysis', *New Left Review*, 131 (January–February 1982).
10. Michèle Barrett, *Women's Oppression Today* (London, 1980), ch.2, pp. 80–3.
11. See Gayle Rubin, 'The Traffic in Women'; and for a critique of the use of Lévi-Strauss on which this reading is based, Elizabeth Cowie, 'Woman as Sign'.
12. Nancy Chodorow, *The Reproduction of Mothering: Psychoanalysis and the Sociology of Gender* (Berkeley, CA, 1978).
13. Ibid., p. 3.
14. Sayers, 'Psychoanalysis and Personal Politics', p. 92.
15. Freud, 'The Dissolution of the Oedipus Complex' (1924); 'Some Psychical Consequences of the Anatomical Distinction Between the Sexes' (1925), SE XIX, PF 7; 'Female Sexuality' (1931).
16. Ernest Jones, 'The Phallic Phase', *IJPA*, 14, Part 1, 1933, p. 265; Karen Horney, 'On the Genesis of the Castration Complex in Women' (1924), *Feminine Psychology* (London, 1967), p. 53.
17. Wilson, 'Reopening the Case – Feminism and Psychoanalysis', opening seminar presentation in discussion with Jacqueline Rose, London 1982. This was the first of a series of seminars on the subject of feminism and psychoanalysis which ran into 1983; see articles by Parveen Adams, Nancy Wood and Claire Buck, *m/f*, 8 (1983).
18. Althusser, 'Freud and Lacan', see publisher's note in *Lenin and Philosophy and Other Essays* (London, 1971), pp. 189–90.
19. For a more detailed discussion of the relative assimilation of Kleinianism through social work in relation to children in this country, especially through the Tavistock Clinic in London, see Rustin, 'A Socialist Consideration of Kleinian Psychoanalysis', p. 85 and note. As Rustin points out, the state is willing to fund psychoanalysis when it is a question of helping children to adapt, but less so when it is a case of helping adults to remember.
20. Judith Walkowitz, *Prostitution and Victorian Society – Women, Class and the State* (London and New York, 1980).
21. Carol Dyhouse, *Girls Growing Up in Late Victorian and Edwardian England* (London, 1981).

22. Angus McLaren, *Birth Control in Nineteenth Century England* (London, 1978).
23. Walkowitz, Prostitution and Victorian Society, p. 69.
24. Ibid., p. 59.
25. Ilza Veith, *Hysteria: the History of a Disease* (London, 1975), p. 229.
26. Freud, *Studies on Hysteria*, p. 122; p. 187.
27. Freud, 'Preface and Footnotes to Charcot's Tuesday Lectures' (1892–94), SE I, p. 137.
28. *Studies on Hysteria*, p. 117; p. 181.
29. Freud, *Three Essays on the Theory of Sexuality*, Part I.
30. Ferdinand de Saussure, *Cours de linguistique générale* (1915), Paris 1972 (tr. Roy Harris, *Course in General Linguistics* (London,1983), pp. 65–70.
31. Jones, 'The Phallic Phase', p. 15.
32. Horney, 'The Flight from Womanhood' (1926), in *Feminine Psychology*, p. 68.
33. *Three Essays*, p. 146n; p. 57n.
34. Shulamith Firestone, *The Dialectic of Sex*.
35. See Mitchell, 'Shulamith Firestone: Freud Feminised', *Psychoanalysis and Feminism*, Part 2, Section 2, ch. 5.
36. Firestone, *Dialectic of Sex*, p. 170.
37. Ibid., introduction by Rosalind Delmar.
38. Sayers quoted by Wilson in 'Reopening the Case'.
39. Michèle Barrett and Mary McIntosh, 'Narcissism and the Family: A Critique of Lasch', *New Left Review*, 135 (September–October 1982).
40. Sheila Rowbotham, Lynne Segal and Hilary Wainwright, *Beyond the Fragments – Feminism and the Making of Socialism* (London, 1979).
41. Sayers, 'Psychoanalysis and Personal Politics', pp. 92–3.

11. JOAN RIVIERE, 'WOMANLINESS AS A MASQUERADE'

(From Victor Burgin, James Donald and Cora Kaplan (eds), *Formations of Fantasy* (London, 1986), pp. 35–44.)

Summary

Although first published in 1929, this essay has become a significant point of reference for late twentieth-century theories of gender. Riviere presents case histories of women who, because of contradictory demands made on them in a particular social context, experience anxieties and instability of identity. (For example, in certain situations, the conventions of feminine behaviour may come into conflict with the need to act as an assertive and competent professional.) These women, she argues, may put on a show or 'masquerade' of disarming girlishness, in order to defuse perceived disapproval from those around them. She cites the examples of a female lecturer who, after an accomplished performance, would anxiously seek reassurance by flirting with men in her audience, and of the housewife who would play down her competence and confidence when dealing with builders in her own home. Riviere goes on to ask how one might distinguish between these masquerades and genuine womanliness, and comes to the intriguing conclusion that they may be, in fact, the same thing. If womanliness is no more or less than a masquerade, then what is behind the mask?

Notes

This article was first published in *The International Journal of Psychoanalysis (IJPA)*, 10 (1929). The author follows the Kleinian practice of spelling 'phantasy'.

1. E. Jones, 'The Early Development of Female Sexuality', *IJPA*, 8 (1927).
2. S. Ferenczi, 'The nosology of male homosexuality', in *Contributions to Psychoanalysis* (1916).
3. I have found this attitude in several woman analysands and the self-ordained defloration in nearly all of them (five cases). In the light of Freud's 'Taboo of virginity', this latter symptomatic act is instructive.
4. M. Klein, 'Early stages of the Oedipus conflict', *IJPA*, 9 (1928).
5. E. Jones, 'Early Development', p. 469, regards an intensification of the oral-sadistic stage as the central feature of homosexual development in women.
6. As it was not essential to my argument, I have omitted all reference to the further development of the relation to children.
7. Cf. M. N. Searl, 'Danger situations of the immature ego', Oxford Congress, 1929.

12. STEPHEN HEATH, 'JOAN RIVIERE AND THE MASQUERADE'

(From Victor Burgin, James Donald and Cora Kaplan (eds), *Formations of Fantasy* (London, 1986), pp. 45–61.)

Summary

Heath provides a useful companion piece to Riviere's essay, helping the reader to contextualise the material and draw out its radical implications. In Riviere's account, Heath points out, gender is understood as a *relation*, and femininity is constructed as subordinate to masculinity. Thus the masquerade is performed for the man, in deference to his expectations. Moreover, since gender is organised in our culture as a binary opposition, to be 'womanly' is specifically about *not* being masculine. 'Womanliness', then, may then be about dissimulating character traits which culture defines as masculine.

However, at the heart of Riviere's paper, Heath points out, is the *question* of feminine identity. Riviere never finally decides what is behind the masquerade: the masquerade at the same time implies and denies the presence of a 'real woman'. Feminine identity is thus constructed not essential, precarious not stable, an ongoing charade, a site of uncertainty – and ultimately is more about representation than reality. Heath also explores ways in which Riviere's arguments might be developed in a modern context: for example, comparing feminine 'masquerade' to masculine 'display', and looking at manifestations and disruptions of these persistent gender charades in cinema.

Notes

References to Riviere's paper 'Womanliness as a masquerade' are given in brackets in the body of the text and are to its reprinting in the present volume.

1. J. Strachey, obituary notice for Joan Riviere, *The International Journal of Psychoanalysis (IJPA)*, 44 (1963), p. 228.
2. J. Riviere, letter to Ernest Jones, 25 October 1918, cit. V. Brome, *Ernest Jones: Freud's Alter Ego* (London, 1982), p. 113; Jones, letter to Freud, 21 January 1921, cit. Brome, p. 131.
3. E. Jones, letter to Freud, 21 January 1921, p. 131.
4. Ibid.
5. See A. Carotenuto, *A Secret Symmetry: Sabina Spielrein Between Jung and Freud* (New York, 1982).
6. E. Jones, letter to Freud, 1 April 1922, cit. Brome, *Ernest Jones*, p. 135.
7. E. Jones, *Sigmund Freud: Life and Work* (London, 1955), vol.II, p. 469.
8. J. Riviere, 'An intimate impression', *The Lancet*, 20 September 1939, p. 768; in E. Jones, *Sigmund Freud: Life and Work*, vol.II, pp. 450–3.
9. See J. Strachey, obituary, p. 228 and P. Heimann, obituary notice for Joan Riviere, *IJPA*, 44 (1963), 232, 233.
10. K. West, *Inner Outer Circles* (London, 1958), p. 26.
11. E. Jones, 'The phallic phase' [1993], in E. Jones, *Papers on Psychoanalysis* (5th edn) (London, 1948), pp. 452–84; reference to Riviere's paper, p. 480.
12. See S. Freud, *Jokes and their Relation to the Unconscious* [1905], *The Standard Edition of the Complete Psychological Works of Sigmund Freud*, ed. J. Strachey (London, 1953–74) (*SE*), VIII, 179; 'A seventeenth-century demonological neurosis' [1922], *SE*, XIX, 104.
13. J. Lacan, 'La signification du phallus' [1958], *Ecrits* (Paris, 1966, pp. 685–95; reference to the masquerade, p. 694; trans. *Ecrits: A Selection* (London, 1977), pp. 281–91, reference p. 290, and J. Mitchell and J. Rose (eds), *Feminine Sexuality: Jacques Lacan and the Ecole Freudienne* (London, 1982), pp. 74–85, reference p. 84.
14. J. Lampl-de Groot, 'The evolution of the Oedipus complex in women', *The International Journal of Psychoanalysis*, 9 (1928), 332–45. See also K. Horney, 'On the genesis of the castration complex in women', *IJPA*, 5 (1924), 50–65; 'The flight from womanhood', *IJPA*, 7 (1926), 324–39; M. Klein, 'Early stages of the Oedipus complex', *IJPA*, 9 (1928), 167–80.
15. E. Jones, letter to Freud, 21 January 1921, p. 132.
16. F. Nietzsche, *Beyond Good and Evil* [1886] (Harmondsworth, 1973), p. 84.
17. Ibid., p. 145.
18. Ibid., p. 144.
19. Ibid., p. 145.
20. F. Nietzsche, *The Gay Science* [1882] (New York, 1974), p. 317.
21. S. Freud, 'Some general remarks on hysterical attacks' [1909], *SE*, IX, 234.
22. I. Diamantis and M. Safouan, 'Entrevue avec Moustapha Safouan', *Ornicar?*, no.9 (1977), 104.
23. J. Lacan, *Ecrits*, p. 710.
24. M. Safauan, *La Sexualité féminine dans la doctrine freudienne* (Paris, 1976), pp. 136–7.
25. J. Lacan, *Le Séminaire, livre XI, Les quatre concepts fondamentaux de la psychanalyse* (Paris, 1973), p. 176; trans. *The Four Fundamental Concepts of Psychoanalysis* (Harmondsworth, 1979), p. 193; *Télèvision* (Paris, 1974), p. 64.
26. J. Lacan, *Ecrits*, p. 825; *Ecrits: A Selection*, p. 322.
27. J. Lacan, *Le Séminaire, livre II, Le moi dans la théorie de Freud et dans la technique de la psychanalyse* (Paris, 1978), p. 261.
28. E. Lemoine-Luccioni, *La Robe* (Paris, 1983), p. 124.

29. J. Lacan, *Le Séminaire, livre II*, p. 261.
30. J. Mitchell, *Feminine Sexuality*, p. 24 (I draw generally here on the introductions by Mitchell and Rose to *Feminine Sexuality*).
31. S. Freud, 'Analysis terminable and interminable' [1937], *SE*, XXIII, 252.
32. Ibid.
33. J. Lacan, *Ecrits*, p. 728; *Feminine Sexuality*, p. 90.
34. M. Montrelay, *L'Ombre et le nom* (Paris, 1977), p. 71; trans. 'Inquiry into femininity', *m/f*, no.1 (1978), 93.
35. M. Safouan, 'Entrevue avec Moustapha Safouan', p. 104.
36. I. Roublef, intervention, *Journées des Cartels de l'Ecole Freudienne de Paris* [1975], *Letters de l'Ecole Freudienne*, no.18 (1976), 211.
37. L. Irigaray, *Ce Sexe qui n'en est pas un* (Paris, 1977), p. 131.
38. M. Plaza, 'Pouvoir "phallomorphique" et psychologie de "la Femme"', *Questions féministes* no.1 (1977), 112; trans. '"Phallomorphique power" and the psychology of "Woman"', *Ideology and Consciousness*, no.4 (1978), 27.
39. 'Entrevue avec Moustapha Safouan', p. 104.
40. S. Freud, *New Introductory Lectures on Psychoanalysis* [1933], *SE*, XXIII, 131.
41. L. Irigaray, *Amante marine* (Paris, 1980), p. 92.
42. V. Woolf, *Three Guineas* [1938] (Harmondsworth, 1977), p. 23.
43. E. Lemoine-Luccioni, *La Robe*, p. 34.
44. S. Freud, *New Introductory Lectures*, p. 119.
45. '*Morocco* de Josef von Sternberg', *Cahiers du cinéma*, no.225 (1970), 5–13; C. Johnston, 'Femininity and the masquerade: *Anne of the Indies*', in C. Johnston and P. Willemen (eds), *Jaques Tourneur* (Edinburgh, Edinburgh Film Festival, 1975), pp. 36–44.
46. S. Bovenschen, 'Is there a feminine aesthetic?', *New German Critique*, no.10 (1977), 129.
47. M. A. Doane, 'Film and the masquerade: theorising the female spectator', *Screen*, 23, no.3–4 (1982), 87.
48. A. Friedberg, 'An interview with filmmaker Lizzie Borden', *Women and Performance*, 1, no.2 (1984), 44. Cf. T. de Lauretis, 'Aesthetic and feminist theory: rethinking women's cinema', *New German Critique*, no.34 (1985), 154–75.
49. For an initial bibliography of Riviere's writings, see *IJPA*, 44 (1963), 235.

13. JUDITH BUTLER, 'CRITICALLY QUEER'

(From Judith Butler, *Bodies That Matter: On the Discursive Limits of 'Sex'* (New York, 1993), pp. 223–242.)

Summary

Since the beginning of the 1990s, Judith Butler has been extraordinarily influential in the field of gender studies. 'Critically Queer' provides an exposition both of her notion of gender as a performative and of the implications of queer theory for our understanding of the relationship between gender and sexuality.

For Butler, the human subject is produced and enabled within social discourses. Gender is neither an essence nor an add-on to a sexed individual: it is a compulsory and repetitive citation of norms or ideals circulated within a culture. One becomes a person by *impersonating* these norms. This performance of gender creates the retrospective *illusion* of an inner or essential sexual identity preceding our acts and our utterances.

Moreover, in our culture, these ideals or norms of gender abide by a heterosexual logic. Heterosexuality, Butler argues, produces hyperbolic versions of man and woman, 'ideals' which are never fully achieved or achievable. Queer theory builds on such insights, developing a range of critical and political strategies which exploit the fact that gender norms are destabilised by homosexual desire.

Notes

This essay was originally published in *GLQ*, 1, no. 1 (Fall 1993). I thank David Halperin and Carolyn Dinshaw for their useful editorial suggestions. This chapter is an altered version of that essay.

1. This is a question that pertains most urgently to recent questions of 'hate speech'.
2. Foucault, *History of Sexuality, Volume One*, pp. 92–3.
3. See Eve Kosofsky Sedgwick's 'Queer Performativity' in *GLQ*, vol. 1, no. 1 (Spring 1993). I am indebted to her provocative work and for prompting me to rethink the relationship between gender and performativity.
4. It is, of course, never quite right to say that language or discourse 'performs', since it is unclear that language is primarily constituted as a set of 'acts'. After all, this description of an 'act' cannot be sustained through the trope that established the act as a singular event, for the act will turn out to refer to prior acts and to a reiteration of 'acts' that is perhaps more suitably described as a citational chain. Paul de Man points out in 'Rhetoric of Persuasion' that the distinction between constative and performative utterances is confounded by the fictional status of both: '. . . the possibility for language to perform is just as fictional as the possibility for language to assert' (p. 129). Further, he writes, 'considered as persuasion, rhetoric is performative, but considered as a system of tropes, it deconstructs its own performance' (pp. 130–1, in *Allegories of Reading* [New Haven, CT, 1987]).
5. In what follows, that set of performatives that Austin terms illocutionary will be at issue, those in which the binding power of the act *appears* to be derived from the intention or will of the speaker. In 'Signature, Event, Context', Derrida argues that the binding power that Austin attributes to the speaker's intention in such illocutionary acts is more properly attributable to a citational force of the speaking, the iterability that establishes the authority of the speech act, but which establishes the non-singular character of that act. In this sense, every 'act' is an echo or citational chain, and it is its citationality that constitutes its performative force.
6. 'Signature, Event, Context', p. 18.
7. The historicity of discourse implies the way in which history is constitutive of discourse itself. It is not simply that discourses are located *in* histories, but that they have their own constitutive historical character. Historicity is a term which directly implies the constitutive character of history in discursive practice, that is, a condition in which a 'practice' could not exist apart from the sedimentation of conventions by which it is produced and becomes legible.
8. My understanding of the charge of presentism is that an inquiry is presentist to the extent that it (a) universalises a set of claims regardless of historical and cultural challenges to that universalisation or (b) takes a historically specific set of terms and universalises them falsely. It may be that both gestures in a given instance are the same. It would, however, be a mistake to claim that all conceptual language or philosophical language is 'presentist', a claim which would

be tantamount to prescribing that all philosophy become history. My understanding of Foucault's notion of genealogy is that it is a specifically philosophical
exercise in exposing and tracing the installation and operation of false universals.
My thanks to Mary Poovey and Joan W. Scott for explaining this concept to me.

9. See Cherry Smyth, *Lesbians Talk Queer Notions* (London, 1922).
10. See Omi and Winant, *Racial Formation in the United States: From the 1960s to the 1980s*.
11. Theatricality is not for that reason fully intentional, but I might have made that
    reading possible through my reference to gender as 'intentional and non-refer-
    ential' in 'Performative Acts and Gender Constitution', an essay published in
    Sue-Ellen Case (ed.), *Performing Feminisms* (Baltimore, MD, 1991), pp. 270–82. I
    use the term 'intentional' in a specifically phenomenological sense. 'Intentional-
    ity' within phenomenology does not mean voluntary or deliberate, but is, rather,
    a way of characterising consciousness (or language) as *having an object*, more
    specifically, as directed toward an object which may or may not exist. In this
    sense, an act of consciousness may intend (posit, constitute, apprehend) an
    imaginary object. Gender, in its ideality, might be construed as an intentional
    object, an ideal which is constituted but which does not exist. In this sense,
    gender would be like 'the feminine' as it is discussed as an impossibility by
    Drucilla Cornell in *Beyond Accommodation* (New York, 1992).
12. See David Román, '"It's My Party and I'll Die If I Want To!"': Gay Men, AIDS,
    and the Circulation of Camp in U.S. Theatre', *Theatre Journal*, 44 (1992),
    305–27; see also by Román, 'Performing All Our Lives: AIDS, Performance,
    Community', in Janelle Reinelt and Joseph Roach (eds), *Critical Theory and
    Performance* (Ann Arbor, MI, 1992).
13. See Larry Kramer, *Reports from the Holocaust: The Making of an AIDS Activist*
    (New York, 1989); Douglas Crimp and Adam Rolston (eds), *AIDSDEMO-
    GRAPHICS* (Seattle, 1990); and Doug Sadownick, 'ACT UP Makes a Spectacle
    of AIDS', *High Performance*, 13 (1990), 26–31. My thanks to David Román for
    directing me to this last essay.
14. See Sedgwick, 'Across Gender, Across Sexuality: Willa Cather and Others'.
15. See Gayle Rubin, 'Thinking Sex: Notes for a Radical Theory of the Politics of
    Sexuality', in Carole S. Vance (ed.), *Pleasure and Danger* (New York, 1984), pp.
    267–319; Eve Kosofsky, *Epistemology of the Closet*, pp. 27–39.
16. Toward the end of the short theoretical conclusion of 'Thinking Sex', Rubin
    returns to feminism in a gestural way, suggesting that 'in the long run, feminism's
    critique of gender hierarchy must be incorporated into a radical theory of sex,
    and the critique of sexual oppression should enrich feminism. But an autonom-
    ous theory and politics specific to sexuality must be developed' (p. 309).

14. DIANE ELAM, 'GENDER OR SEX?'

(From Diane Elam, *Feminism and Deconstruction: Ms. En Abyme* (London, 1994),
pp. 42–58.)

Summary

This piece critically evaluates a range of recent debates on gender. Elam's exposition
of the Lacanian parable of the girl and the boy on a train is particularly helpful,

reprising and reinforcing a number of points about sex and gender which have already arisen in different contexts in this anthology: for example, that ideologies of gender control us in ways we are not necessarily conscious of, that both sex and gender are conceived in binary oppositional terms, and that gender differences are established in the language we use rather than decreed by nature. However, what Elam is most interested in is the possible outcomes of a dialogue between feminism and deconstruction – a dialogue which, she feels, opens up many exciting questions and challenges. She proposes that sex should no longer be seen as a foundational category in feminist analyses, and insists that this loss of the fixed and definitive category 'women' should not be seen as a problem for feminism. If gender were freed from the binarism of our current understandings of sex, it is suggested, this would make possible a greater diversity of sex/gender combinations and a proliferation of sexualities and gender differences.

Notes

1. For detailed and thoughtful analyses of Freud's account of the subject of women, see: Sarah Kofman, *The Enigma of Woman: Woman in Freud's Writings*, trans. Catherine Porter (Ithaca, NY, 1985); Luce Irigaray, *Speculum of the Other Woman*, trans. Gilliam C. Gill (Ithaca, NY, 1985); and *This Sex Which is Not One*, trans. Catherine Porter (Ithaca, NY, 1985).
2. Jacques Lacan, 'The Agency of the Letter in the Unconscious', *Ecrits: A Selection* (New York, 1977), p. 152.
3. Jane Gallop, *The Daughter's Seduction* (Ithaca, NY, 1982), p. 11. Gallop also provides an excellent analysis of the same passage that I am discussing.
4. For detailed accounts and perceptive analyses of cases of 'mistaken' identity, see Holly Devor, *Gender Blending: Confronting the Limits of Duality* (Bloomington, IN, 1989).
5. For an extended consideration of the relationship between sex/gender and division of labour see Gayle Rubin, 'The Traffic in Women: Notes on the "Political Economy" of Sex', *Toward an Anthropology of Women*, ed. Rayna Rapp Reiter (New York, 1975); and Luce Irigaray, 'Women on the Market', *This Sex Which is Not One* (Ithaca, NY, 1985).
6. Jacqueline Rose, 'Introduction II', *Feminine Sexuality: Jacques Lacan and the école freudienne*, ed. Juliet Mitchell and Jacqueline Rose (New York), p. 42.
7. Joan Wallach Scott, *Gender and the Politics of History* (New York), p. 50. See also especially pp. 28–50.
8. Teresa de Lauretis, *Technologies of Gender* (Bloomington, IN, 1987), p. 4. Further references to this text will be cited parenthetically by page number.
9. This is not to be understood as the same thing as Derridean deconstruction. De Lauretis believes that Derrida is guilty of 'displacing the question of gender onto an ahistorical, purely textual figure of femininity'. According to her, 'this kind of deconstruction of the subject is effectively a way to recontain women in femininity (Woman) and to reposition female subjectivity *in* the male subject, however that will be defined' (*Technologies of Gender*, p. 24).
10. Judith Butler, *Gender Trouble: Feminism and the Subversion of Identity* (New York, 1990).
11. Judith Butler, 'Imitation and Gender Insubordination', *Inside/Out: Lesbian Theories, Gay Theories*, ed. Diana Fuss (New York and London, 1991). p. 28.
12. Paul de Man, *Allegories of Reading* (New Haven, CT, 1979). p. 249.

13. Suzanne J. Kessler, 'The Medical Construction of Gender: Case Management of Intersexed Infants', *Signs* 16, 1 (1990). Further references to this text will be cited parenthetically by page number. I would like to thank Elizabeth Kuhlmann for calling my attention to Kessler's essay. A more well-known case is that of Herculine Barbin, now famous thanks to Foucault's presentation of it in *Herculine Barbin: Being the Recently Discovered Memoirs of a Nineteenth-Century Hermaphrodite*, trans. Richard McDougall (New York, 1980). See also Anne Fausto-Sterling, *Myths of Gender: Biological Theories about Women and Men* (New York, 1985).

14. It is also worth noting Kessler's point that 'after the infant's gender has been assigned, parents generally latch onto the assignment as the solution to the problem' (p. 21). Just to make sure that family and friends also understand that the problem has been solved, physicians routinely advocate that the mother will allow some of 'her women friends' to take a look at the baby's reconstructed genitals (p. 22). Seeing is believing, apparently.

15. Devor, *Gender Blending*, pp. 11–12. I do not want to leave the impression, however, that gender stereotypes only dog a couple of isolated aspects of medical and biological science. To turn to another kind of example, it seems worth noting that the descriptions of reproductive organs, as well as the relationship between eggs and sperm, noticeably rely on a number of similar gender stereotypes. As Emily Martin thoroughly demonstrates in 'The Egg and the Sperm: How Science has Constructed a Romance Based on Stereotypical Male-Female Roles', *Signs* 16, 3 (1991), 485–501, typically both scientific textbooks and journal articles represent sperm as valuable commodities which actively pursue and penetrate eggs. By contrast, eggs are described as passive receptacles which are both inefficiently produced and badly stored. That recent research indicates that this is far from an accurate description of events only further calls attention to the force of gender stereotypes within the medical and biological sciences.

16. Devor, *Gender Blending*, p. 43.

17. Ibid., p. 50.

18. Elizabeth Grosz, *Jacques Lacan: A Feminist Introduction* (London and New York, 1990), p. 190.

19. Jacques Lacan, 'God and the *Jouissance* of The Woman. A Love Letter', *Feminine Sexuality*, p. 144. Further references to this text will be cited parenthetically by page number.

20. Grosz also makes this claim and argues the case at some length in *Jacques Lacan: A Feminist Introduction*.

21. Irigaray, 'Così Fan Tutti', *This Sex Which is Not One*, pp. 90–1. In suggesting that Lacan would have more to learn from Saint Theresa's own writings, Irigaray seems to be stressing the value of women's own experience as recalled in autobiographical writings. This move is not without its own problems, as I will hope to make clear later.

22. See Irigaray, 'Così Fan Tutti', *This Sex Which is Not One*, pp. 96–7.

23. Derrida, 'Le Facteur de la vérité', *The Post Card*, trans. Alan Bass (Chicago, 1987), pp. 441–2. For an excellent discussion of Derrida's engagement with Lacanian psychoanalysis, see Drusilla Cornell, *Beyond Accommodation* (New York and London, 1991); and Barbara Johnson, *The Critical Difference* (Baltimore and London, 1980).

24. Monique Wittig, 'The Mark of Gender', *The Poetics of Gender*, ed. Nancy K. Miller (New York, 1986), p. 64; 'The Category of Sex', *Feminist Issues* 2, 2 (Spring 1982), 66.

25. Wittig, 'The Mark of Gender', p. 67.
26. Butler, *Gender Trouble*, p. 20.
27. Derrida discusses this point, drawing a distinction between Hegel's and Heidegger's notion of Being. On the one hand, the Hegelian movement of the speculative dialectic neutralises Being in order to ensure phallocentric mastery. On the other hand, Heidegger's *Dasein* is neutral (as opposed to neutralising) in that it neither carries the marks of binary sexual opposition nor denies sexual difference. See. 'Choreographies', pp. 72, 74, and '*Différence sexuelle, différence ontologique (Geschlect I)', Heidegger et la question: de l'esprit et autres essais* (Paris, 1990).
28. Cornell, *Beyond Accomodation*, p. 182.
29. Ibid., p. 110.
30. Marjorie Garber provides an excellent analysis of transsexual and transvestite gender constructions in 'Spare Parts: The Surgical Construction of Gender', *Vested Interests: Cross-Dressing and Cultural Anxiety* (New York and London, 1992). It is worth noting that Garber concludes:

> The transsexual body is not an absolute insignia of anything. Yet it makes the referent ('man' or 'woman') seem knowable. Paradoxically it is to transsexuals and transvestites that we need to look if we want to understand what gender categories mean. For transsexuals and transvestites are *more* concerned with maleness and femaleness than persons who are neither transvestite nor transsexual. (p. 110)

31. Devor, *Gender Blending*, p. viii.
32. Ibid., p. 154.
33. Jacques Derrida with Geoff Bennington, 'On Colleges and Philosophy', *Postmodernism: ICA Documents*, ed. Lisa Appignanesi (London, 1989), p. 227.
34. Derrida, 'Restitutions', *The Truth in Painting*, p. 268.
35. Ibid., p. 306.
36. To demonstrate his point, Derrida even plays around with the symbolic significance of the shoes and goes on to ask: 'could it be that, like a glove turned inside out, the shoe sometimes has the convex "form" of the foot (penis) and sometimes the concave form enveloping the foot (vagina)?' ('Restitutions', *The Truth in Painting*, p. 267).
37. Derrida, 'Choreographies', p. 76.
38. Irigaray, 'Così Fan Tutti', *This Sex Which is Not One*, p. 95. Hélène Cixous also argues that one cannot talk about *a* female sexuality, any more than one can speak of a general or typical woman. Instead, she appeals to bisexuality as a notion that articulates a multiplicity of possible sites for desire and pleasure. According to Cixous, bisexuality 'doesn't annul differences but stirs them up, pursues them, increases their number' ('Laugh of the Medusa', trans. Keith Cohen and Paula Cohen, *New French Feminisms*, ed. Elaine Marks and Isabelle de Courtivron [New York, 1981], p. 254).

Cixous's use of the term 'bisexuality' has led some feminists to conclude that she is doing nothing more than returning us to the binary oppositions of phallogocentric sexual difference, of male and female. That is certainly what Julia Kristeva maintains when she argues that bisexuality, no matter what qualifications accompany the term, always privileges 'the totality of one of the sexes' and thus effaces difference ('Women's Time', *The Kristeva Reader*, ed. Toril Moi [New York, 1986], p. 209).

I would like to take both sides here. Kristeva correctly identifies both a problem with the use of the term 'bisexuality' and the inevitable reduction that follows in Cixous's argument. However, Cixous is actually trying to increase rather than efface the possibility for sexual multiplicity. I want to hold on to this possibility of multiplicity and leave behind the term 'bisexuality', which all too easily leads back to the reinscription of binary sexual difference.

39. For examples of this type of critique, see: Rosi Braidotti, *Patterns of Dissonance* trans. Elizabeth Guild (New York, 1991); Margaret Whitford, *Luce Irigaray: Philosophy in the Feminine* (London and New York, 1991); Nancy K. Miller, *Getting Personal: Feminist Occasions and Other Autobiographical Acts* (New York and London, 1991). Miller reads Derrida's reference to the multiplication of sexual difference as somehow a 'degendered dream' (p. 78). She then goes on to argue that it is 'the exclusive emphasis in deconstructive and feminist rhetorics on a radically decontextualised sexual difference that has papered over – with extremely serious consequences – both the institutional and political differences between men and women and the equally powerful social and cultural differences between women' (p. 80) . . . I think Miller is wrong on this count. I will argue that feminism and deconstruction do not 'decontextualise' sexual difference but instead carefully consider the political roles institutions play. I will even go so far as to suggest that feminism and deconstruction together give rise to an ethical activism, addressing the very questions that concern Miller most.

40. Cornell, *Beyond Accommodation*, p. 19.

41. Ibid., p. 169.

Suggestions for Further Reading

Armstrong, Isobel (ed.), *New Feminist Discourses: Critical Essays on Theories and Texts* (London and New York, 1992).

Belsey, Catherine, *Desire: Love Stories in Western Culture* (Oxford, 1994).

Belsey, Catherine and Jane Moore (eds), *The Feminist Reader: Essays in Gender and the Politics of Literary Criticism*, second edn (London, 1997).

Butler, Judith, *Gender Trouble: Feminism and the Subversion of Identity* (New York, 1990).

Butler, Judith, *Bodies That Matter: On the Discursive Limits of 'Sex'* (New York, 1993).

Butler, Judith and Joan W. Scott (eds), *Feminists Theorize the Political* (New York, 1992).

Coward, Rosalind, *Female Desire: Women's Sexuality Today* (London, 1984).

Derrida, Jacques, *Spurs: Nietzsche's Styles*, trans. Barbara Howe (Chicago, 1978).

Devor, Holly, *Gender Blending: Confronting the Limits of Duality* (Bloomington, IN, 1989).

Elam, Diane and Robyn Wiegman (eds), *Feminism Beside Itself* (New York, 1995).

Fausto-Sterling, Anne, *Myths of Gender: Biological Theories About Women and Men* (New York, 1985).

Freud, Sigmund, *The Essentials of Psychoanalysis*, selected and introduced by Anna Freud (Harmondsworth, 1986).

Garber, Marjorie, *Vested Interests: Cross-Dressing and Cultural Anxiety* (New York, 1992).

Garber, Marjorie, *Vice Versa: Bisexuality and the Eroticism of Everyday Life* (London, 1996).

Haraway, Donna, *Simians, Cyborgs and Women: The Reinvention of Nature* (New York, 1991).

hooks, bell, *Yearning: Race, Gender and Cultural Politics* (Boston, 1990).

Jacobus, Mary, *Reading Women: Essays in Feminist Criticism* (London, 1986).

Jardine, Alice A., *Gynesis: Configurations of Woman and Modernity* (Ithaca, NY, 1985).

Jordan, Glenn and Chris Weedon, *Cultural Politics: Class, Gender, Race and the Postmodern World* (Oxford, 1994).

Kessler, Suzanne J., 'The Medical Construction of Gender: Case Management of Intersexed Infants', *Signs*, 16.1 (1990).

Landry, Donna and Gerald MacLean (eds), *The Spivak Reader* (New York, 1996).

Laqueur, Thomas, *Making Sex: Body and Gender from the Greeks to Freud* (Cambridge, MA, 1990).

Marks, Elaine and Isabelle de Courtivron, *New French Feminisms: An Anthology* (Hemel Hempstead, 1981).

211

Moi, Toril, *Sexual/Textual Politics: Feminist Literary Theory* (London, 1985).

Parker, Andrew and Eve Kosofsky Sedgwick (eds), *Performativity and Performance* (New York and London, 1995).

Riley, Denise, *'Am I That Name?': Feminism and the Category of 'Women' in History* (Minneapolis, 1988).

Rutherford, Jonathan, *Men's Silences: Predicaments in Masculinity* (New York, 1994).

Scott, Joan Wallach, *Gender and the Politics of History* (New York, 1988).

Sedgwick, Eve Kosofsky, *The Epistemology of the Closet* (Hemel Hempstead, 1991).

Sedgwick, Eve Kosofsky and Andrew Parker (eds), *Performance and Performativity* (London, 1994).

Silverman, Kaja, *Male Subjectivity at the Margins* (New York, 1992).

Weedon, Chris, *Feminist Practice and Poststructuralist Theory* (Oxford, 1987).

Weedon, Chris, *Feminism, Theory and the Politics of Difference* (Oxford, 1999).

Woolf, Virginia, *Three Guineas* (London, 1943).

Notes on Contributors

Catherine Belsey chairs the Centre for Critical and Cultural Theory at Cardiff University. Books include *Critical Practice* (1980), *The Subject of Tragedy: Identity and Difference in Renaissance Drama* (1985), *John Milton: Language, Gender, Power* (1988) and *Desire: Love Stories in Western Culture* (1994).

Homi K. Bhabha is Professor of Literary and Cultural Theory at the University of Chicago. Books include (ed.) *Nation and Narration* (1990) and *The Location of Culture* (1994).

Judith Butler is Professor of Rhetoric and Comparative Literature at the University of California at Berkeley. Books include *Gender Trouble: Feminism and the Subversion of Identity* (1990), *Bodies That Matter: On the Discursive Limits of 'Sex'* (1993) and *Excitable Speech: A Politics of the Performative* (1997).

Diane Elam is Professor of English and Critical and Cultural Theory at Cardiff University. Books include *Romancing the Postmodern* (1992), *Feminism and Deconstruction: Ms. en Abyme* (1994), and (ed. with Robyn Wiegman) *Feminism Beside Itself* (1995).

Stephen Heath is a Fellow of Jesus College, Cambridge. He was an important contributor to the British film journal *Screen* in the 1970s, and is author of *The Sexual Fix* (1982).

Anne Fausto-Sterling is Professor of Medical Sciences in the Division of Biology and Medicine at Brown University. She is the author of *Myths and Gender: Biological Theories about Women and Men* (1992).

Chandra Talpade Mohanty is Associate Professor of Women's Studies at Hamilton College, New York, and Core Faculty at the Union Institute Graduate School, Cincinnati. Books include (ed. with Ann Russo and Lourdes Torres) *Third World Women and the Politics of Feminism* (1991) and (ed. with M. Jacqui Alexander) *Feminist Genealogies, Colonial Legacies, Democratic Futures* (1997).

Adrienne Rich is a North American poet and essayist. Books include *The Fact of a Doorframe: Poems Selected and New 1950–1984 (1984)*, *An Atlas of the Difficult World: Poems 1988–1991* (1991), *Dark Fields of the Republic* (1996), *Blood, Bread and Poetry: Selected Prose 1950–1984* (1996) and *What is Found There: Notebooks on Poetry and Politics* (1993).

Joan Riviere (1883–1962). A contemporary of Sigmund Freud's, Riviere collaborated with Melanie Klein in the development of child analysis, translated Freud's *Collected Papers*, worked for the *International Journal of Psychoanalysis* and wrote for *The Lancet*.

Jacqueline Rose is Professor of English at Queen Mary and Westfield College, London. Books include *The Case of Peter Pan, Or, The Impossibility of Children's*

Fiction (1984), *Sexuality in the Field of Vision* (1986), *The Haunting of Sylvia Plath* (1991) and *States of Fantasy* (1996).

Jonathan Rutherford teaches cultural studies at Middlesex University. Books include *Forever England: Reflections on Race, Masculinity and Empire* (1997), *Young Britain* (1998), *I Am No Longer Myself Without You: An Anatomy of Love* (1999) and *Art of Life* (2000).

Lynne Segal is Professor of Gender Studies at Middlesex University. Books include *Is the Future Female? Troubled Thoughts on Contemporary Feminism* (1987), *Slow Motion: Changing Masculinities, Changing Men* (1990), (ed. with Mary McIntosh) *Sex Exposed: Sexuality and the Pornography Debate* (1992) and *Why Feminism? Gender, Psychology and Politics* (2000).

Anna Tripp is a Lecturer in Literature at the University of Hertfordshire.

Virginia Woolf (1882–1941) was a British author. Novels include *The Voyage Out* (1915), *Mrs Dalloway* (1925), *To the Lighthouse* (1927) and *Orlando* (1928). Her most famous critical works are *A Room of One's Own* (1929) and *Three Guineas* (1938).

Index

Index